EARLY CELTIC MASTERPIECES FROM BRITAIN

IN THE BRITISH MUSEUM

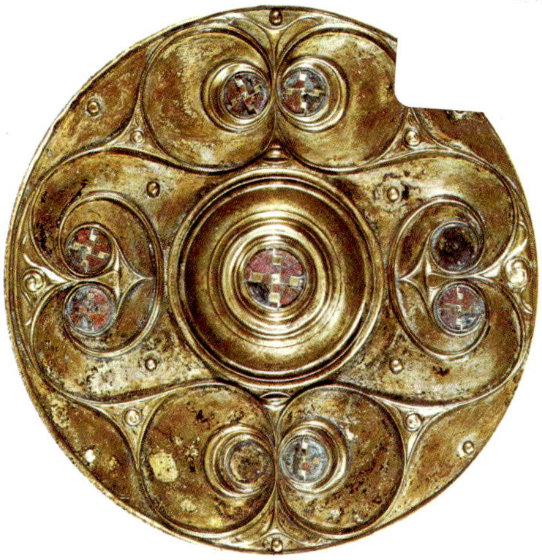

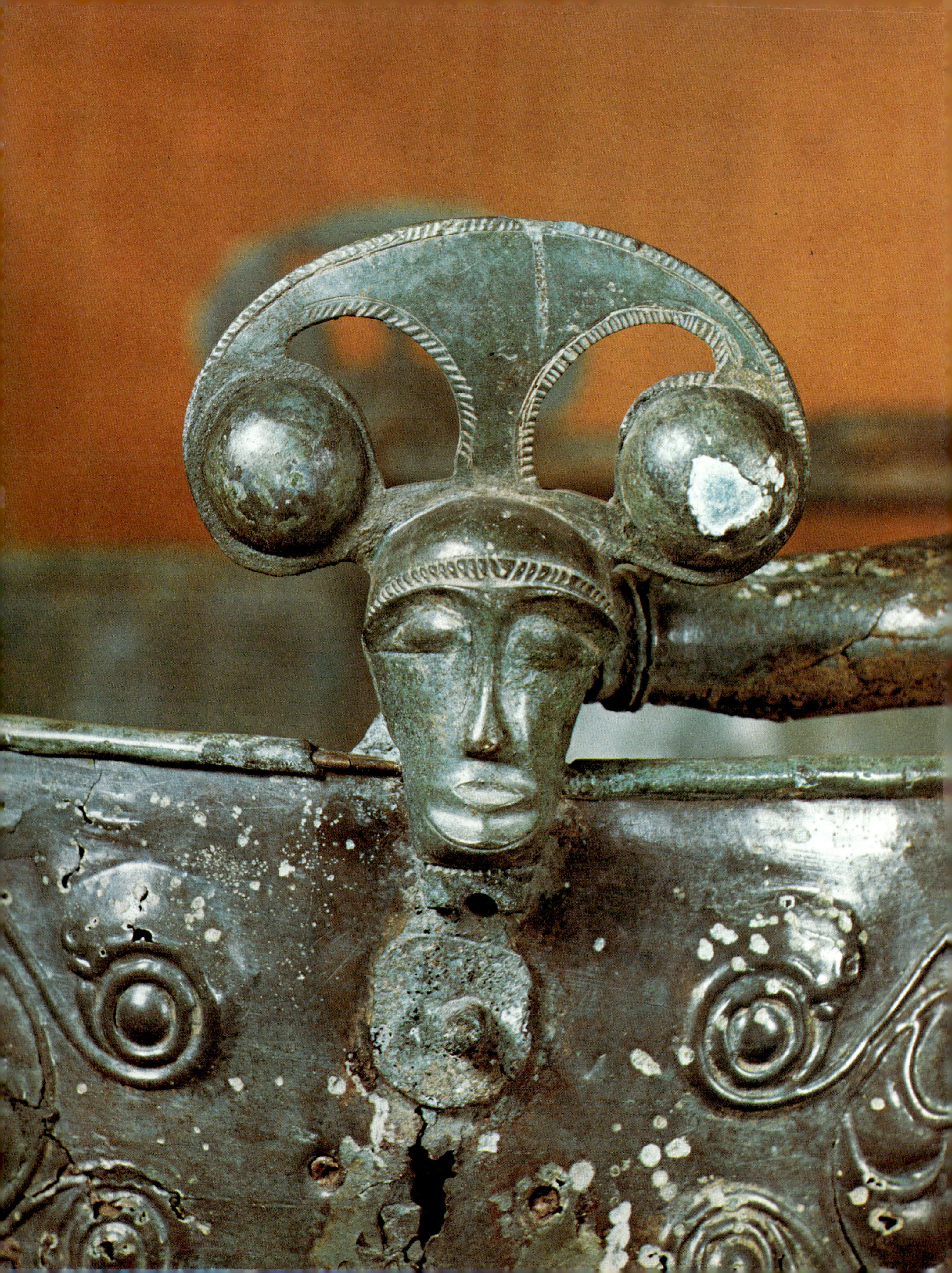

EARLY CELTIC MASTERPIECES FROM BRITAIN
IN THE BRITISH MUSEUM

JOHN BRAILSFORD

formerly Keeper of Prehistoric and Romano–British Antiquities in the British Museum

Published for THE TRUSTEES OF THE BRITISH MUSEUM

by BRITISH MUSEUM PUBLICATIONS LIMITED

Acknowledgements

All the drawings are by Philip Compton.
The photographs are also by Philip Compton with the following exceptions: numbers 11, 12 and 13 are by P. Jacobsthal; numbers 97, 105, 114, 122, 132–135, and all the colour plates are by the British Museum Photographic Service.

ISBN 0 7141 1362 X cased
ISBN 0 7141 1363 8 paper
Published by British Museum Publications Ltd
6 Bedford Square, London WC1B 3RA

Designed by Patrick Yapp
Filmset in 12 point Bembo
Printed Offset Litho in Great Britain by
Cox & Wyman Ltd, London Fakenham and Reading

CONTENTS

LIST OF ILUSTRATIONS

COLOUR PLATES

MONOCHROME

INTRODUCTION

The world of Early Celtic Art is a haunted region where little human faces may be seen peering out of a tangle of plant ornament on torcs and bracelets and even the precise pattern ornament on the Battersea Shield suddenly reveals stags' heads with great spreading antlers and also owl-like faces with great round squinting eyes (Ill. 33). Other similar examples are the ornament on the Wandsworth Long Shield Boss, its terminal formed by a grotesque human face with a row of teeth just visible resting on its lower lip, and 'birds' heads' with long curving toothed beaks (Ill. 17). The attachment of the handle of the Holcombe mirror is another case among our present examples where what at first glance may be taken for abstract ornament resolves itself on a closer look into an animal face (Ill. 94).

Professor Stuart Piggott has described the ancient Celts as 'swaggering, belching, touchy chieftains and their equally impossible warrior crew, hands twitching to the sword-hilt at the imagined hint of an insult . . . wiping the greasy moustaches that were a mark of nobility' (*Ancient Europe*, Edinburgh, 1965, p. 229). Inevitably one wonders how such a barbarous people could produce such sophisticated and accomplished works of art. It may go some way towards solving the problem when one remembers the status of the Celtic artist–craftsman who was credited with a sacred character and therefore had full scope to exercise his imaginative gifts in a world where 'that distinction between natural and supernatural which is the consequence of civilized thought had not yet been clearly drawn' (K. H. Jackson, *A Celtic Miscellany*, London, 1951, pp. 153–4).

From about the middle of the fifth century BC there developed in continental Europe the accomplished and distinctive school of Early Celtic Art associated with the La Tène culture. By the first century BC this tradition had declined and it was finally extinguished by the spread of the Roman Empire. As the continental tradition declined, however, there grew up in Britain a distinctive insular school of Early Celtic Art and this was at its maximum development during the first century BC and the first century AD. Early Celtic Art of the British Isles is well represented in the British Museum and a selection of outstanding examples is presented in this book. Its purpose is primarily to make easily available good and detailed drawings and photographs of the objects. It is believed that this will meet a special need among scholars as well as introducing this school of British art to a wider public. The objects provide a series of landmarks in the development of Early Celtic Art in Britain and the select bibliographies lead to studies dealing more fully with their stylistic and historical background.

La Tène art had various roots and this diversity is reflected in the varied nature of examples of the Early Style. This first phase is not represented in Britain but one of its finest masterpieces, a pair of decorated flagons from Basse-Yutz in the Moselle department of France, may be seen exhibited in the British Museum. These flagons are Italic in form and their decoration includes the classical palmette, while the hounds on the handles are oriental in character and the ducks on the spout are derived from the preceding Hallstatt culture of Central Europe. The fully developed La Tène style is characterized by swirling patterns and is named after the rich find from Waldalgesheim. Examples of this style are very rarely found in Britain and the third-century 'Plastic' style, with its exuberant three-dimensional treatment and grotesque human and animal heads, representing what has been called a 'Disney'-school, does not occur in these islands at all. However, the delicate engraved decoration of the Eastern European 'Sword' style of the third and second centuries BC may have inspired comparable ornament on the earliest examples of Early Celtic Art in the British Isles, such as certain scabbards and also on such pieces as the Wandsworth Round Shield Boss (Ills. 8, III).

CHAPTER ONE

THE WITHAM SHIELD AND THE WANDSWORTH SHIELD BOSSES

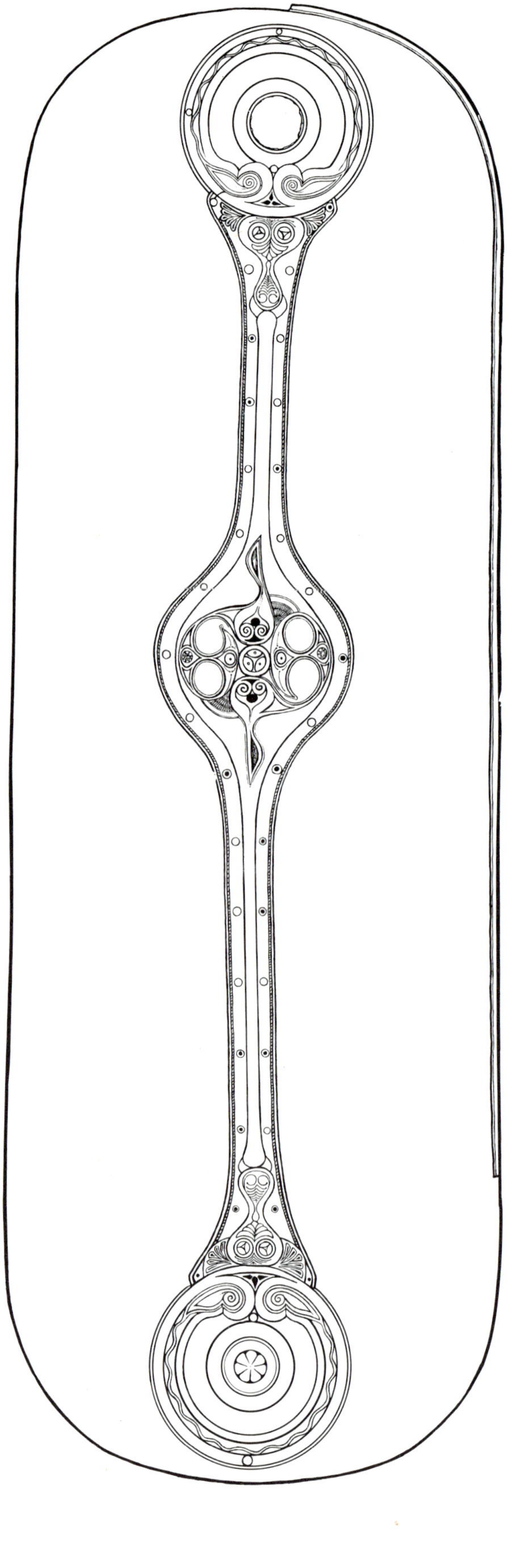

1

THE WITHAM SHIELD

II The Witham Shield was found in the River Witham near Lincoln. It was originally in the Meyrick Collection, and was presented to the British Museum in 1872 by A. W. (later Sir Wollaston) Franks, who was a notable benefactor to many of the Departments in the Museum.

Strictly speaking the Witham 'Shield' is the
1, 3 bronze facing for a wood or leather shield measuring 1·25 m. long with curved ends and parallel sides. The body is made up of two longitudinal plates and there is a U-section binding round the edge. The spine and end roundels are attached by rivets through the flange and the length of these indicates that the original wood or hide backing was about 0·6 cm. thick. Domed washers held the rivets in place at the back. The central boss, the spine and the end roundels are all made in one piece, a remarkable example of Iron Age craftsmanship. Originally there had been the outline of
2 the figure of a boar applied to the front of the shield, and the holes for the pins which held it in place still remain. The present central boss, spine and end roundels may be a second stage in the ornament of the shield, having replaced the boar emblem.

4 Unfortunately the upper end roundel is damaged. Its outer border consists of a repoussé, wavy, raised line between ridges which ends in a pair of comma-shaped recesses, each of which encloses a 'snail-shell' boss with a tail. There is an inner flat zone engraved with scroll and spiral ornament. The lower end boss is similar but is complete, retaining its central roundel with dished centre which has a raised rosette. At the junction of each end roundel
4, 5 with the centre spine is a grotesque animal head formed by a pair of domed eyes decorated with an engraved or chased triangle. An elongated bulbous snout extends along the spine and this, together with the brow and the area under the eyes of each head, is decorated with engraved or chased lines which give the appearance of wrinkles. The upper part of the head is flanked by a pair of ear-like palmettes.

Delicate scroll ornament executed by engraving or chasing extends some way along the spine from the snout of each head and each edge of the central spine is bordered by a fine zig-zag ridge within a groove.

The oval central boss is richly decorated with *6*
repoussé ornament. This consists of two complexes, one on either side of a diagonal axis. Each has a pair of circular areas to one side which are enclosed by ridges. In the angles formed at the intersection of these there is a rosette on the outer side and a coral stud on the inner side. These ridges are connected by 'snail-shell' bosses with a tongue that extends along the central spine. The other most important element in the central boss ornament consists of three segments of coral which together form a central circular stud. These are attached to the shield by fine pins and enclosed within a circular raised border. Between each pair of 'snail-shell' bosses are a circular and a triangular opening which may originally have revealed a backing of some material colour-contrasted with the surface of the shield for visual effect.

The three red decorative studs on the central boss have usually been identified as coral. A recent examination by Dr Brian Rosen of the Coelenterata and Bryozoa Section, Department of Palaeontology, the Natural History Museum, has confirmed this identification. Dr Rosen concludes: 'There is no reason to suppose that the studs are anything but precious coral. The dimensions and character of the grain pattern and the general colouration strongly favour this. The grain represents the ridged structure of the coral surface after removal by polishing.'

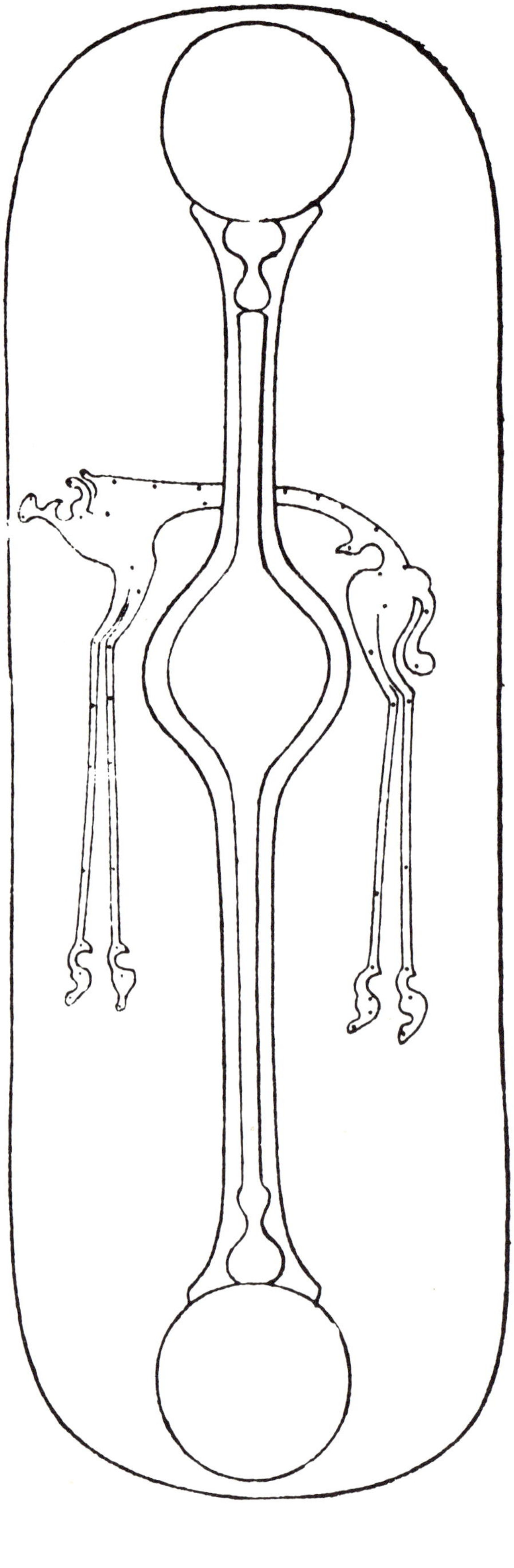

2

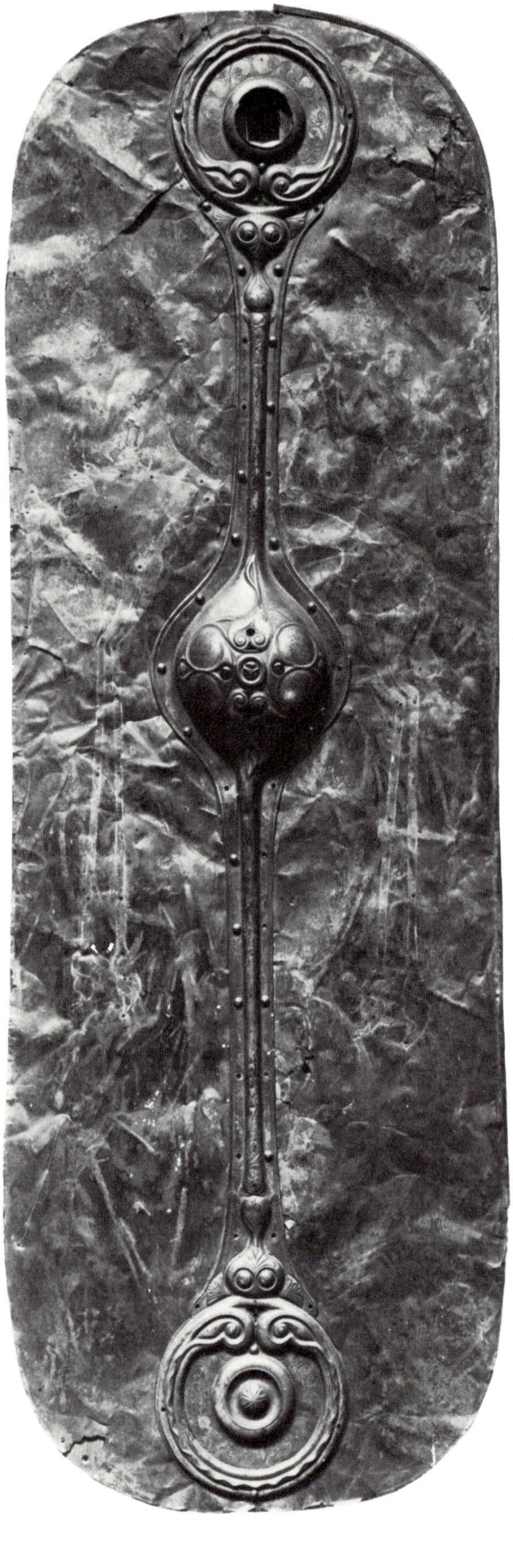

3

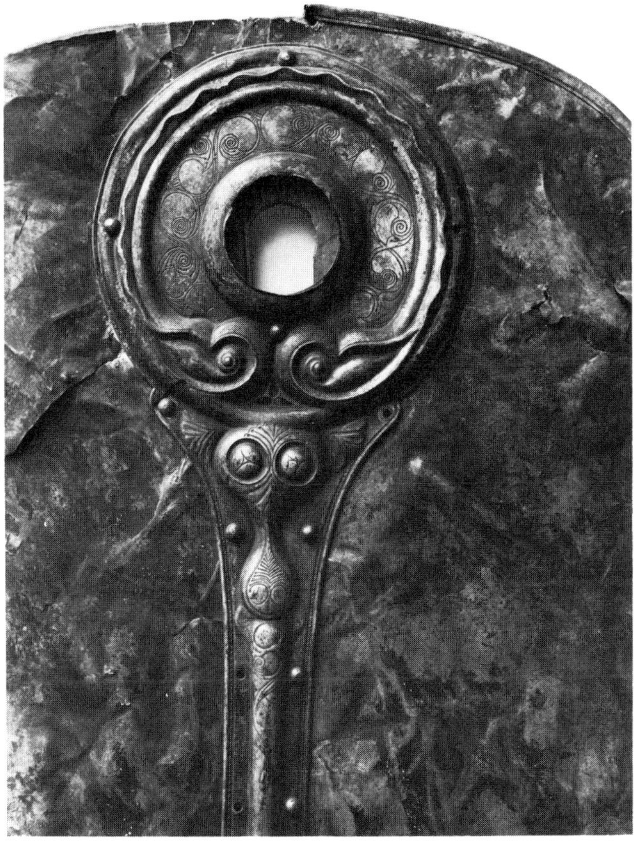

4

6

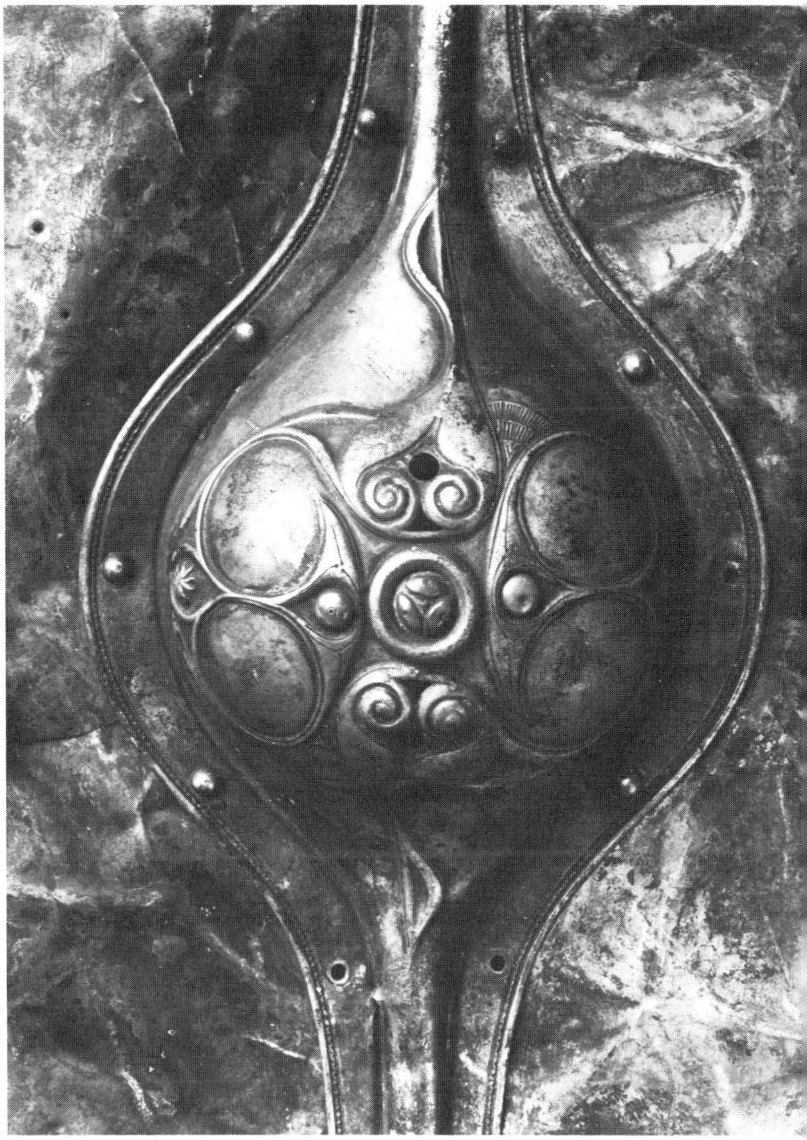

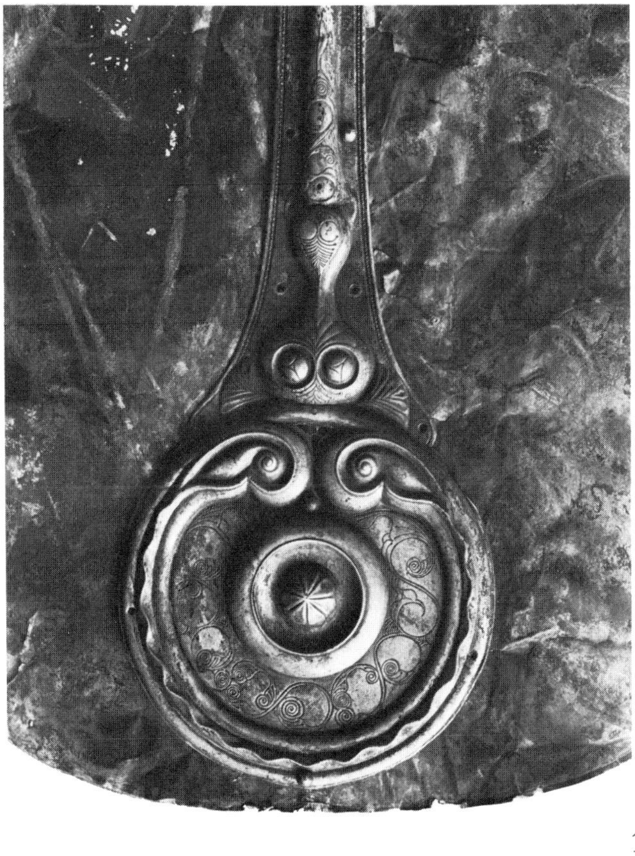

5

THE ROUND WANDSWORTH SHIELD BOSS

III This is one of two shield bosses which were found in the Thames near Wandsworth and both were presented to the British Museum by the Archaeological Institute in 1858.

7 The boss, 36·5 cm. in diameter, consists of a broad decorated flange with a relatively small central domed boss. The ornament on the
flange has a bold design in repoussé which is 8, 9
basically a scroll pattern with two 'birds' head' motifs. Ornament in a different style, finely
executed by chasing or engraving, occurs in 13
the spaces of the repoussé design and also on the central boss. The motifs used in the fine
ornament include dragon-like figures with 12
'birds' heads' and varieties of trumpet-form 11

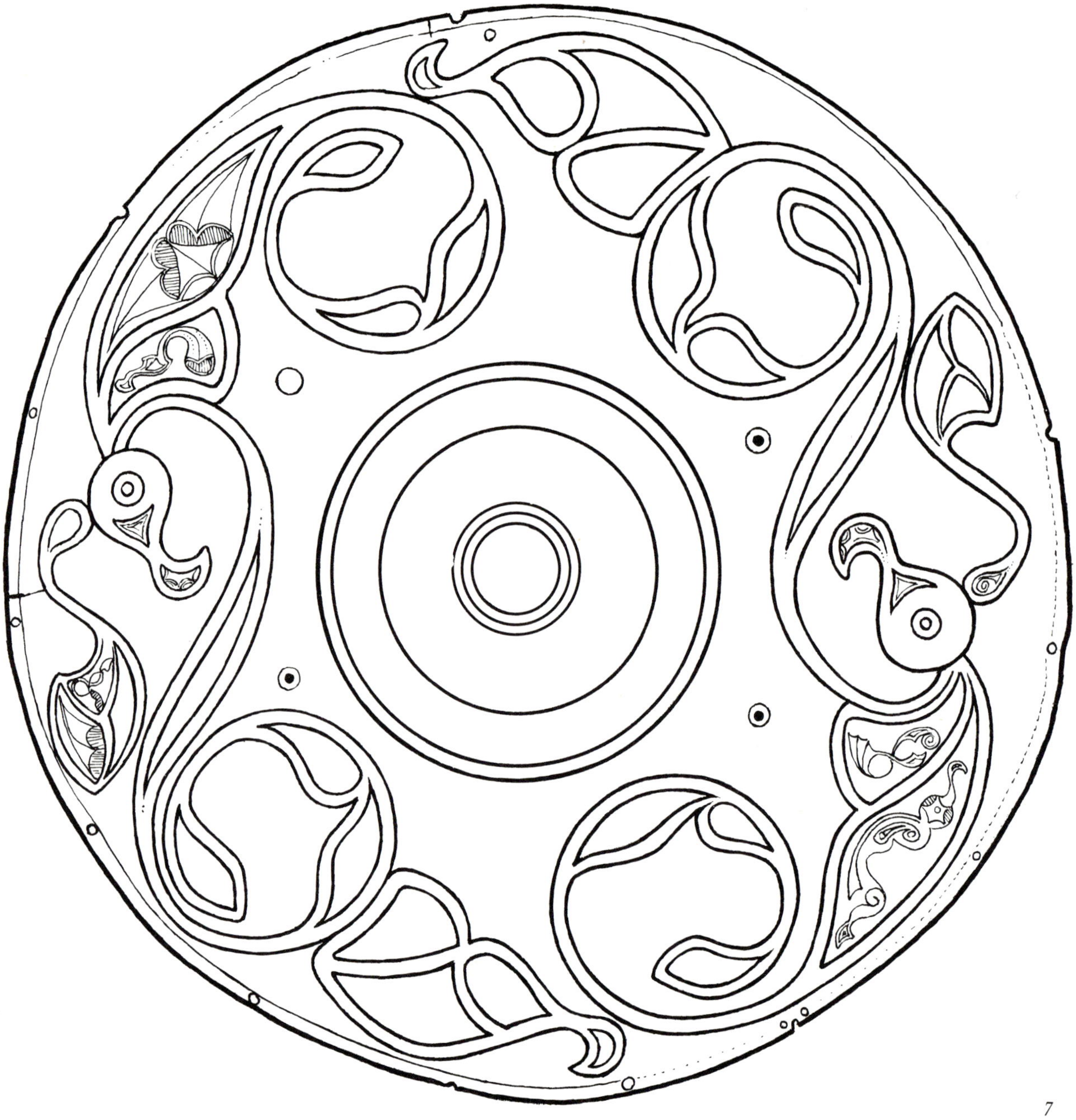

7

with a pair of hatched semi-circles in the
mouth.

In the eyes of the two repoussé 'birds' heads'
10 on the flange are still the small pins which
must originally have held inlays of coral or
glass. A small perforation in the centre of
10 the boss must also originally have had a
similar pin. Surrounding the central umbo is
a circular repoussé ridge. A broad punch was
used on this to produce a zig-zag effect along 8, 9
the crest of the ridge.

The four large rivets which fastened the
boss to the shield were located in the space
between the ridge which surrounds the central
domed boss and the running decoration on
the flange; only one rivet remains, 0·8 cm. in 10
length. Around the outer edge of the flange
is a line of small perforations, approximately 8, 9

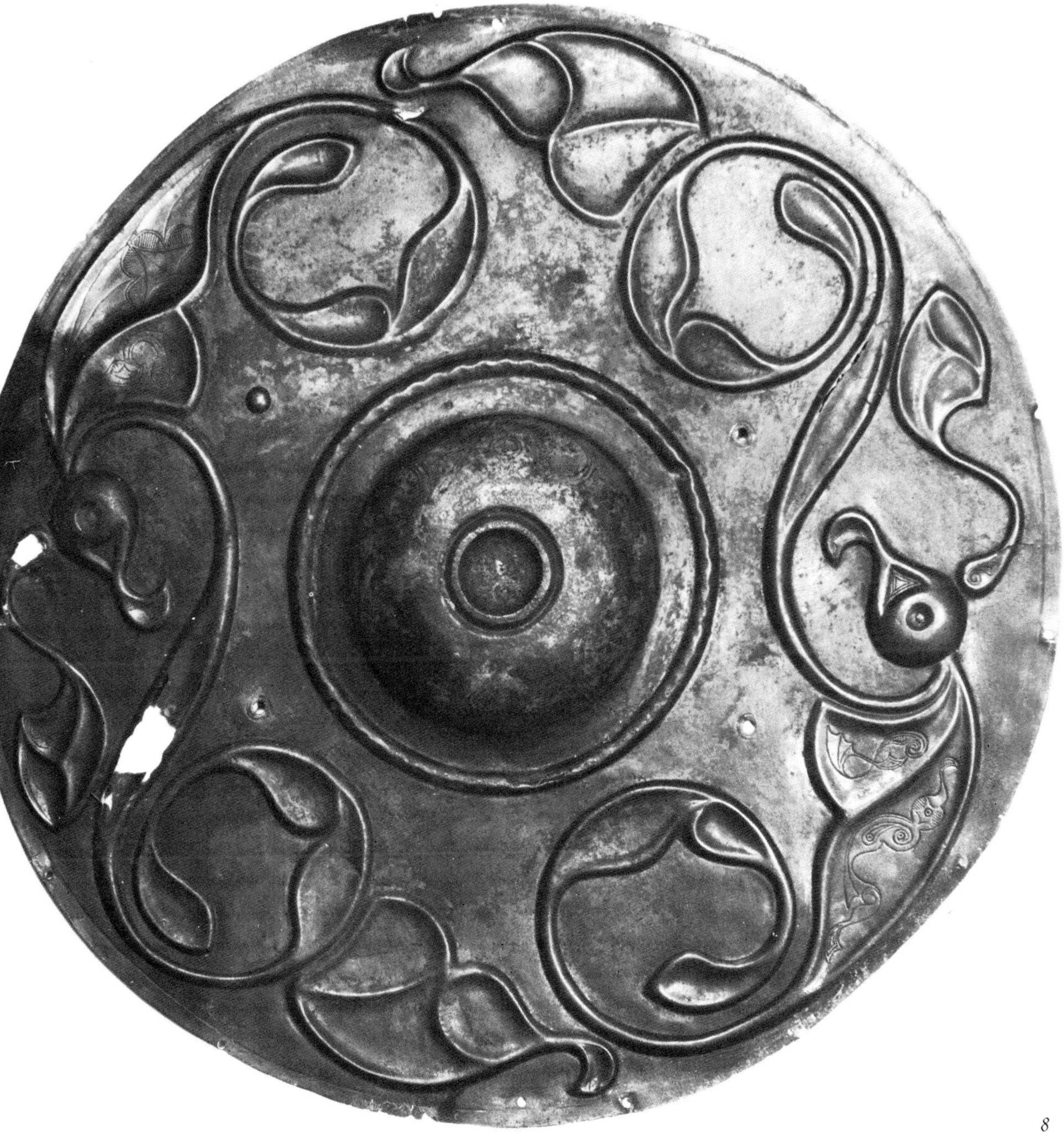

8

6·2 cm. apart, with a roughly engraved line immediately within them. In one segment of the flange these small holes are missing, giving the impression that the edge had been pared off in this part. Presumably small nails through these perforations held the edge of the boss down to the surface of the shield and gave it greater stability.

9

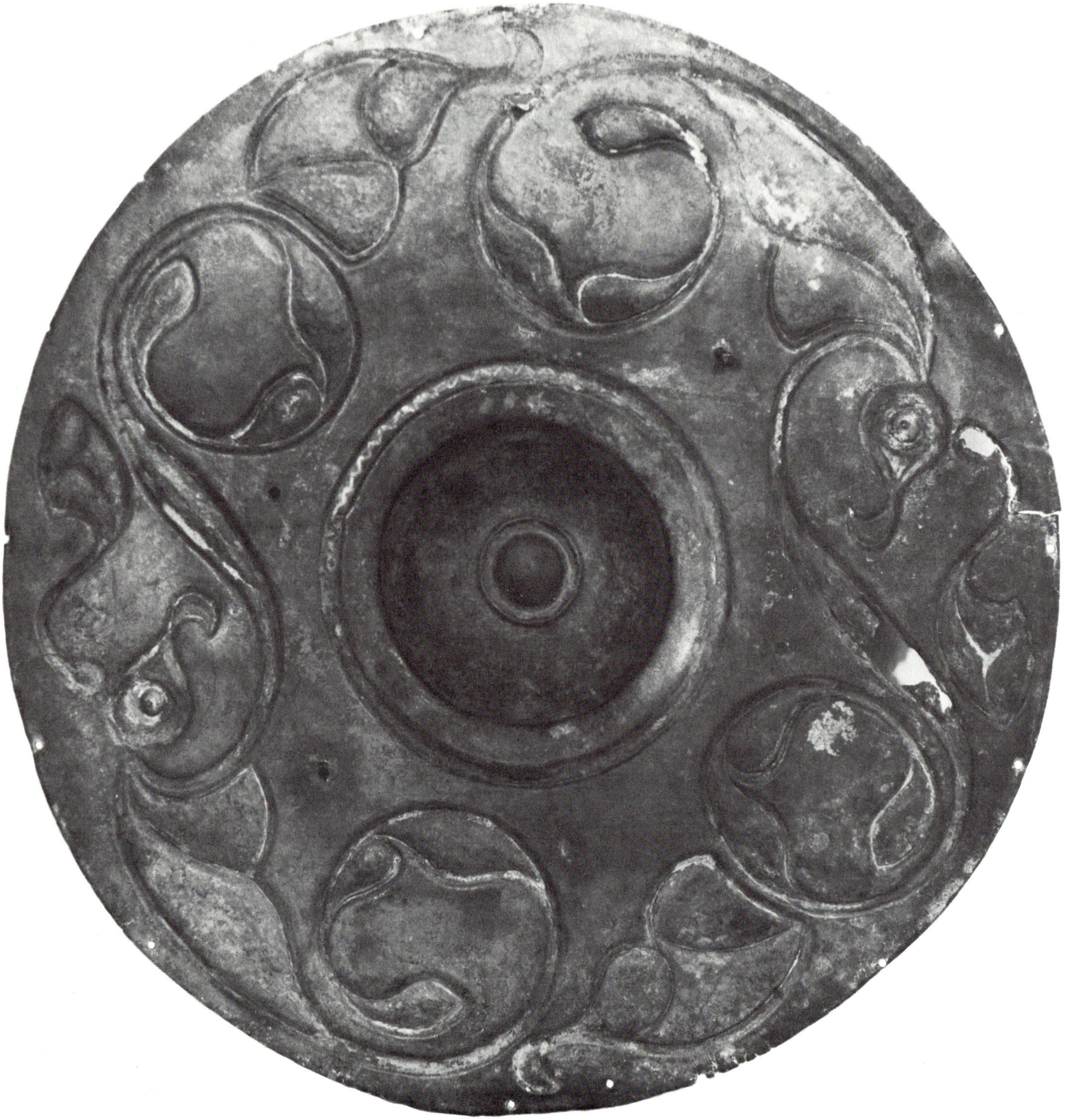

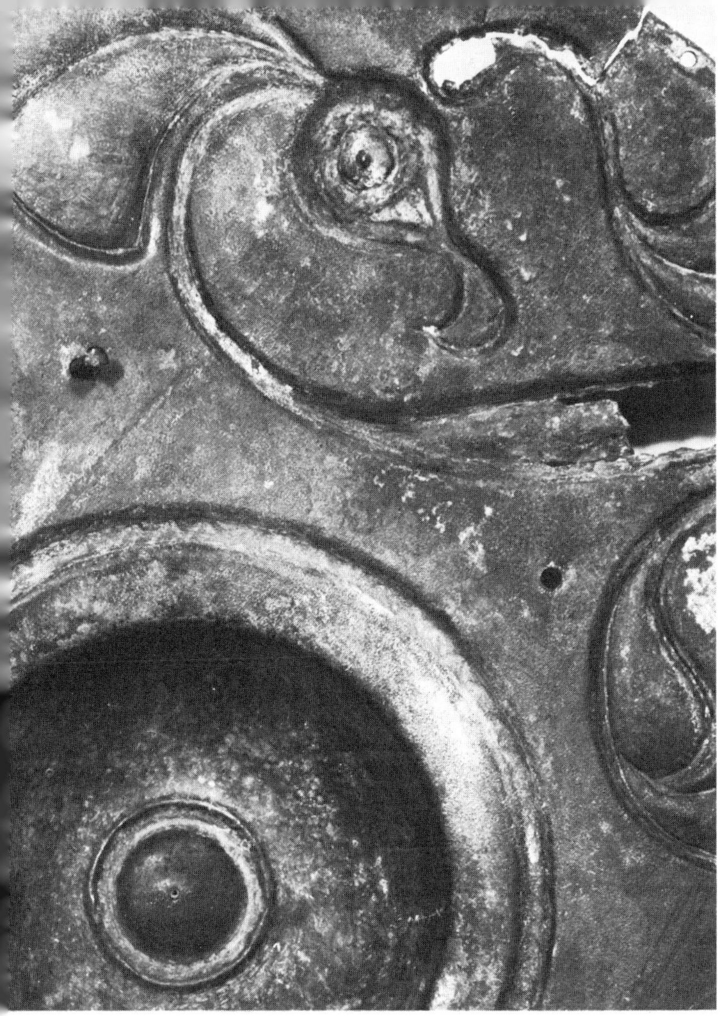
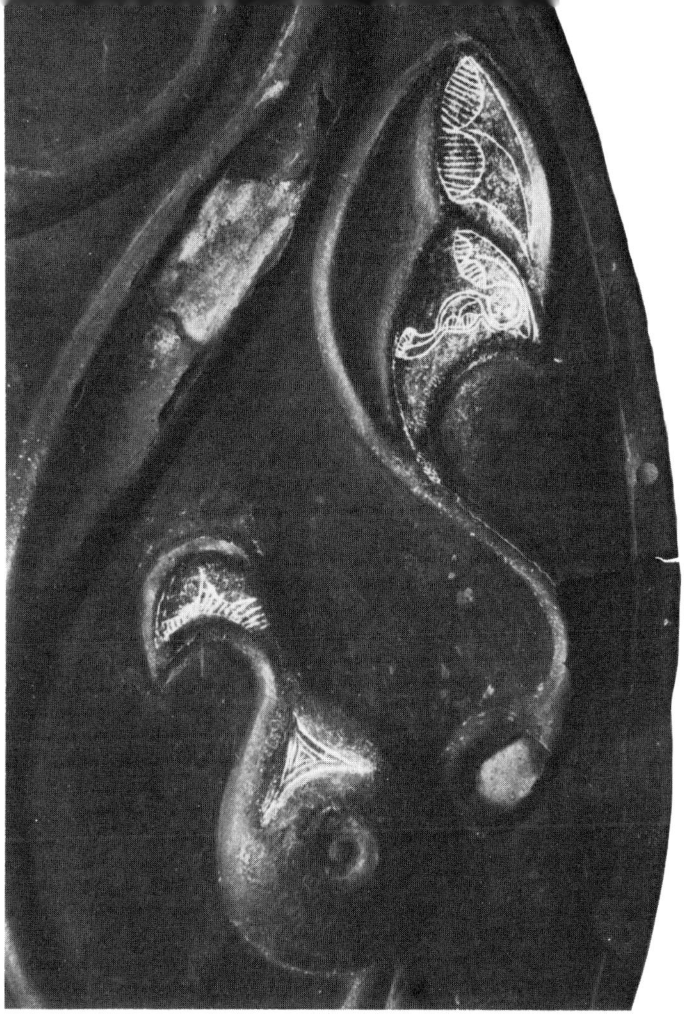

10, 11

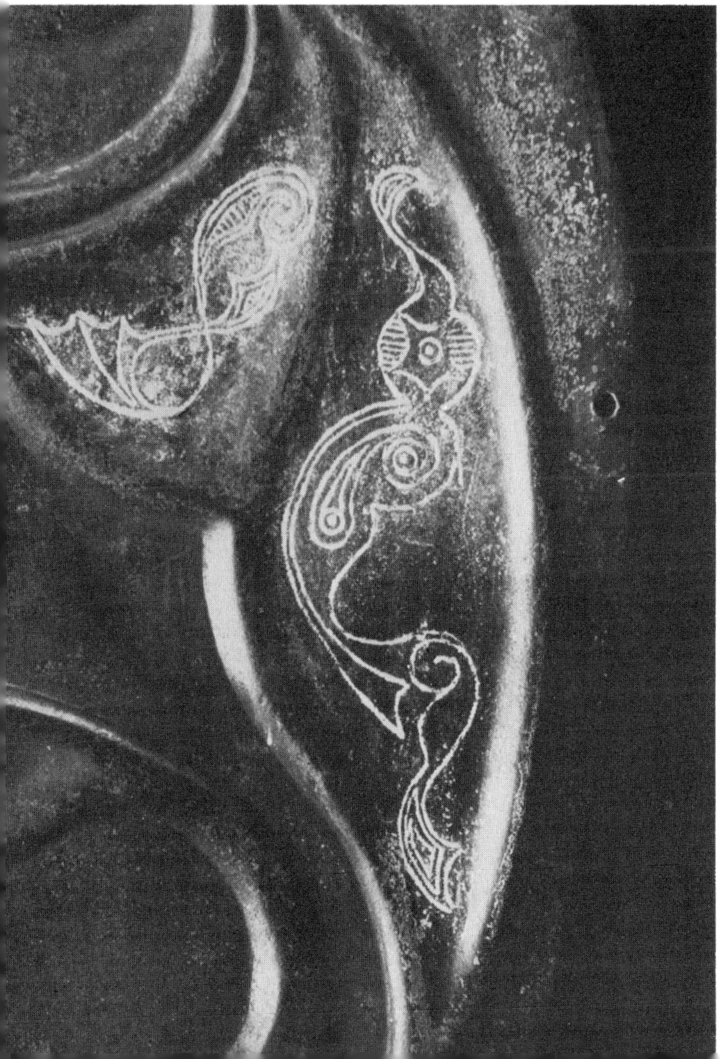
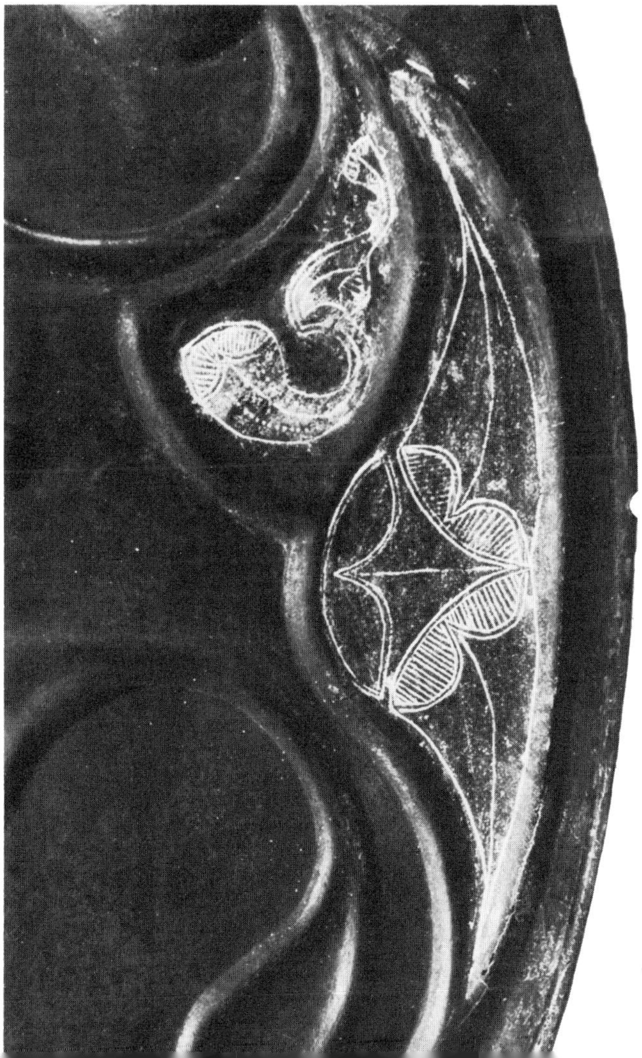

12, 13

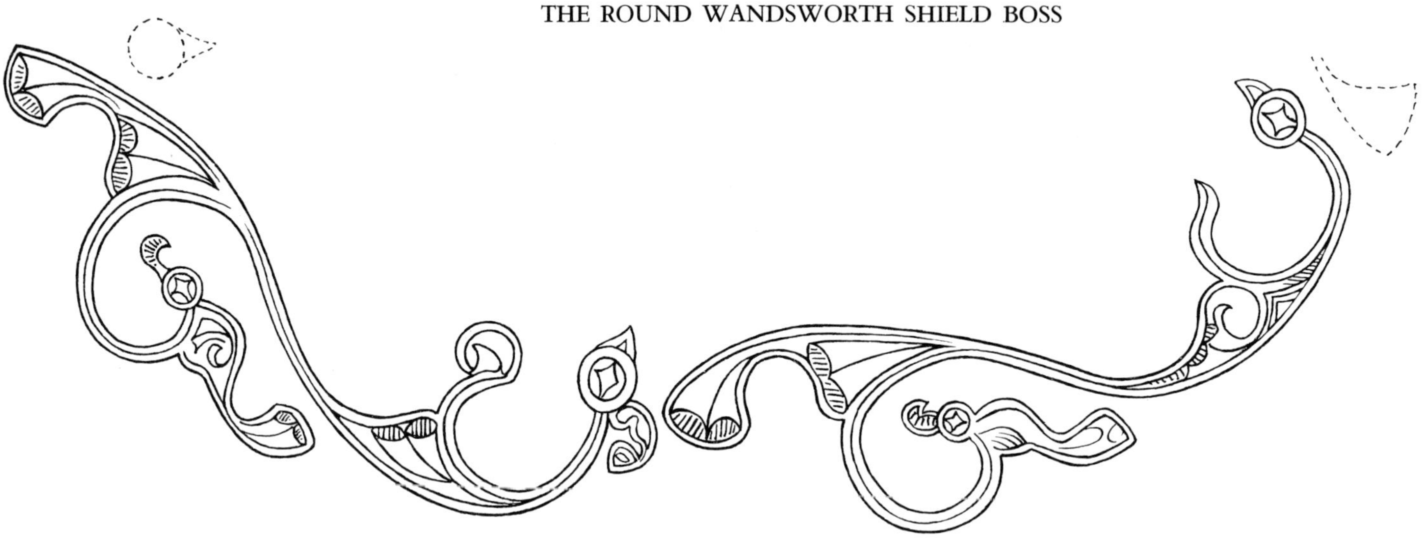

14

15

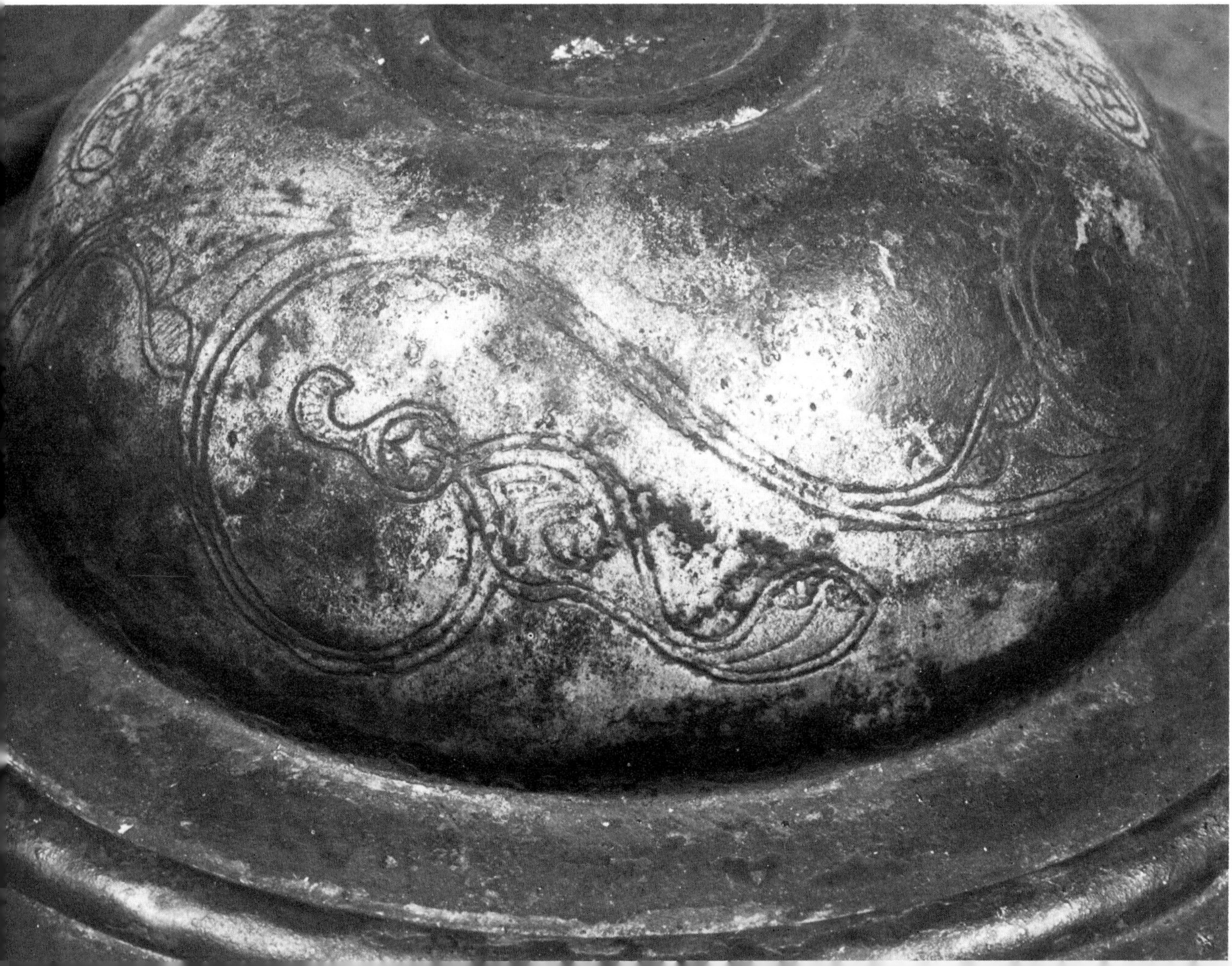

II

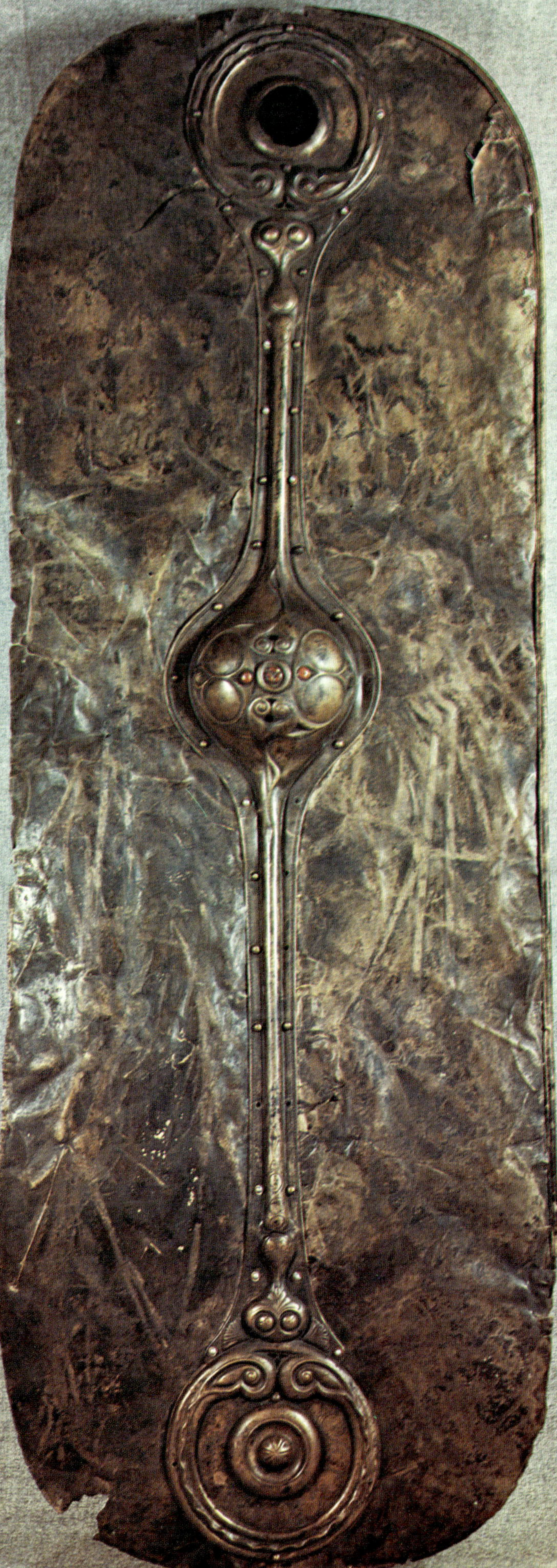

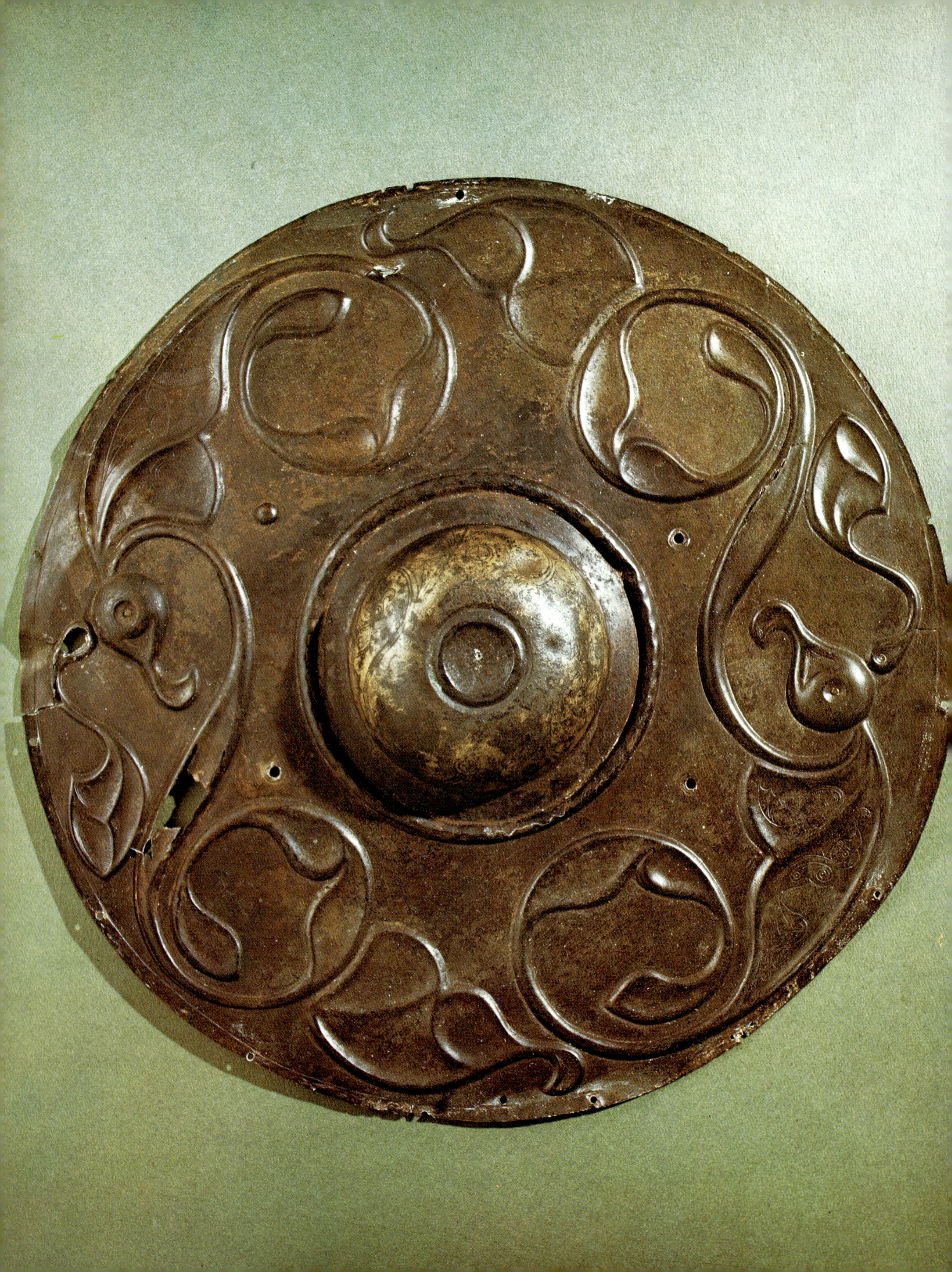

THE LONG WANDSWORTH SHIELD BOSS

The second of the two shield bosses which were found in the Thames near Wandsworth and presented to the British Museum by the Archaeological Institute in 1858 (p. 14). It
16, 17 consists of a central boss approximately 15·8 cm. long by 11·5 cm. wide which continues at each end into a spine, one end of which terminates in a grotesque human face, giving a total distance of 19·7 cm. from the centre of the boss. Both boss and spine are surrounded by a flange which is pierced at intervals by rivet-holes and six round-headed rivets survive in place. The length of these indicates that the thickness of the wood or hide backing of the boss was 1·1 cm. The upper end of the grotesque head terminal is concave and there is a narrow flange above it with a small hole in the centre. The boss was no doubt attached to the centre of the shield in the same way as that on the Witham Shield (p. 11) and there would have been a further pair of bosses at each end, overlying the flange above the grotesque head which survives at only one end. The diameter of such bosses must have been approximately 18 cm.

The principal decoration on the central boss is boldly executed in repoussé and includes
22, 23 a pair of 'birds' heads'. These are separated by a diagonal ridge made with a broad punch which produces a modified zig-zag effect. This ridge then runs out along the spine with a tongue-like terminal at each end. Very fine ornament, executed by chasing or engraving, decorates the terminals and similar ornament also appears in two places on the 'birds' head'
20 pattern as well as on the nose of the grotesque human head. The fine ornament is made up mostly of delicate spirals, left in relief against a sunk background. Along the 'beaks' of the 'birds' heads', on the lip of the terminal mask and along one margin of each tongue terminal are rows of dentate depressions, leaving lines *19*
of raised tooth-like projections. This treatment is a characteristically Celtic conventional decorative motif used to suggest some feature of a human being or animal—spirals for nostrils *20*
on the terminal mask, and rows of dentate lines to suggest teeth on the terminal mask and on the 'beaks' of the 'birds' heads'.

NOTE: The fine detailed ornament on the Wandsworth Long Boss (Ill. 17) is not clearly visible on the original but has been revealed on an electrotype made by Peter Shorer, where it was possible to polish the decorated area and thus reveal details not clearly visible on the original.

THE DATING OF THE WITHAM SHIELD AND WANDSWORTH SHIELD BOSSES

Professors Piggott and Atkinson, in their publication of the Torrs Chamfrein in 1955, argued that the style found on the Witham Shield and Wandsworth Bosses developed in Britain during the late third century BC on the basis of the continental Waldalgesheim and 'Hungarian-sword' styles. An important recent commentary to this has been provided by Mansel Spratling in his note on the shield boss decorated in Torrs-Wandsworth style which was found at South Cadbury hill-fort in Somerset. This boss was excavated stratified in a context dating from the first century BC, or the early first century AD, suggesting that this style may have continued rather later than had previously been thought. Spratling quotes Continental parallels of the first century AD to the Witham and Wandsworth bosses.

◄ *III*

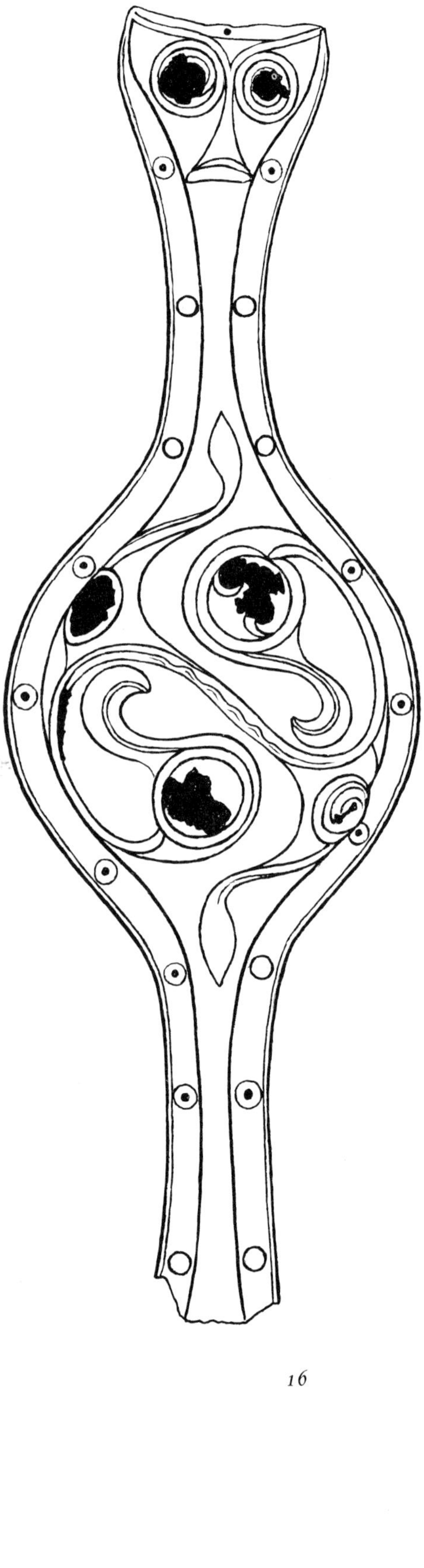

16

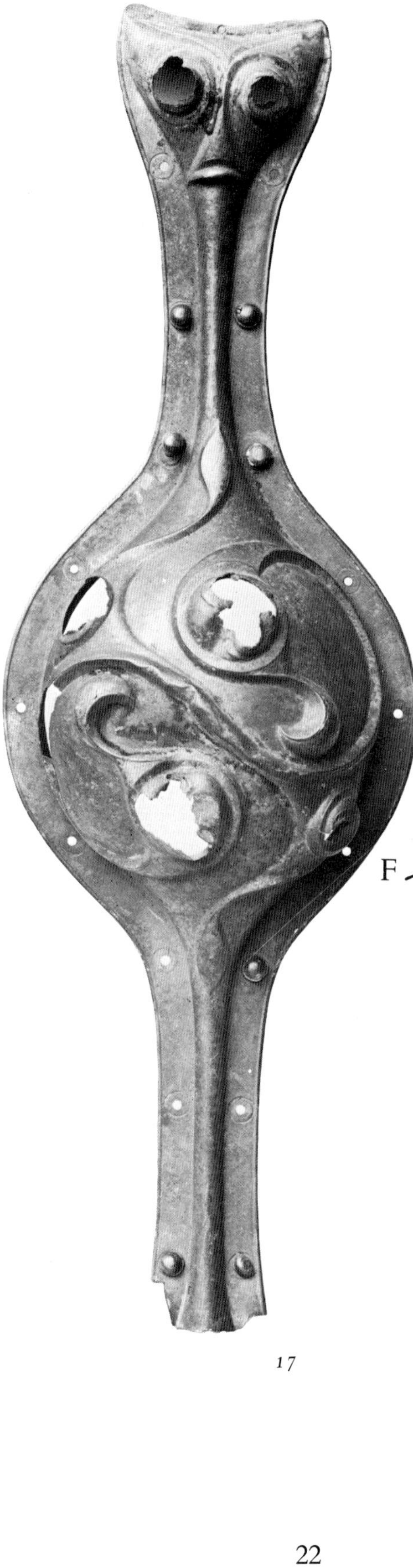

17

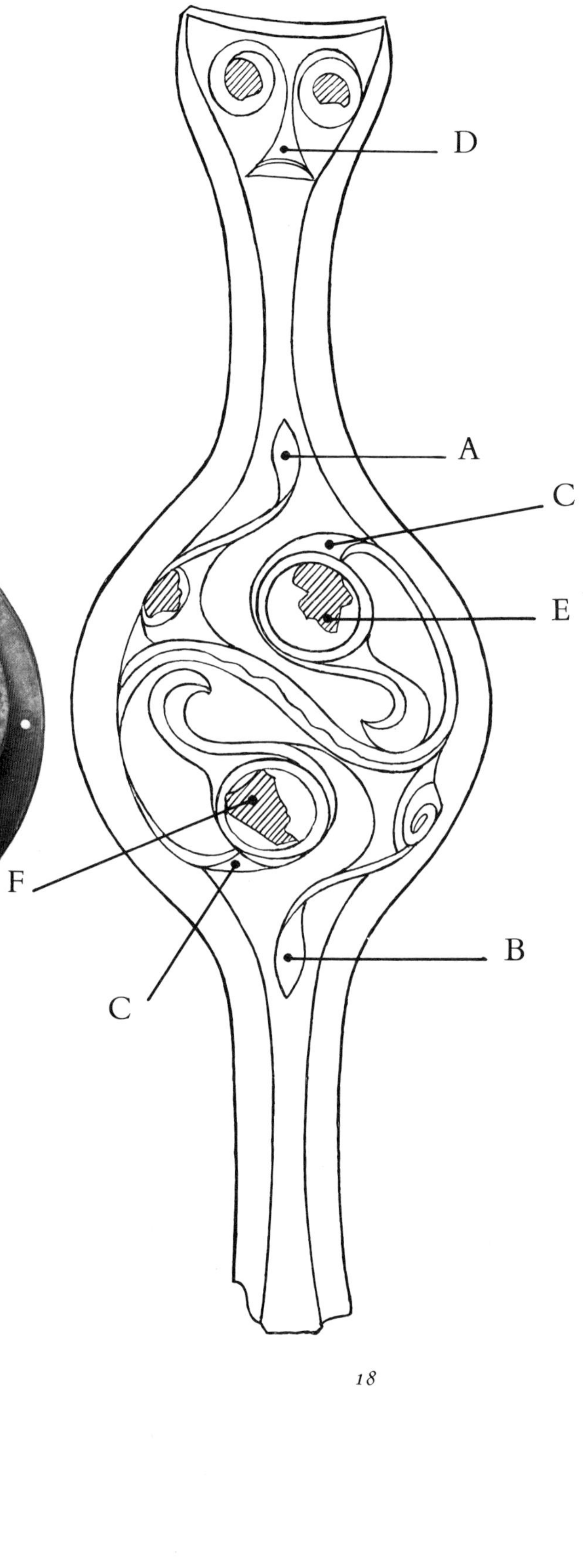

18

19

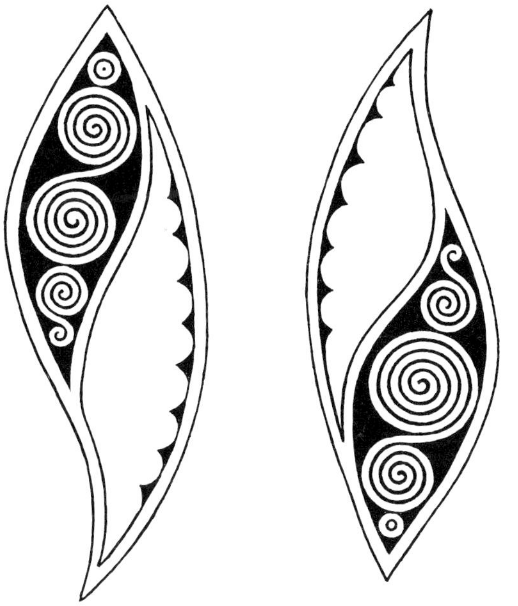

A B

20

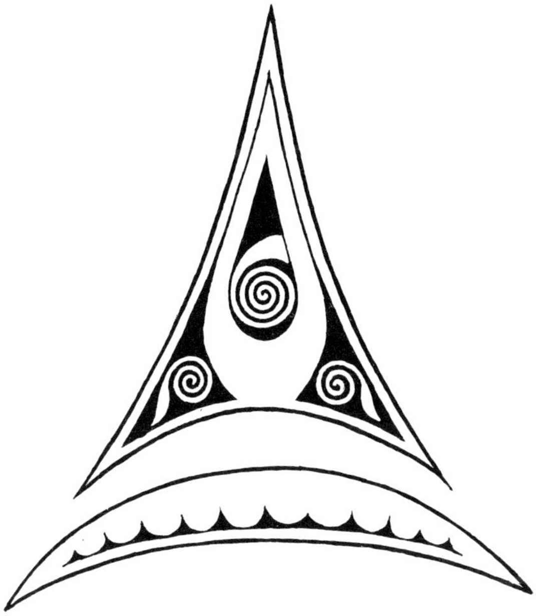

D

21

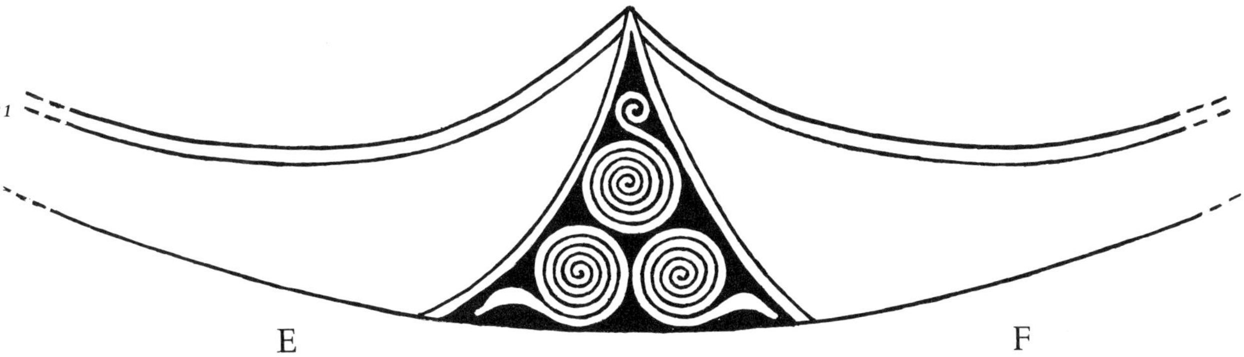

C

E

22

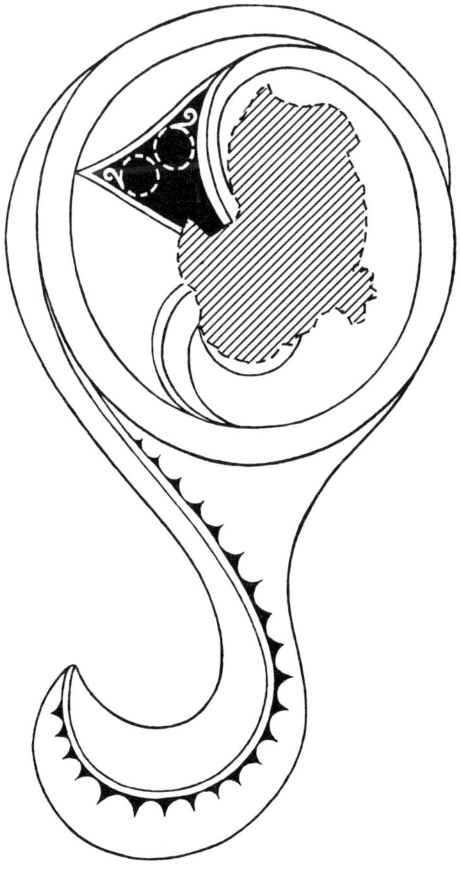

F

23

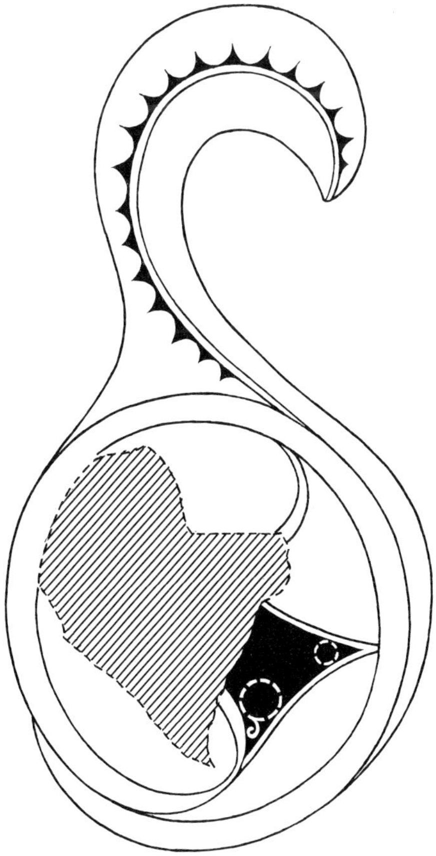

Bibliography

Guide to Antiquities of the Early Iron Age in the Department of British and Mediaeval Antiquities, British Museum, London, 1925. Witham Shield: pp. 101, 105, figs. 113–15. Wandsworth Bosses: p. 106.

Later Prehistoric Antiquities of the British Isles in the British Museum, London, 1953. Witham Shield: p. 68, No. 1, pl. xix, 1. Wandsworth Bosses: p. 70, pl. xx, 1–2.

C. Fox, *Pattern and Purpose*, Cardiff, 1958. Witham Shield: pp. 26–7, frontispiece, pl. 15. Wandsworth Bosses: pp. 25–6, pls. 13, 14b.

P. Jacobsthal, *Burlington Magazine*, 1939, pp. 28–9, pls. B, D (Wandsworth Round Boss only).

J. M. Kemble, *Horae Ferales*, London, 1863. Witham Shield: p. 190, pl. xiv. Wandsworth Bosses: p. 191, pl. xvi.

J. V. S. Megaw, *Art of the European Iron Age*, Bath, 1970. Witham Shield: no. 252, pl. 7. Wandsworth Bosses: no. 247 (Round); no. 255 (Long).

S. R. Meyrick, *Archaeologia* 23 (1831) pp. 92–7, pl. xiii (Witham Shield).

S. Piggott and R. J. C. Atkinson, 'The Torrs Chamfrein', *Archaeologia* 96 (1955), pp. 197–235.

T. G. E. Powell, *Prehistoric Art*, London, 1966. Witham Shield: p. 236, illus. 241–2. Wandsworth Round Boss: p. 234, illus. 238.

N. Sandars, *Prehistoric Art in Europe*, Harmondsworth, 1968, pp. 261–6, pls. 288–91.

M. Spratling, 'The Smiths of South Cadbury', *Current Archaeology* 18 (Jan. 1970), p. 188–91.

CHAPTER TWO

THE BATTERSEA SHIELD

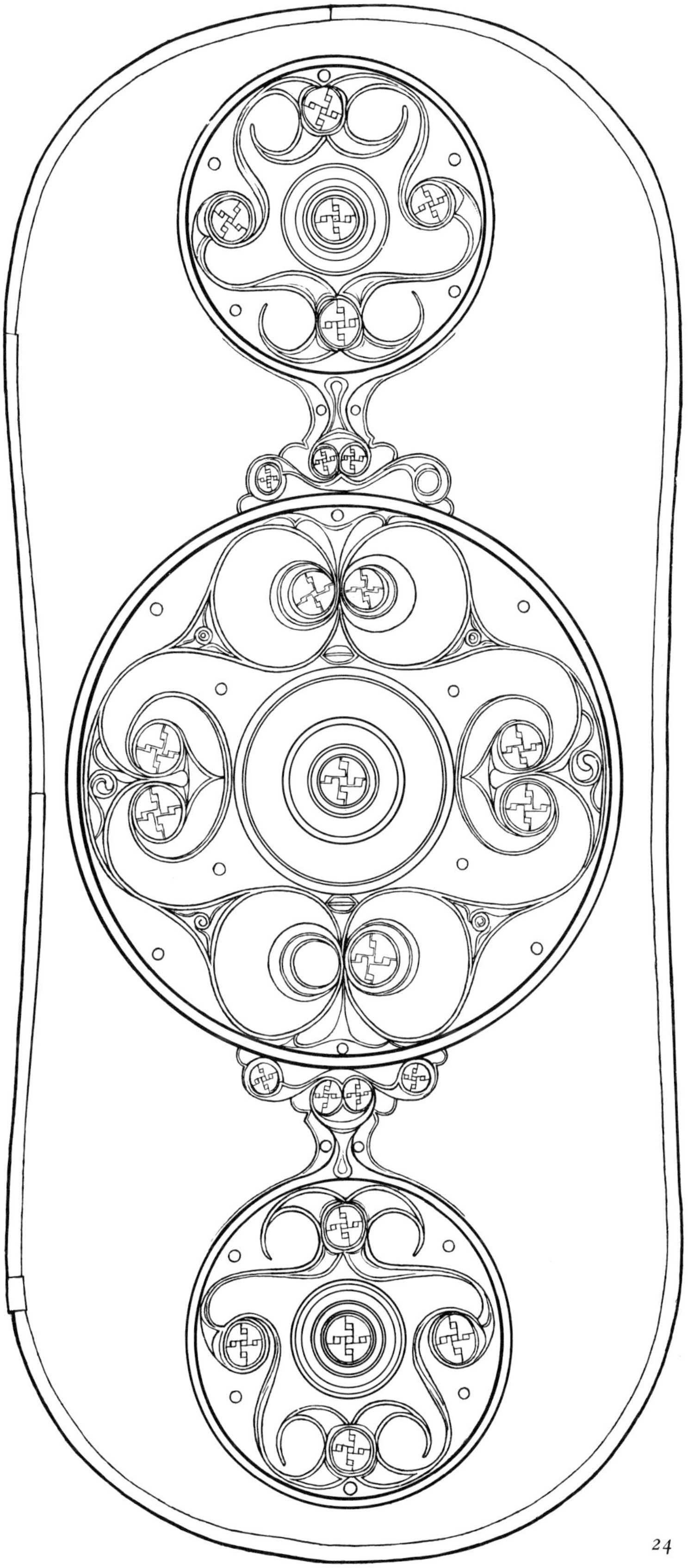

24

X This shield, perhaps the best-known piece of
Early Celtic craftsmanship from Britain, was
recovered from the River Thames at Battersea
in 1857.

What is preserved is the decorated bronze
24, 25 facing for a backing of wood or leather. Its
overall length is 84·5 cm. The main sheet of
bronze is in four quarters, and was secured to
the backing by a U-sectioned binding in five
pieces. The central roundel and each of the
terminal roundels (with its extension joining
it to the central roundel) is a separate piece.
These were secured to the backing by rivets.

32 An openwork bronze plate was found with
the shield, and must have been the covering for
a handle. It is pierced with thirteen small holes
for pins or rivets to hold it to the wood or
leather backing, but these perforations do not
continue through the central roundel. The
length across the grip and the two lateral
openings in the plate is slightly more than the
diameter of the opening at the back of the
central boss; in fact the plate fits the shield.
The grip and openings, however, would only
accommodate a hand of a relatively small
size.

It was at one time suggested that the
Battersea Shield had been gilded, but a recent
careful examination in the British Museum
Research Laboratory has established that no
evidence exists to support this supposition.

The three-roundel layout of the Battersea
25, 3 Shield is shared with the Witham Shield.
Such an arrangement was also undoubtedly
a feature of the shield from which the Wands-
17 worth Long Boss came, and perhaps of the

Polden Hill shield too (p. 63). Moreover, the stylized animal heads placed in corresponding positions on the Battersea and Witham Shields are decorative features which emphasize their common tradition. On the Battersea Shield
28 the heads face outwards and are placed between the central and terminal roundels; on the Witham Shield they face inwards and are placed at the point of contact between the central rib and each terminal boss. On the Witham Shield the heads are embossed, whilst
28 on the Battersea Shield they are part embossed and part represented by a pair of red glass studs, with another pair perhaps representing horns. Other features common to both shields
35 are the snail bosses and ornamentation by red-coloured studs (though of very different types). The pairs of studs on the axis of the Battersea
25 Shield within the central roundel surely represent the eyes in owl-like faces.

X The type of glass used for the studs on the Battersea Shield cannot have been melted or fused into place because if it is heated to a temperature sufficiently high for it to flow easily, the red colour disappears and a green glass is formed. The red glass also changes colour from red to black unless it is heated out of contact with the air. Dr A. E. Werner and Miss M. Bimson of the British Museum Research Laboratory reported that, 'with these limitations in mind it is easy to visualize how the studs on the shield were made. A circular domed fretted piece of metal was made and fitted into a similarly shaped hemispherical depression in a mould of suitable composition (fired clay). The mould was then filled with fragments of the opaque red glass and heated in a reducing atmosphere until the glass just began to soften. The mould was then removed from the furnace and the glass pressed into the fretted piece of metal from the back by means of a suitably shaped tool, perhaps a piece of bronze or even hard charcoal. After cooling, the glass would be backed with pitch or bitumen, a hole drilled through the centre, and the resulting stud riveted into place on the shield. The red material cannot be regarded as a true enamel, nor as glass cut to shape and inserted using a cloisonné technique'.

The studs on the Battersea Shield are made in the same way as those from the Hertford Heath and Lexden burials, both of which must date from the middle of the first century AD. These very distinctive features must be of prime importance in dating the shield, and a date during the first half of the first century AD would be consistent both with the evidence of the studs and with that of its style of ornament.

The embossed ornament on the roundels *26–28*
includes scrolls and palmette derivatives familiar from other pieces of Celtic craftsmanship, and technically is superbly accomplished. Nevertheless, its almost mechanical quality of *25*
precision and its linear nature may be considered alien to the main British tradition of the first century BC and the first century AD. Roman influence may even be discerned, and one expects the Battersea Shield to come very late in the sequence of Early Celtic art in Britain.

If the dating proposed by Piggott and Atkinson (p. 21) is accepted for the Witham and Wandsworth pieces, and if the dating here proposed for the Battersea Shield is also accepted, an interval of some two centuries must be allowed between the manufacture of the Witham Shield and the Wandsworth Long Boss and that of the Battersea Shield. A persistence of basic shield design in the South-east over this period is surely not impossible. Indeed, the difference in detail between the pieces demands a fairly long time-range.

Technical Note

An examination of the red ornamental inlays on bronze objects of the British Iron Age has recently been made by M. J. Hughes of the British Museum Research Laboratory. Thirty-three specimens were analysed in order to determine the percentage of cuprous oxide (which gives the red colour) and of lead

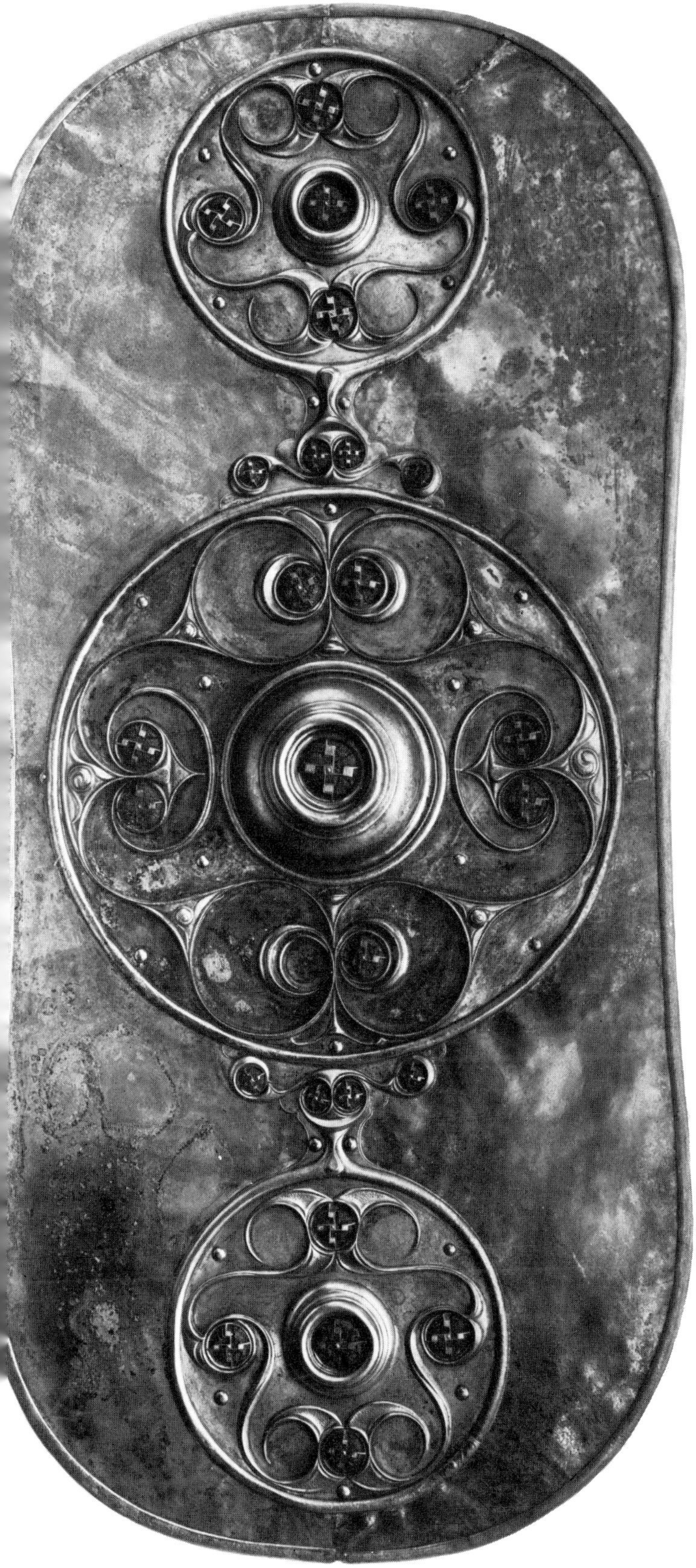

26

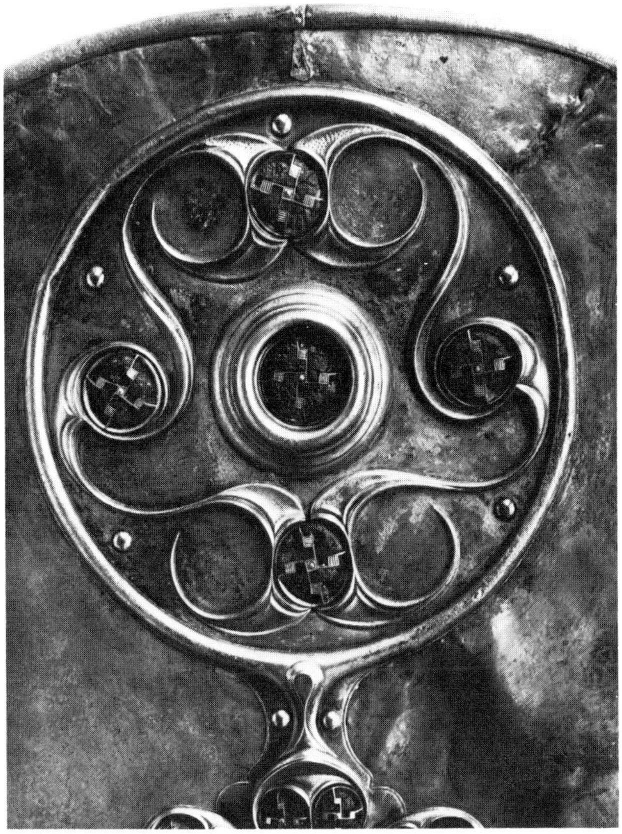

27

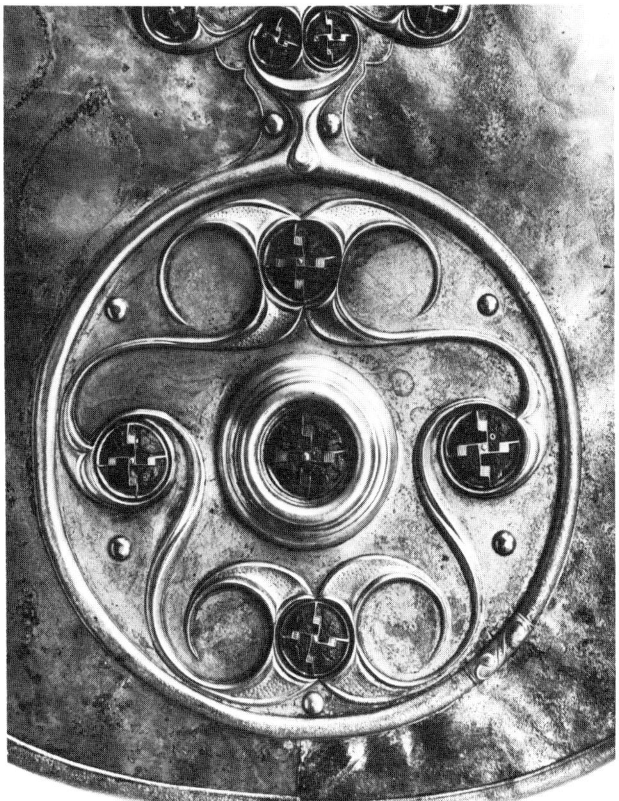

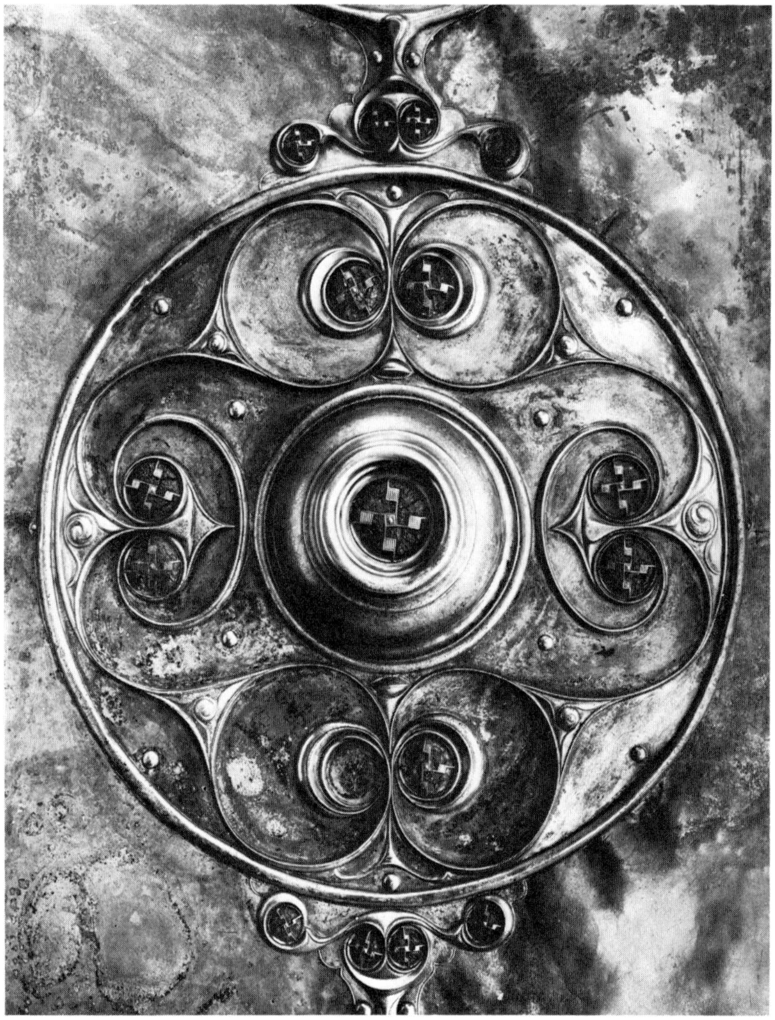

28

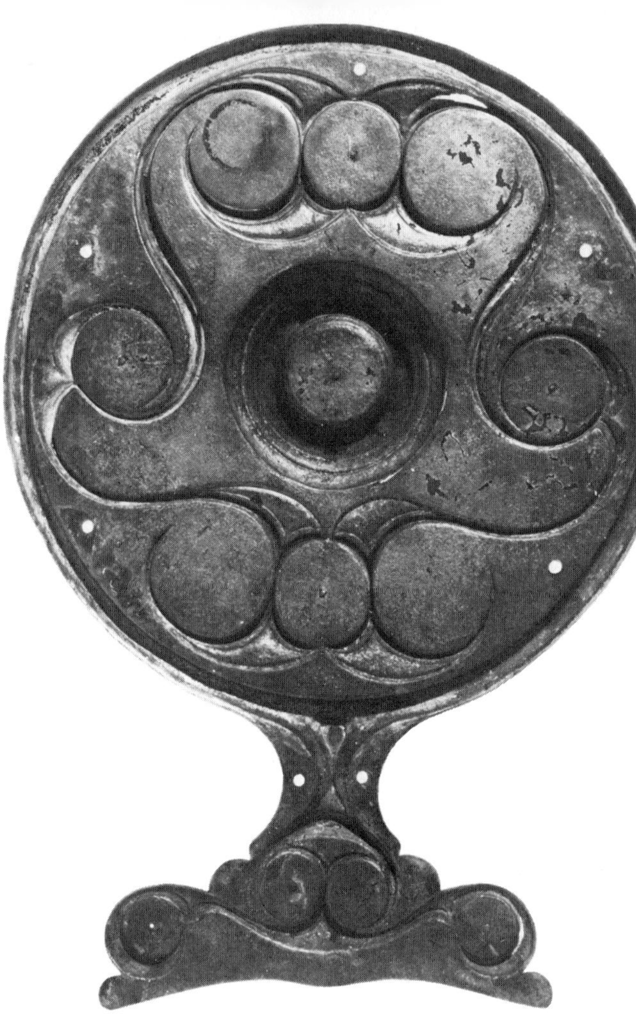

29

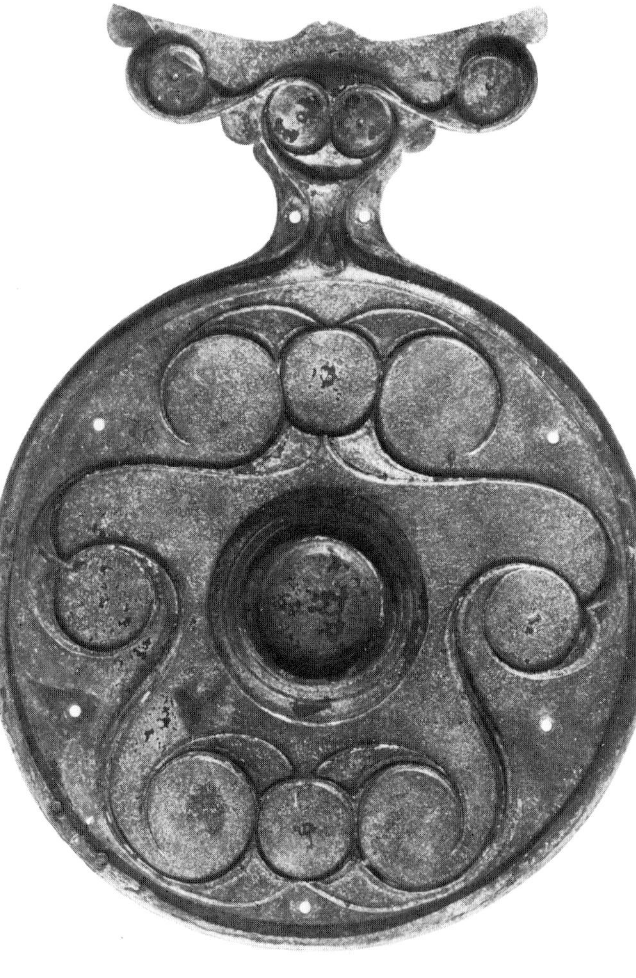

30

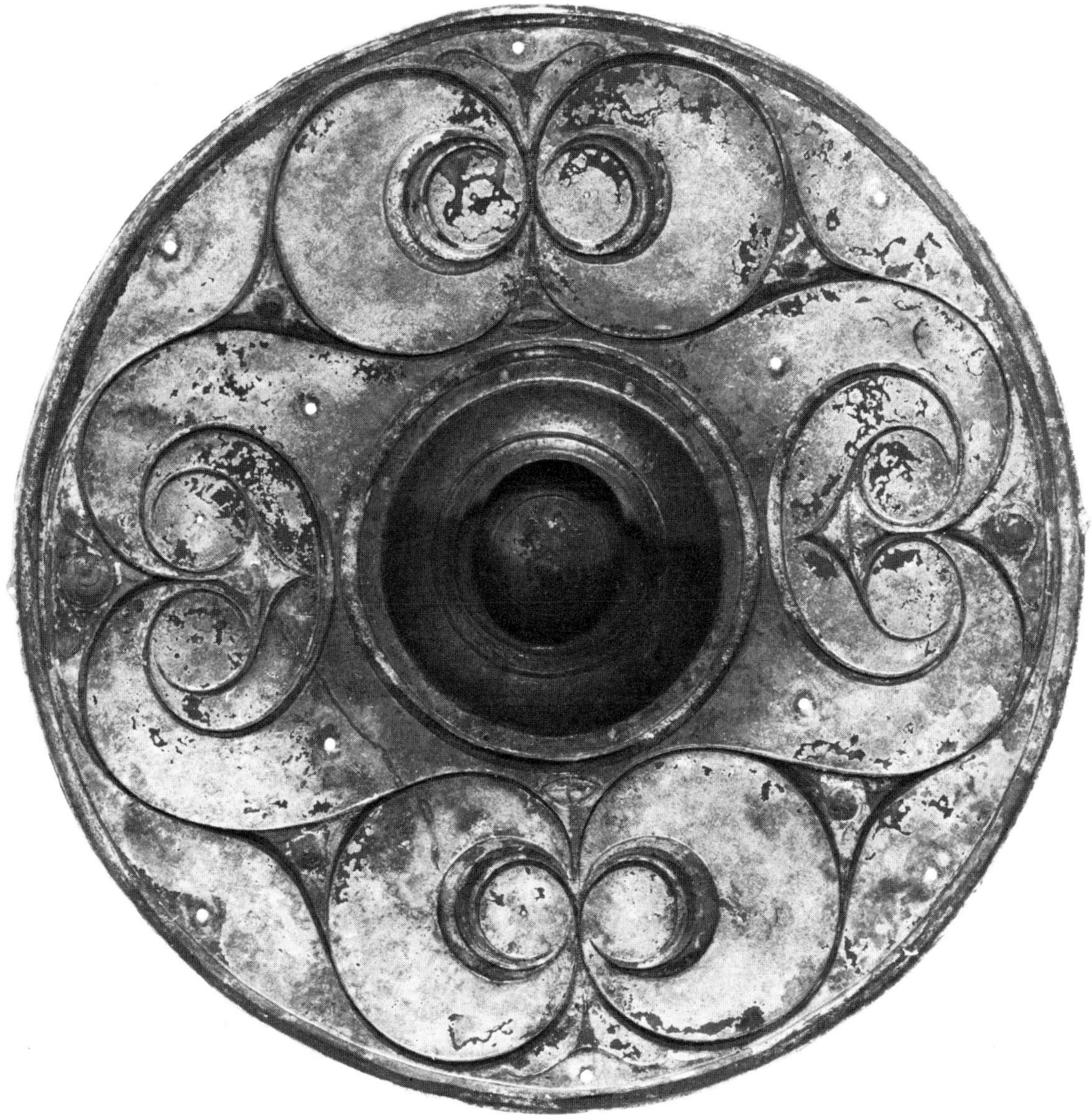

31

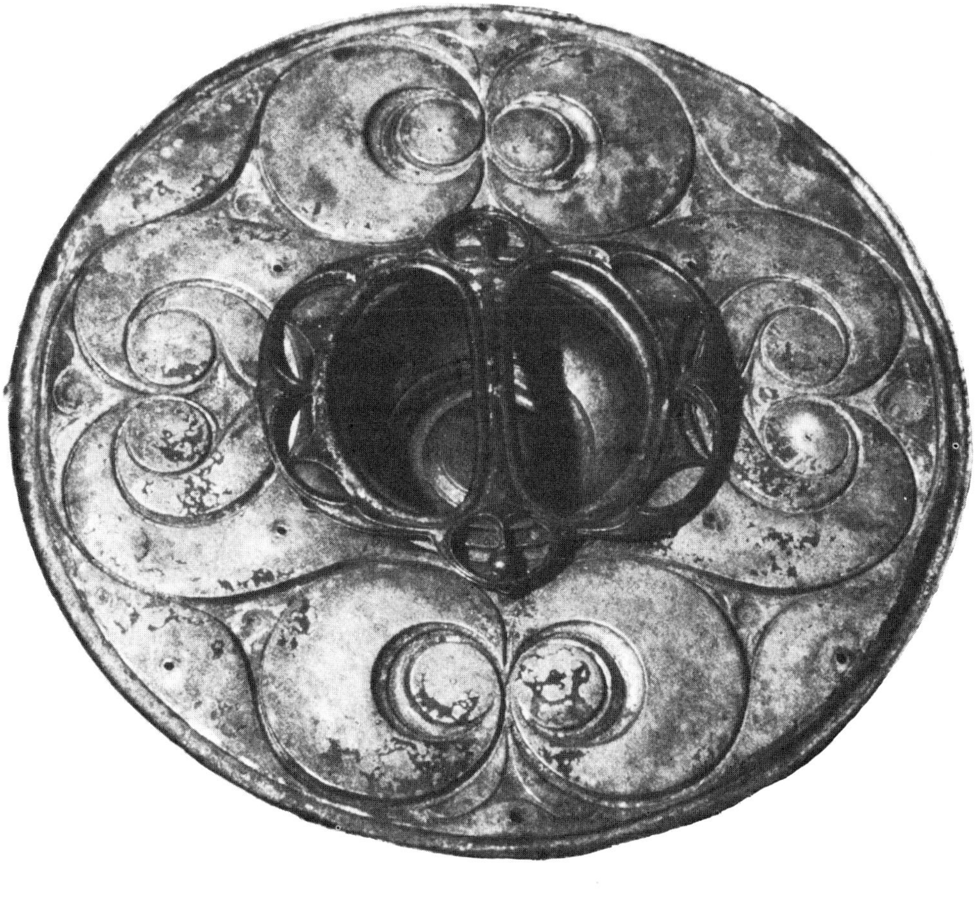

32

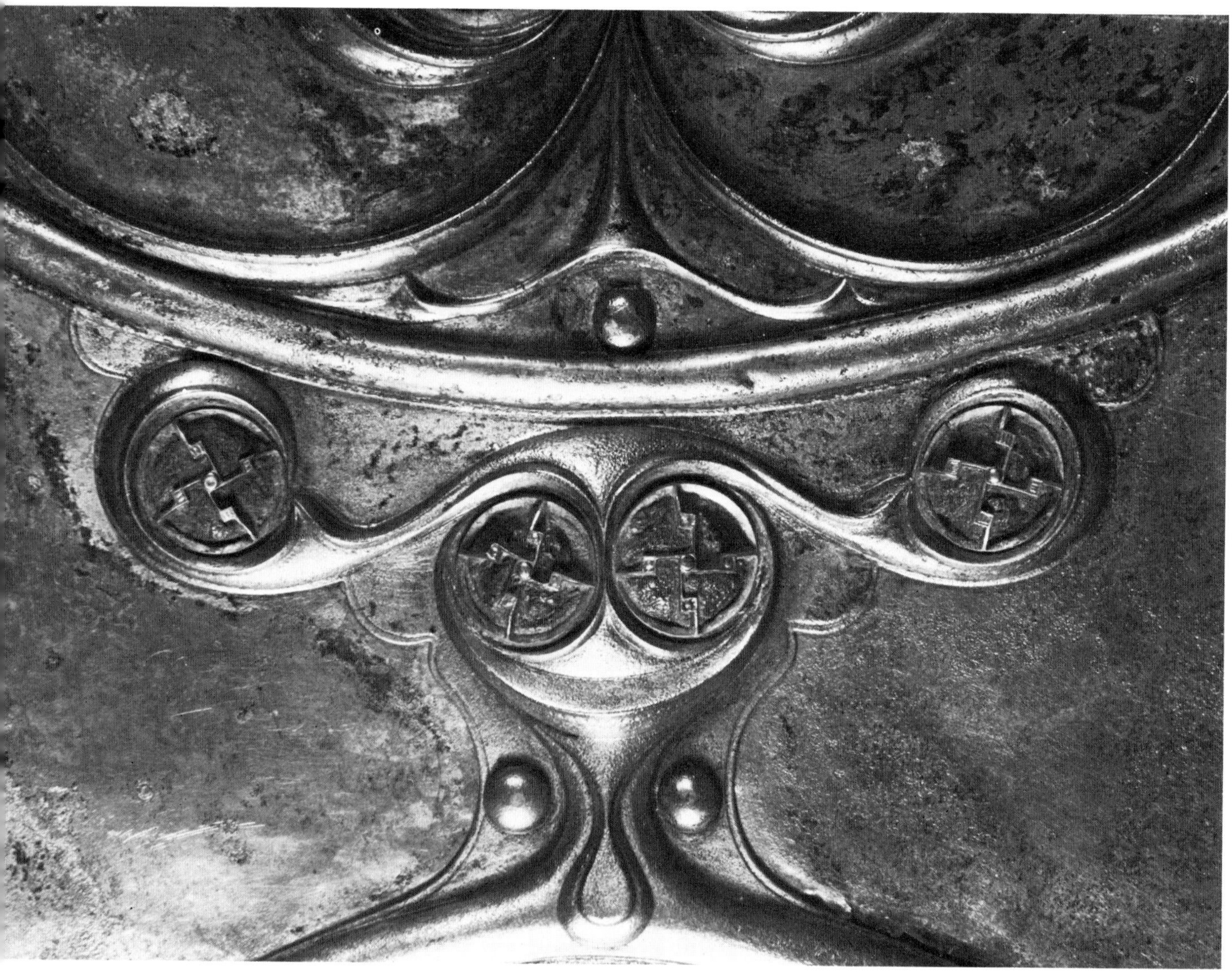

33

oxide in each. The composition of all the examples followed a uniform pattern with average values of about 7 per cent cuprous oxide and 25 per cent lead oxide. This constancy in composition must be deliberate. A block of raw glass found at Tara Hill is of the same chemical composition as the samples from Iron Age bronzes and it is significant that the lead isotope ratios in the Tara Hill glass suggest that the lead in it came from Italy.

The uniformity in composition of specimens of red glass in the British Iron Age suggests that its production was concentrated in a limited number of centres. Such centres were probably in the Mediterranean area. 'The raw glass would then have reached Britain and Northern Europe through trade, where it could be broken down into smaller lumps and used by a glassworker to decorate the bronzes of this period'.

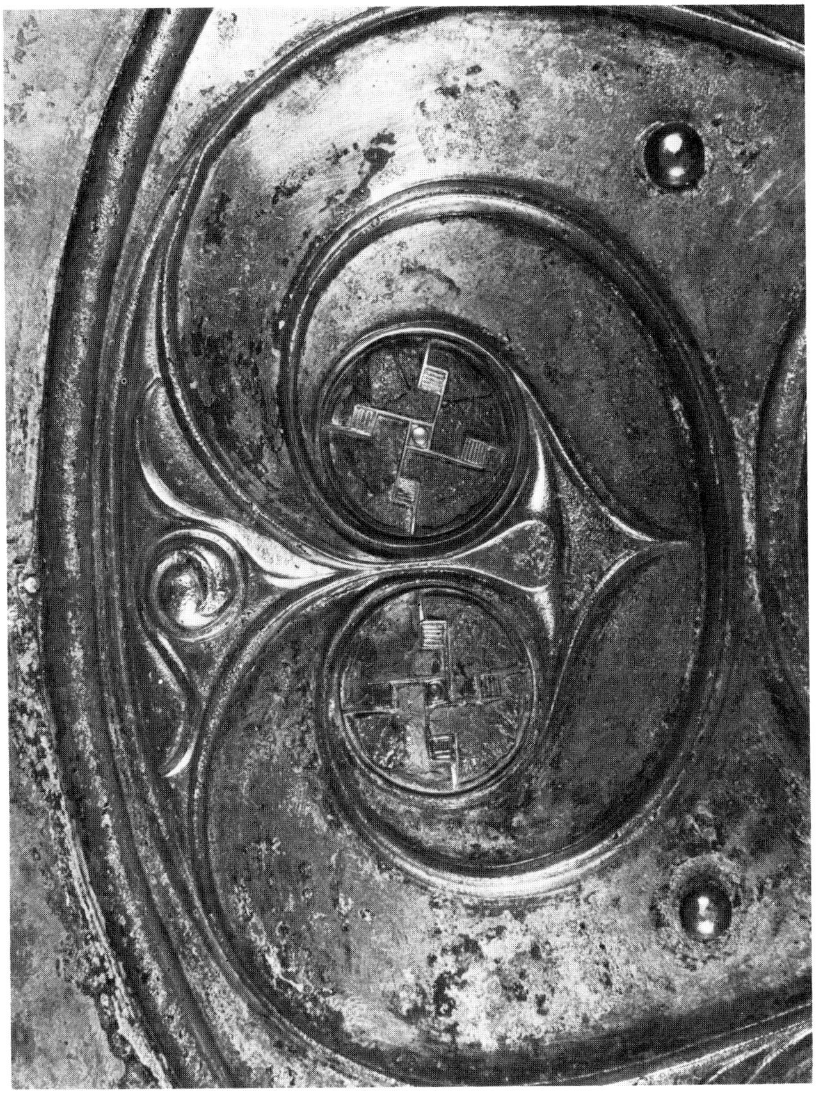

34

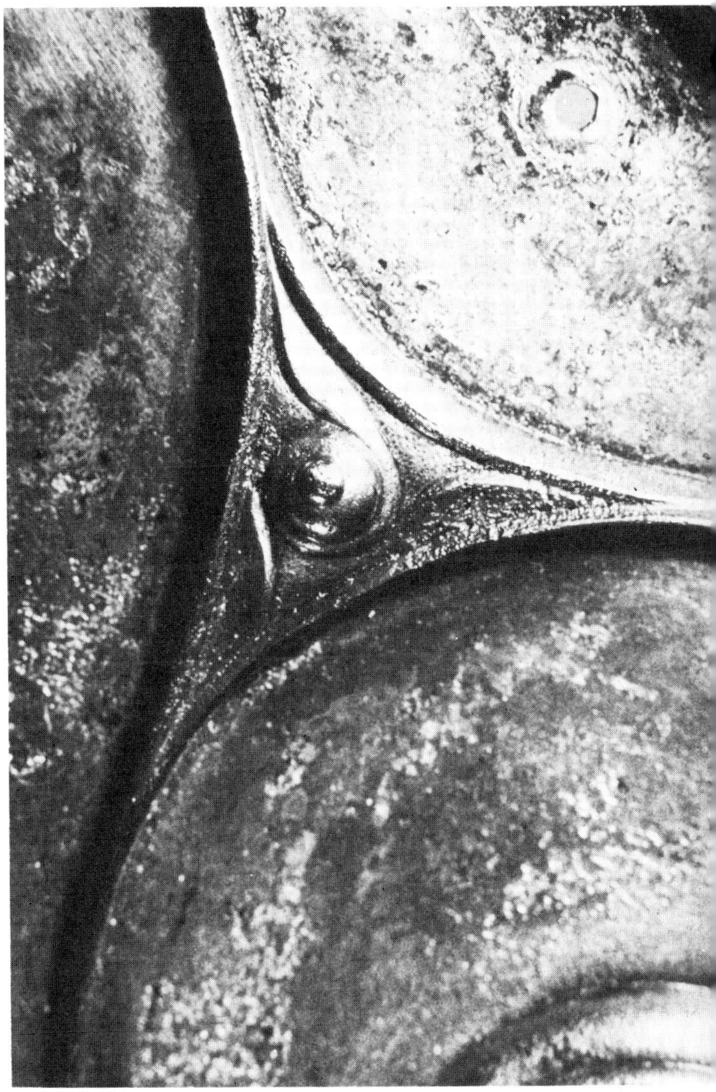

35

Bibliography

Guide to Antiquities of the Early Iron Age in the Department of British and Mediaeval Antiquities, British Museum, London, 1925, p. 106, frontispiece.

Later Prehistoric Antiquities of the British Isles, London, 1953, p. 68, pl. xix (2).

C. Fox, *Pattern and Purpose*, Cardiff, 1958, pp. 27ff., pls. 14a, 16–17.

J. V. S. Megaw, *Art of the European Iron Age*, Bath, 1970, no. 253.

J. M. Kemble, *Horae Ferales*, London, 1863, pl. xv, pp. 190–91.

M. J. Hughes, 'A technical study of opaque red glass of the Iron Age in Britain', *Proc. Prehist. Soc.* 1972, pp. 98ff.

CHAPTER THREE

THE THAMES HELMET

This famous horned helmet was recovered *36*
from the River Thames at Waterloo Bridge, and was deposited in the British Museum on loan by the Thames Conservancy in 1868.

The cap is made from two pieces of bronze sheet, front and rear, riveted together, while below the front part extends a separate cres- *37, 38*
cent-shaped piece. The edge is strengthened with a U-section binding held in position by riveted clips. Each horn consists of a cone of bronze sheet riveted up the side, with terminal *37, 39,*
knobs cast in position (the distance between the knobs is 42·5 cm.). One horn has been *48, 49*
broken away and replaced. At each side is a ring fitting for a chin-strap or cheekpiece and, *40, 41*
running up from these round the base of each horn and along the junction between the two main parts of the cap, is a decorative strip embellished with a row of rivets or cast studs with ball heads; most of these are solely decorative in purpose, and the ornamental strip is secured to the cap of the helmet by flat-headed rivets.

The strip overlies part of the repoussé ornament. Small holes irregularly spaced round the edge of the cap were perhaps to secure a lining.

The ornament of the helmet consists of five (originally six) bronze studs, cross-scored to *42, 43*
take red enamel, and a repoussé design on the front and back. This design is of the same type as that on the great torc from Snettisham (p. 57). On each the same elements are employed, and on each the design is asymmetric. Whereas on the Snettisham torc, however, the design is compact, on the helmet it is drawn out and includes 'birds' head' and 'leaf' motifs *51, 52*
reminiscent of the Wandsworth Round Boss (p. 14).

A date in the first century BC for the Thames helmet is endorsed by its cross-scored and enamelled studs; such studs are characteristic of the La Tène III period on the Continent. One wonders whether there may be a parallelism between these studs and the roundels of concentric ridges on the Snettisham torc and the Cairnmuir terminal.

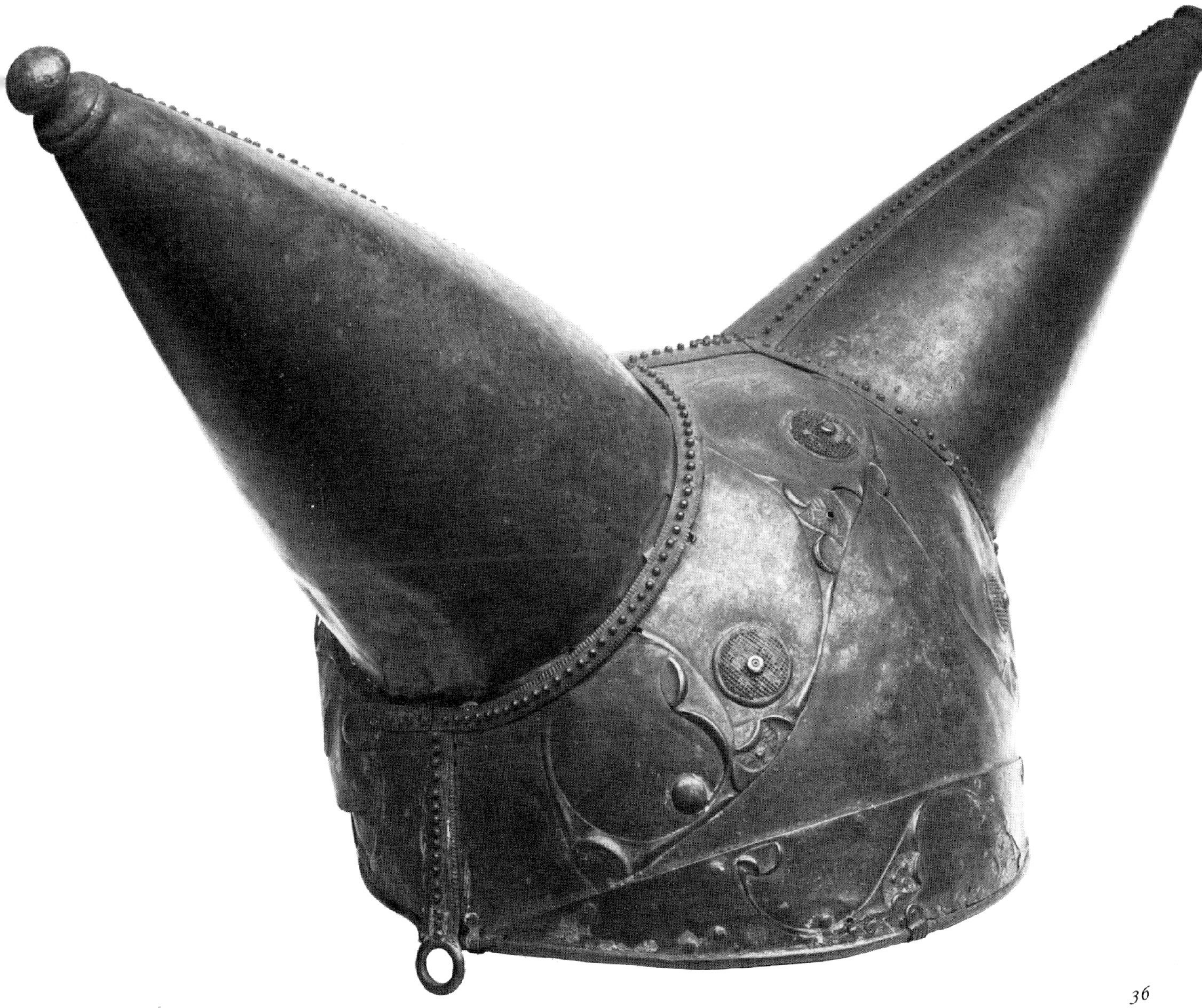

36

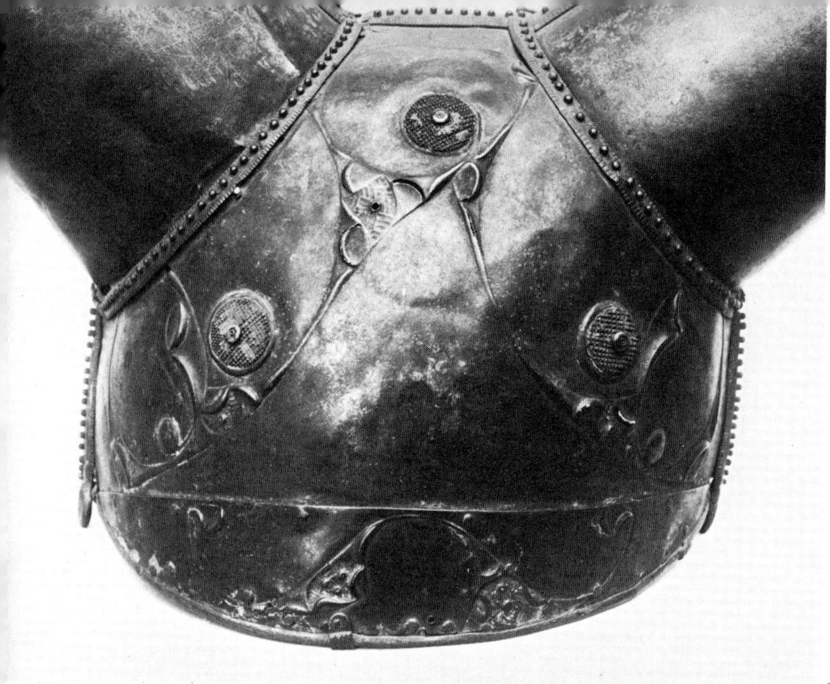

37

42 43

▶

44 45

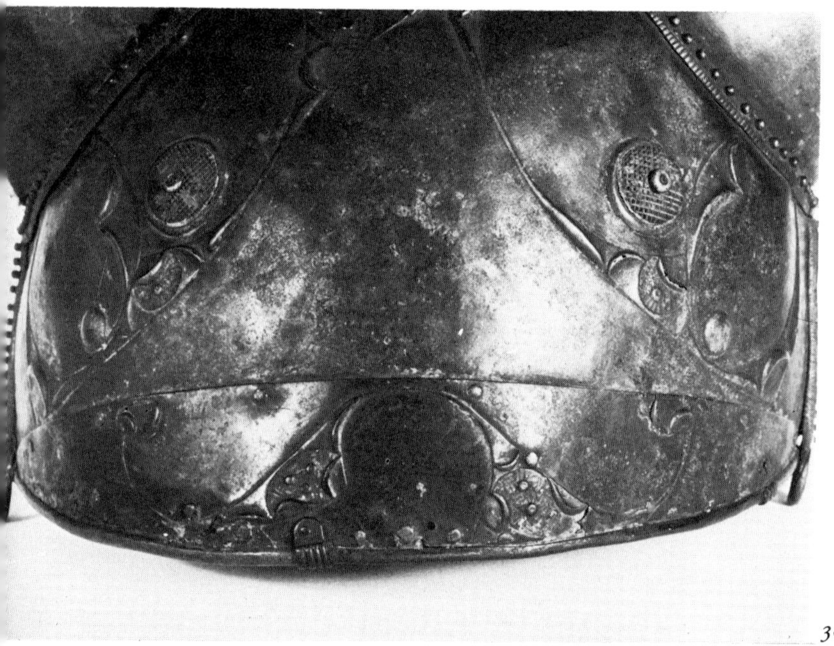

38

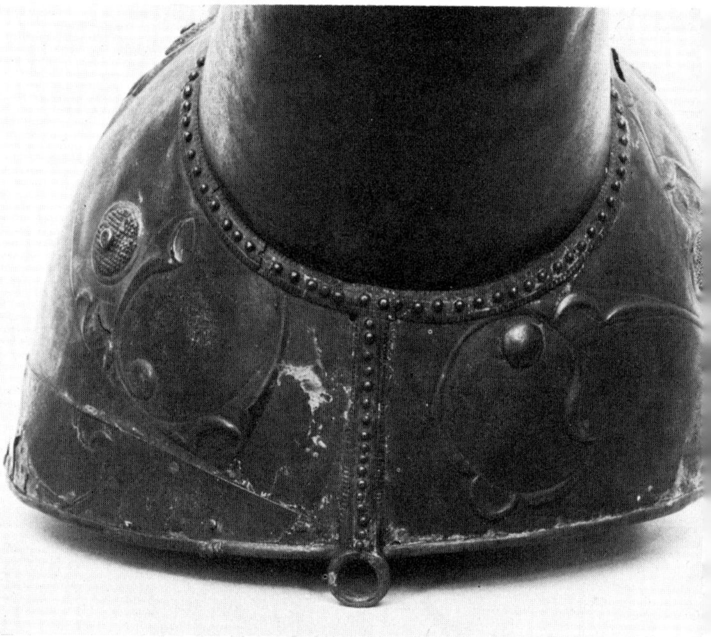

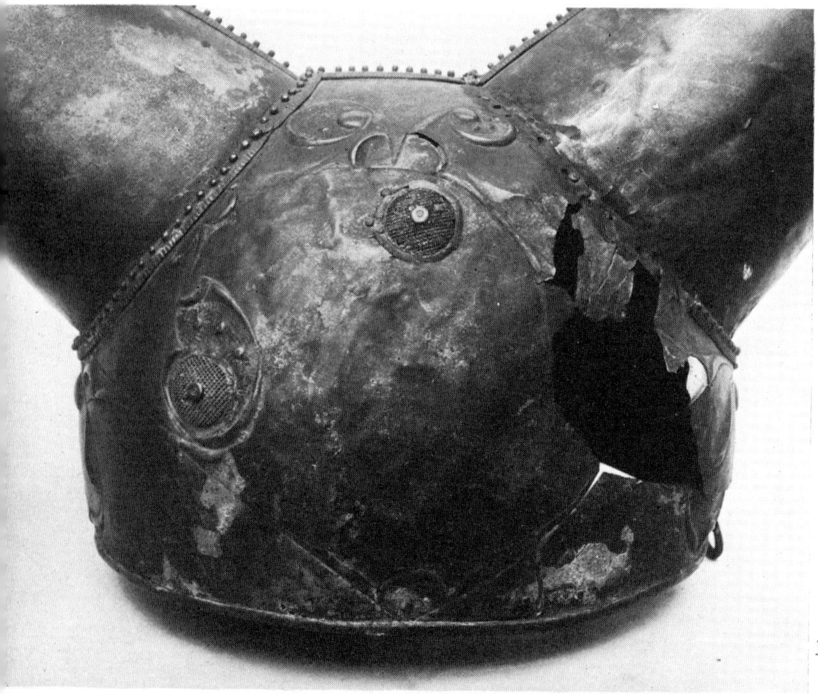

39

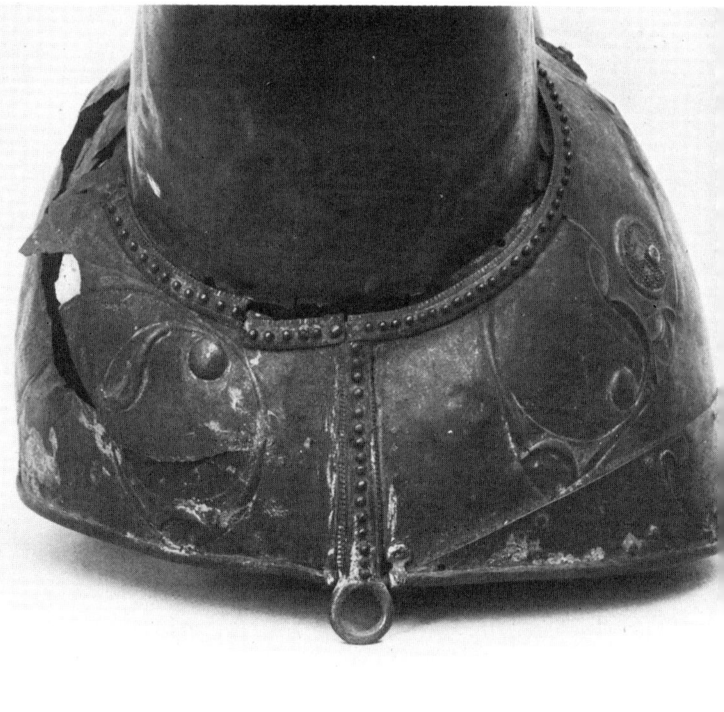

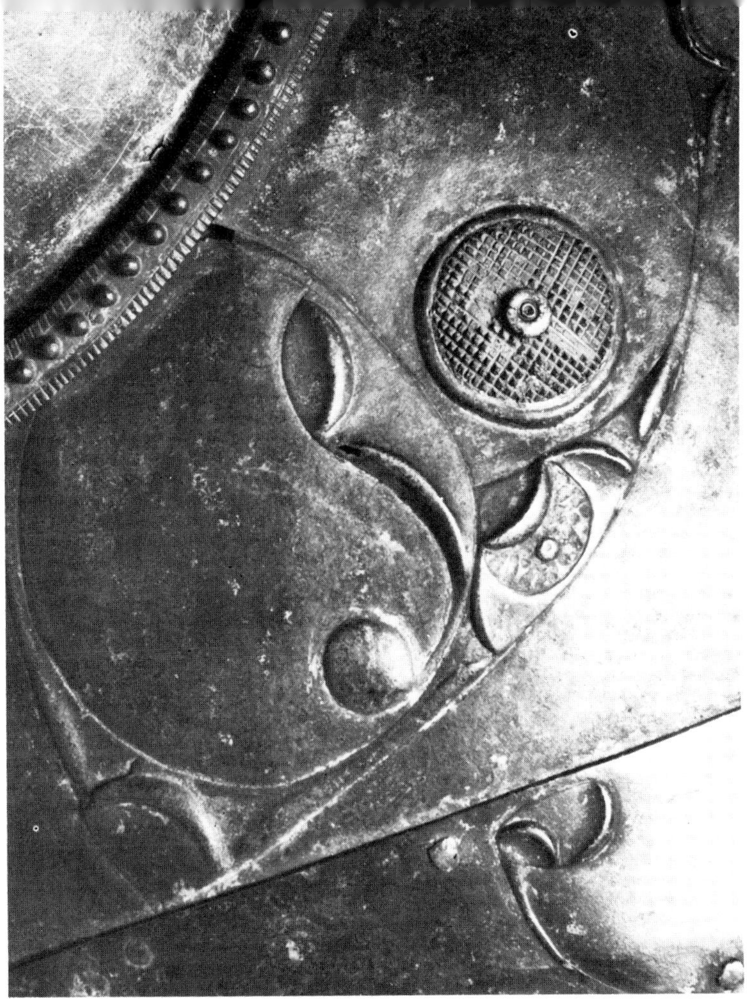
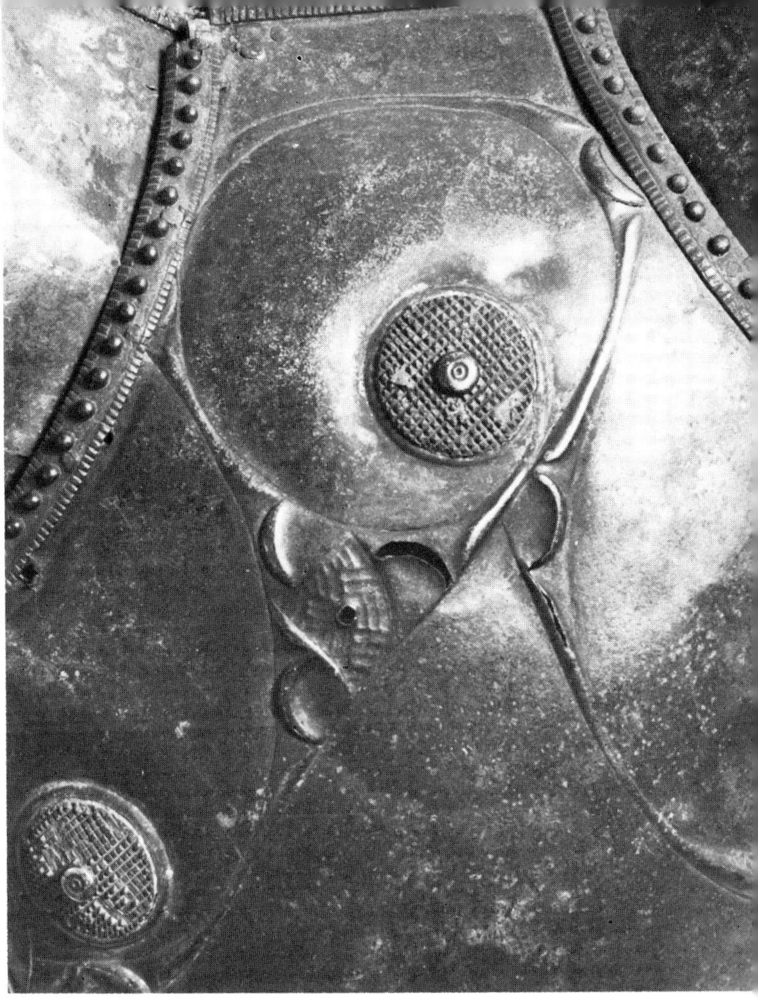
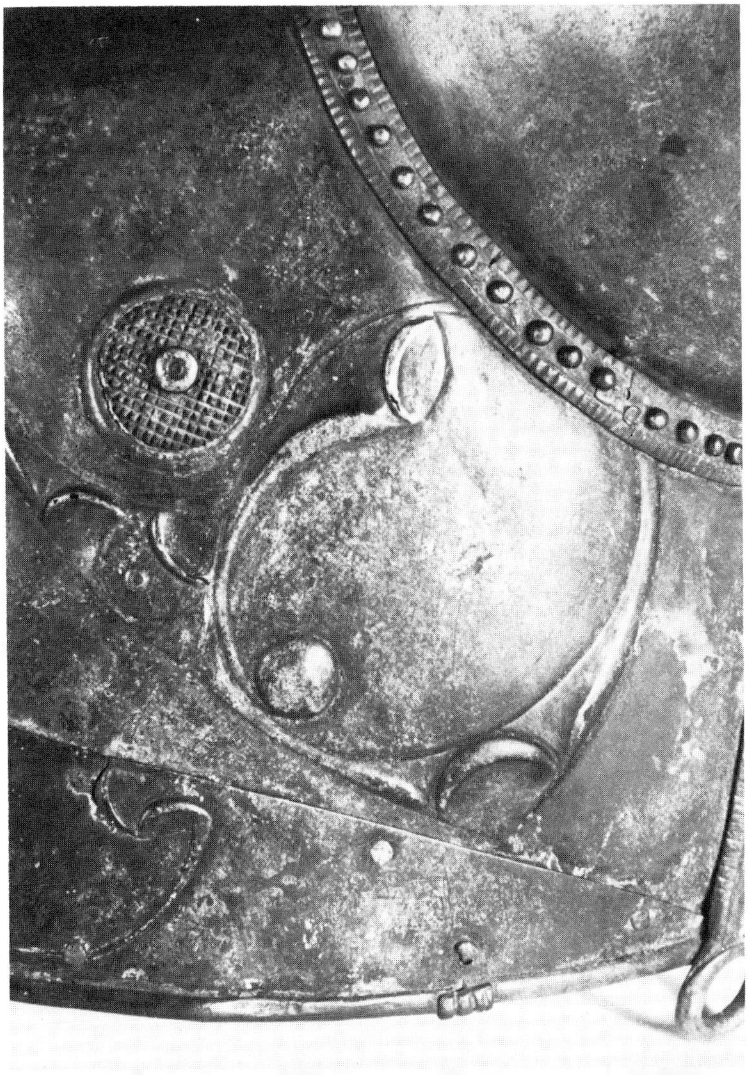
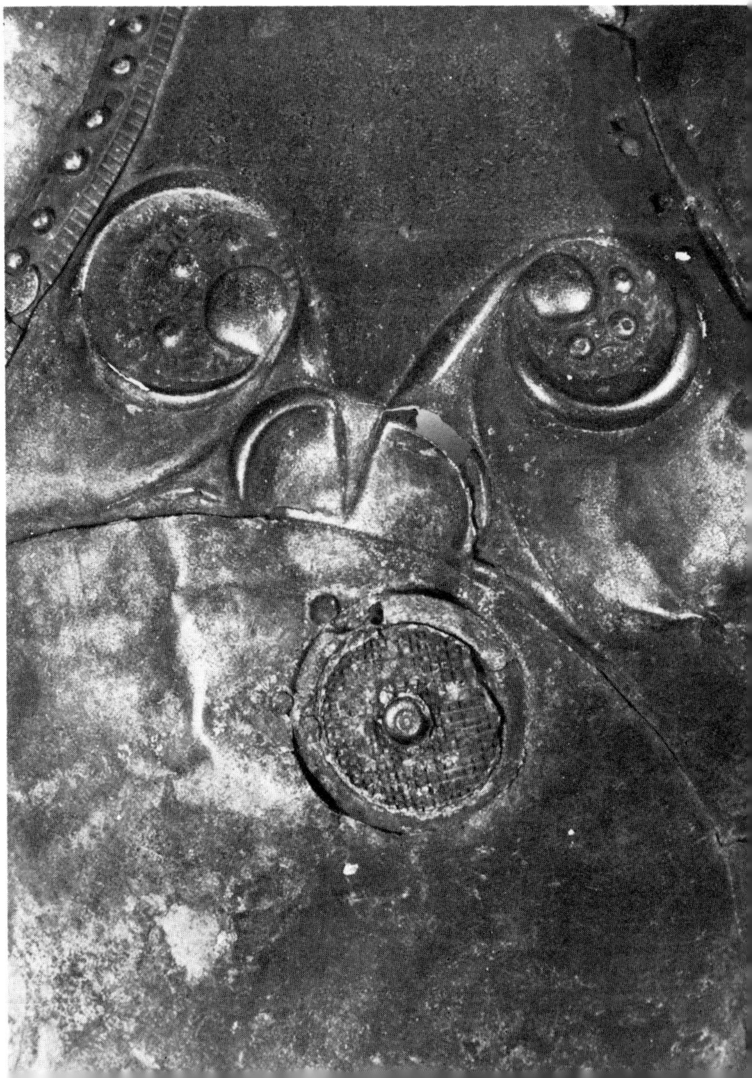

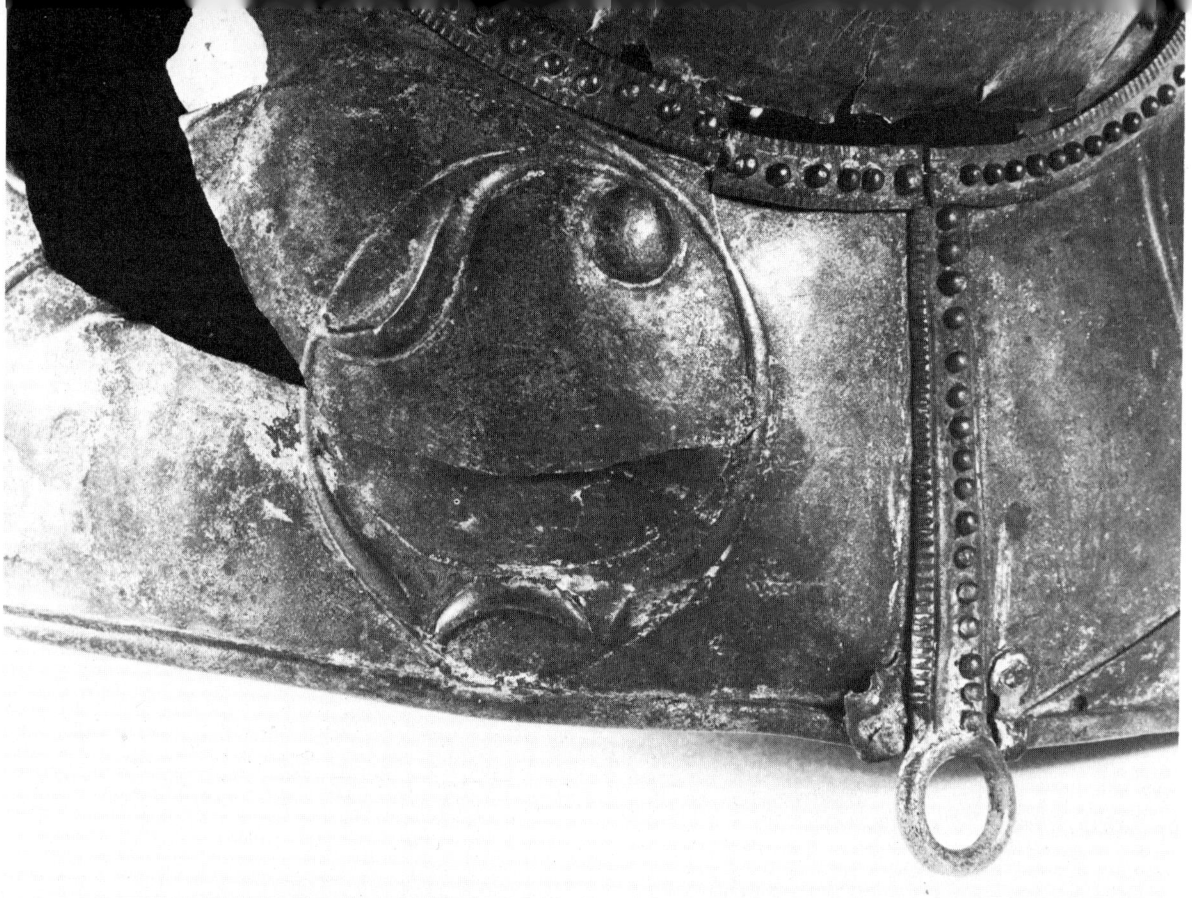

46

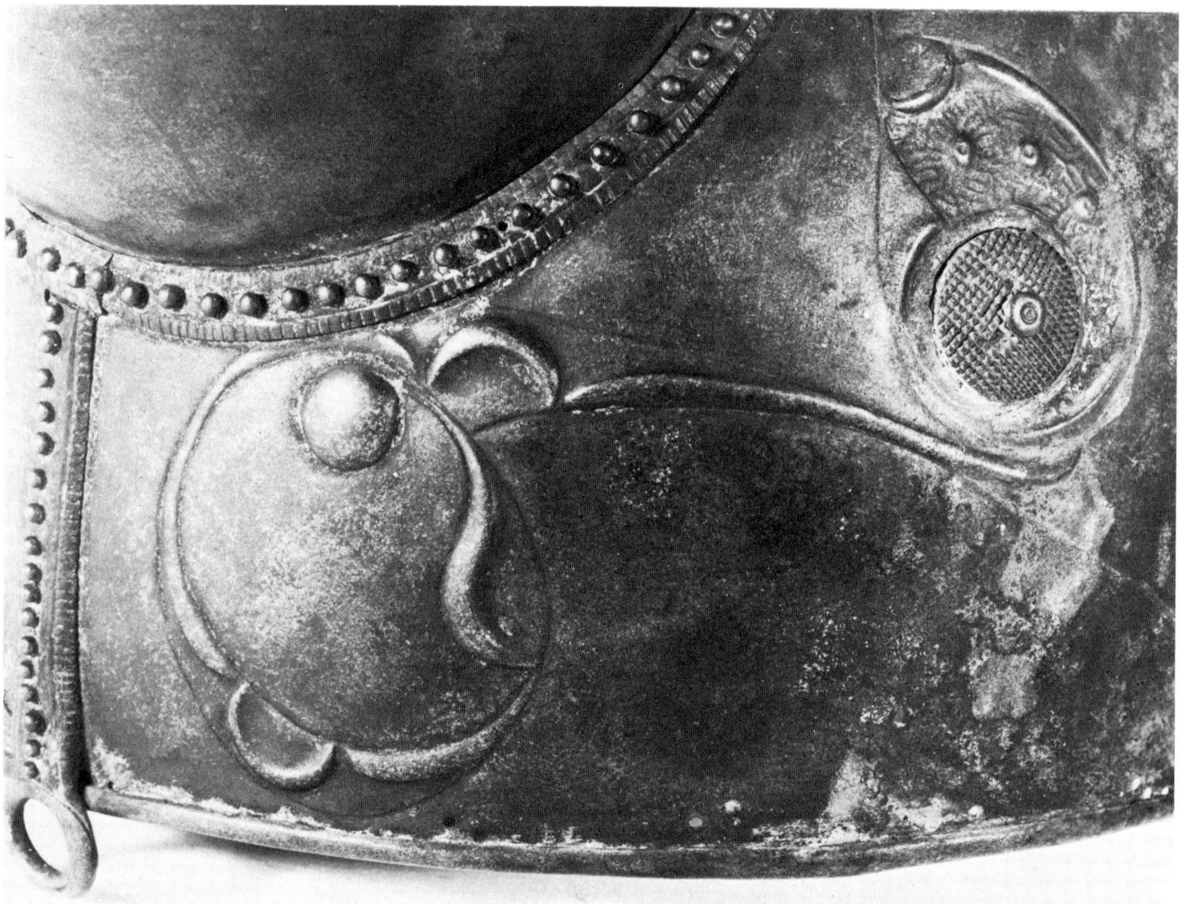

47

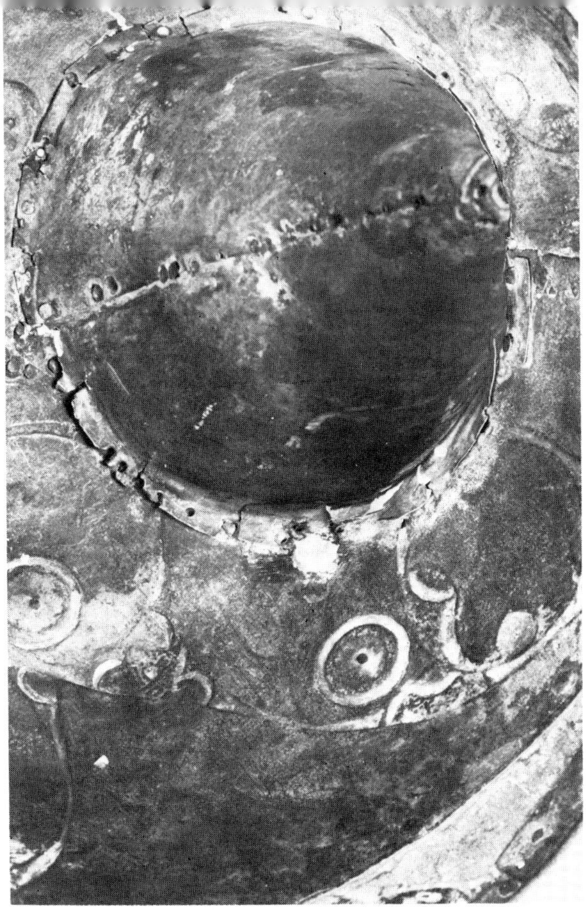
48

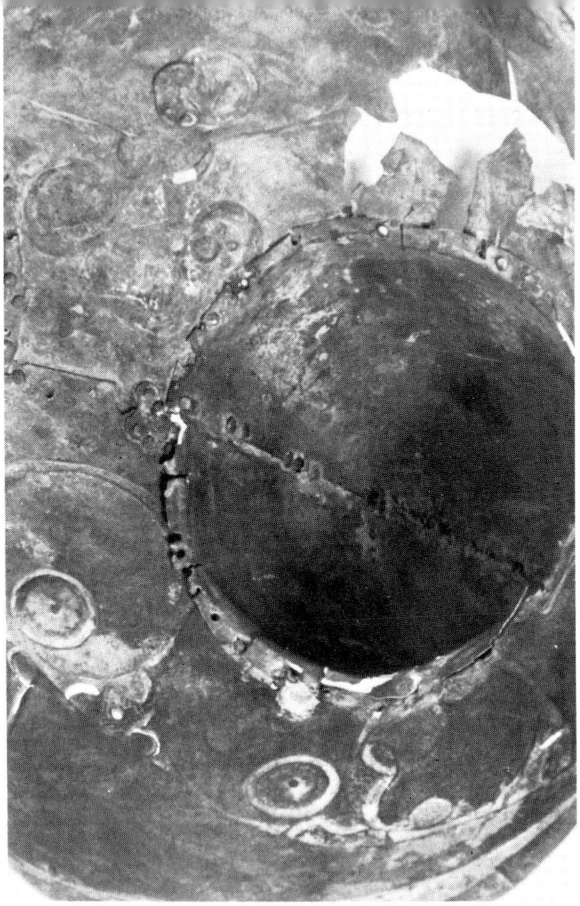
49

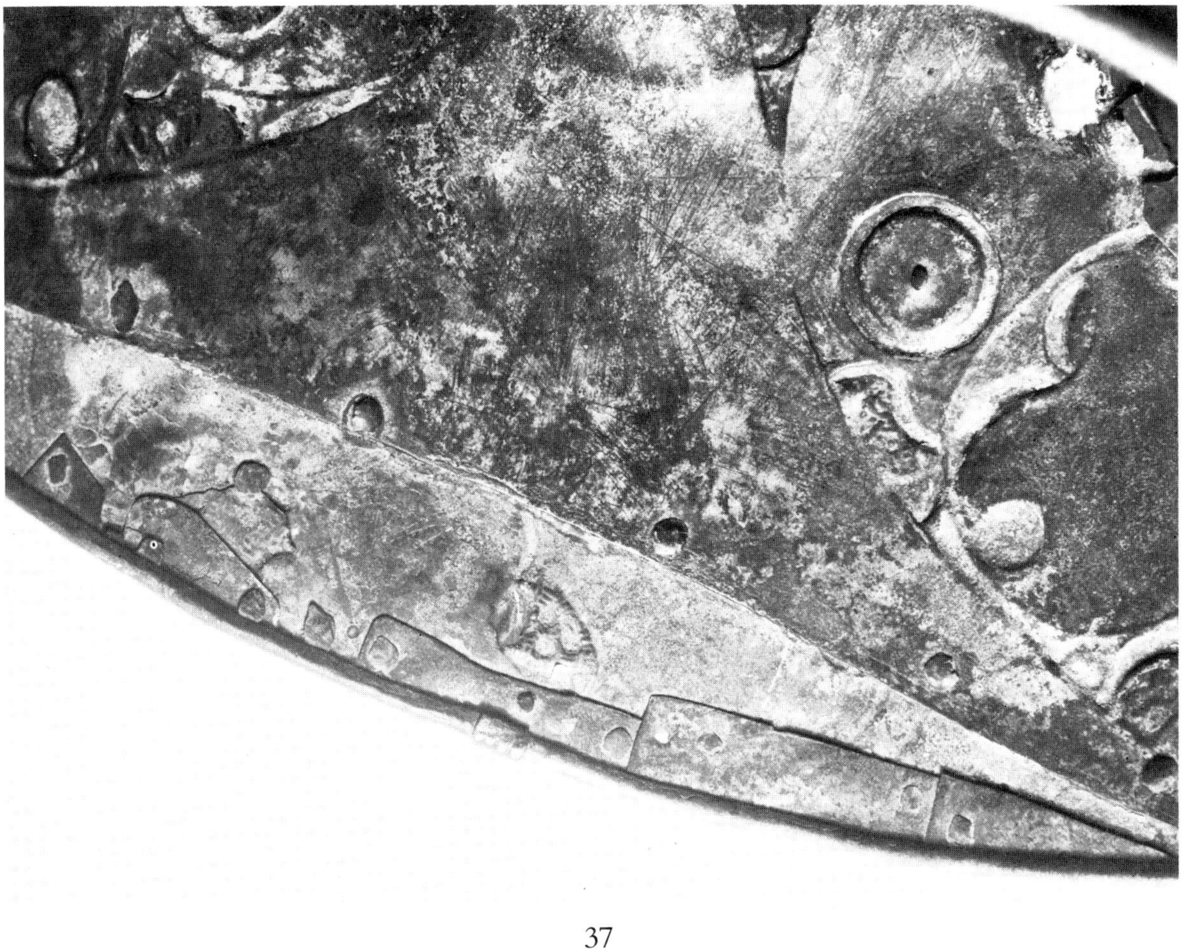
50

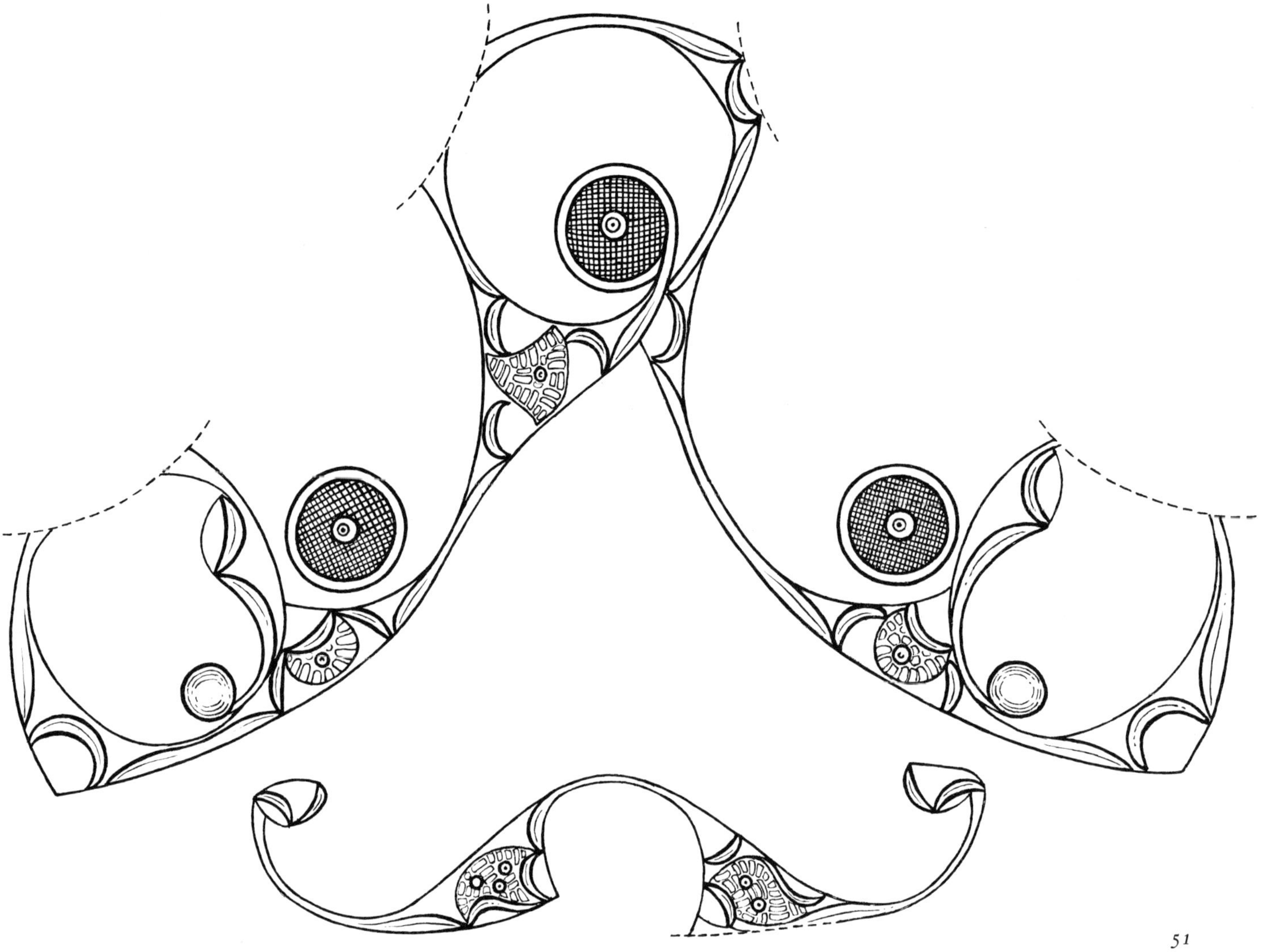

51

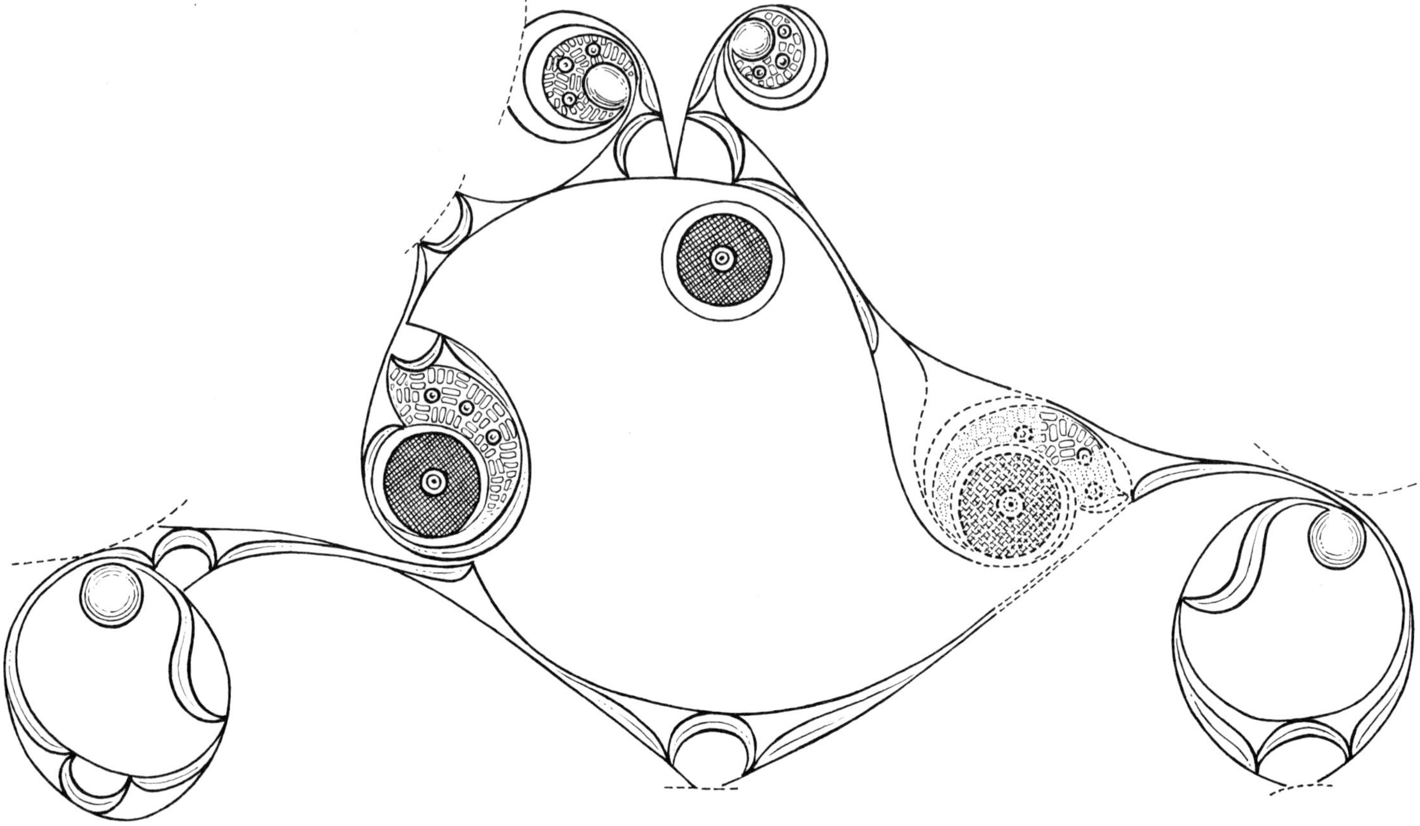

52

OTHER HORNED HELMETS

In considering very briefly other horned helmets which may be related to the Thames helmet, I have to acknowledge the help given by Dr Graham Ritchie, who has very kindly allowed me to read his unpublished doctoral thesis on *Celtic Defensive Weaponry in Britain and its Continental Background.*

Diodorus Siculus, writing in the first century BC describes horned helmets worn by Celtic warriors. The actual helmets do not survive (perhaps because they were made of leather), but their use in La Tène times is confirmed by a number of representations, notably on Roman monuments of the first century BC in the south of France at Orange, La Brague, or in a sculpture from St Remy which is in the Vatican Museum. A bronze figurine of the third century BC from near Rome shows a Celtic barbarian wearing a horned helmet at an even earlier date than the sculptures. The Gundestrup cauldron (in the Danish National Museum, Copenhagen) demonstrates, from a native point of view, the use of horned helmets among the Celts around 100 BC.

It is difficult to accept the Thames helmet as a functional piece of battle equipment. It is of frail construction and does not fit the head satisfactorily: it was surely intended as a ritual article. This character is endorsed by its finding in the river, where it most likely came as a votive deposit.

Bibliography

J. W. Brailsford, 'Notes on the Battersea Shield and two Iron Age helmets from Britain', *Acts of the IV International Congress of Pre- and Protohistoric Sciences*, Madrid, 1954, p. 759.

Guide to Antiquities of the Early Iron Age in the Department of British and Mediaeval Antiquities, British Museum, London, 1925, p. 107, fig. 116.

Later Prehistoric Antiquities of the British Isles, London, 1953, p. 68, pl. xviii.

C. Fox, *Pattern and Purpose*, Cardiff, 1958, p. 49, fig. 36a, b.

A. W. Franks, *Proc. Soc. Ants.*, 2 ser. 3, 1864–7, pp. 342ff.

J. V. S. Megaw, *Art of the European Iron Age*, Bath, 1970, no. 294.

CHAPTER FOUR

THE MEYRICK HELMET

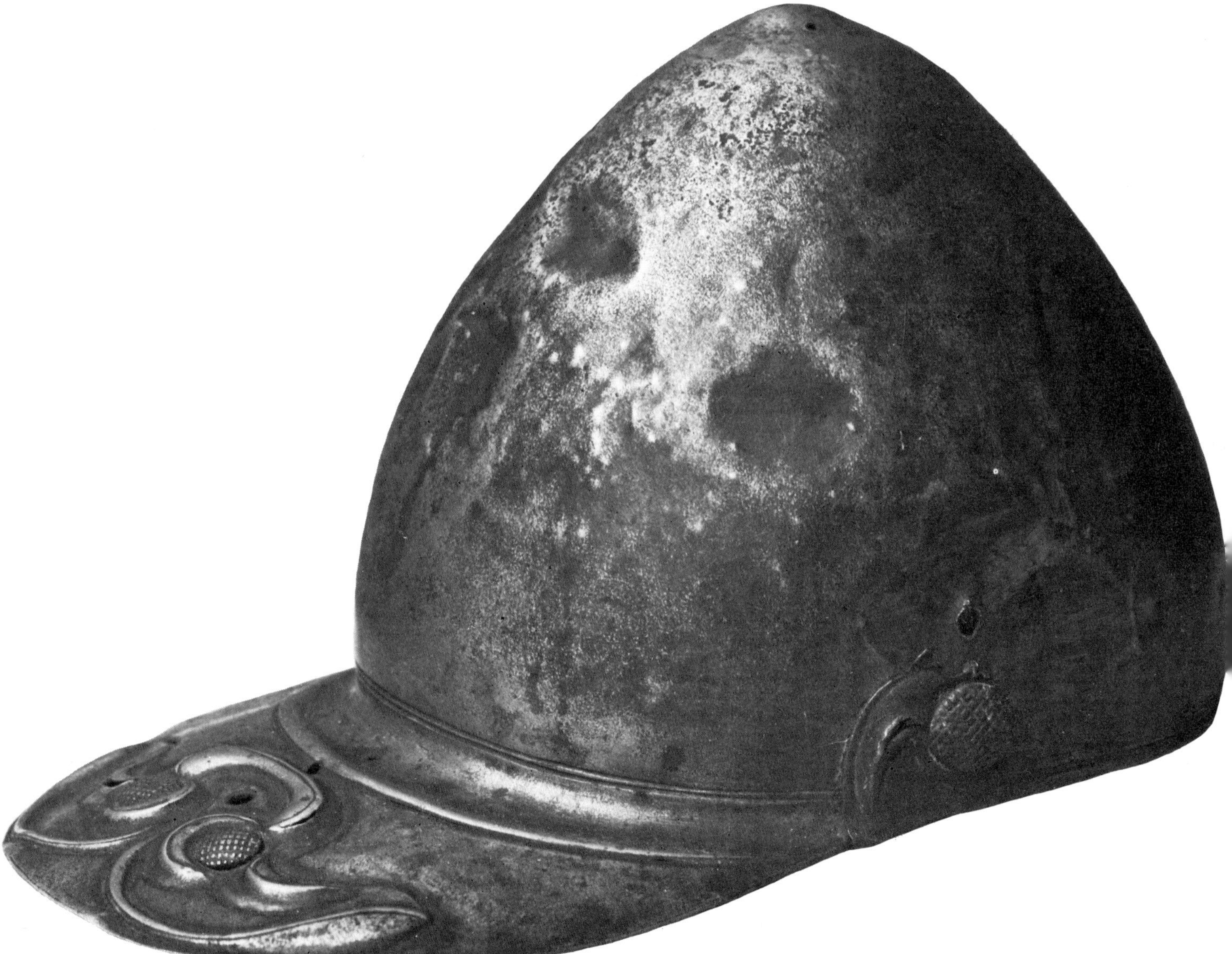

53

Details of the findings of this helmet are not recorded. It was acquired by the British Museum in 1872 and had previously been in the Meyrick Collection.

53 The Meyrick Helmet is of a common ancient
54 type having a domed cap, a broad neck-guard
57, 58 and originally carrying cheekpieces. In this
case the cap is not hemispherical but steep-
sided rising to a relatively pointed apex. The
cap is 30·5 cm. long, by 17·1 cm. wide, by
15·9 cm. high.

The width of the flange on the longitudinal
axis of the helmet is 8·9 cm. A knob or other
54 fitting was originally riveted on the top and
has left a circular mark 4·5 cm. in diameter. It
was secured by four rivets, one at the apex and
three in an equilateral triangle round it. In the
centre of the neck-guard are two holes which
may have supported the bottom of a crest or
have been used to fasten a carrying cord or
strap.

The general form of the helmet is very close
to that of a Roman legionary helmet but the
form is found in a Celtic context in Italic
helmets which were imported into Gaul and
copied during the La Tène I period. The
54 repoussé ornament on the neck-guard and on
55–58 the side-plates is entirely Celtic in character
and is combined with large studs, cross-scored
to take red enamel. Such studs are character-
istic of the continental La Tène III period.

'It is not easy to find exact parallels to the embossed ornament on the neck-guard, but its 'broken backed' curves, the placing of the enamelled bosses at nodal points and the heaviness of the general treatment all seem to belong to the school of North British art, flourishing in the first century AD, which is represented by pieces such as the Elmswell panel and the Balmaclellan mirror.

'Although not necessarily modelled on
the Roman legionary helmet which it so
closely resembles, the helmet has at some
time been in Roman hands. This is demon-
strated by the Roman numeral II which was 56
incised in antiquity on the right-hand side,
like the figure XII incised on the Roman
parade helmet from the River Wensum.
The number probably indicates the unit to
which the owner belonged. The owner
may well have been a Roman auxiliary
soldier and the quality of workmanship on
the helmet suggests that it is more likely to
have been worn by an officer than an
ordinary soldier.'

Graham Ritchie in his unpublished thesis compares the Meyrick Helmet to one found in the River Meuse at Buggenum dating from about AD 70 and with a XIIIth Legion inscription. He quotes parallels to the shape of the helmet among native helmets from Tongern and Mainz and suggests the origin of the type in the Tungrian district. The inference is that although of British workmanship, the Meyrick Helmet may have been made for one of the Tungrian troops serving in Agricola's army, and that its form was decided by the preference of the customer.

55

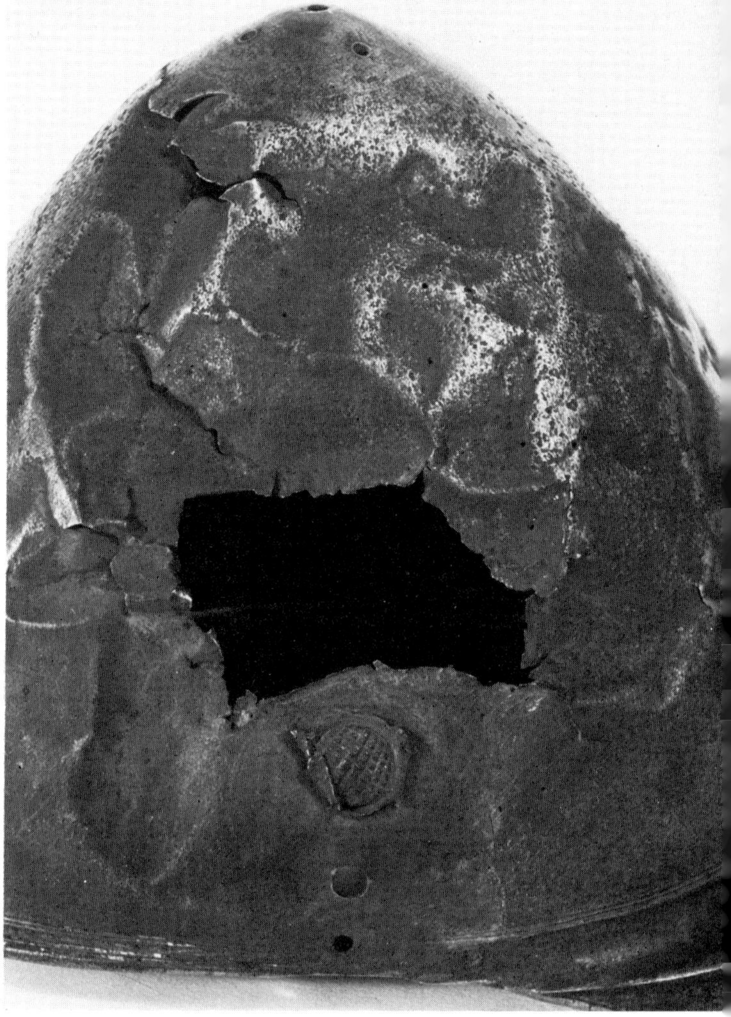

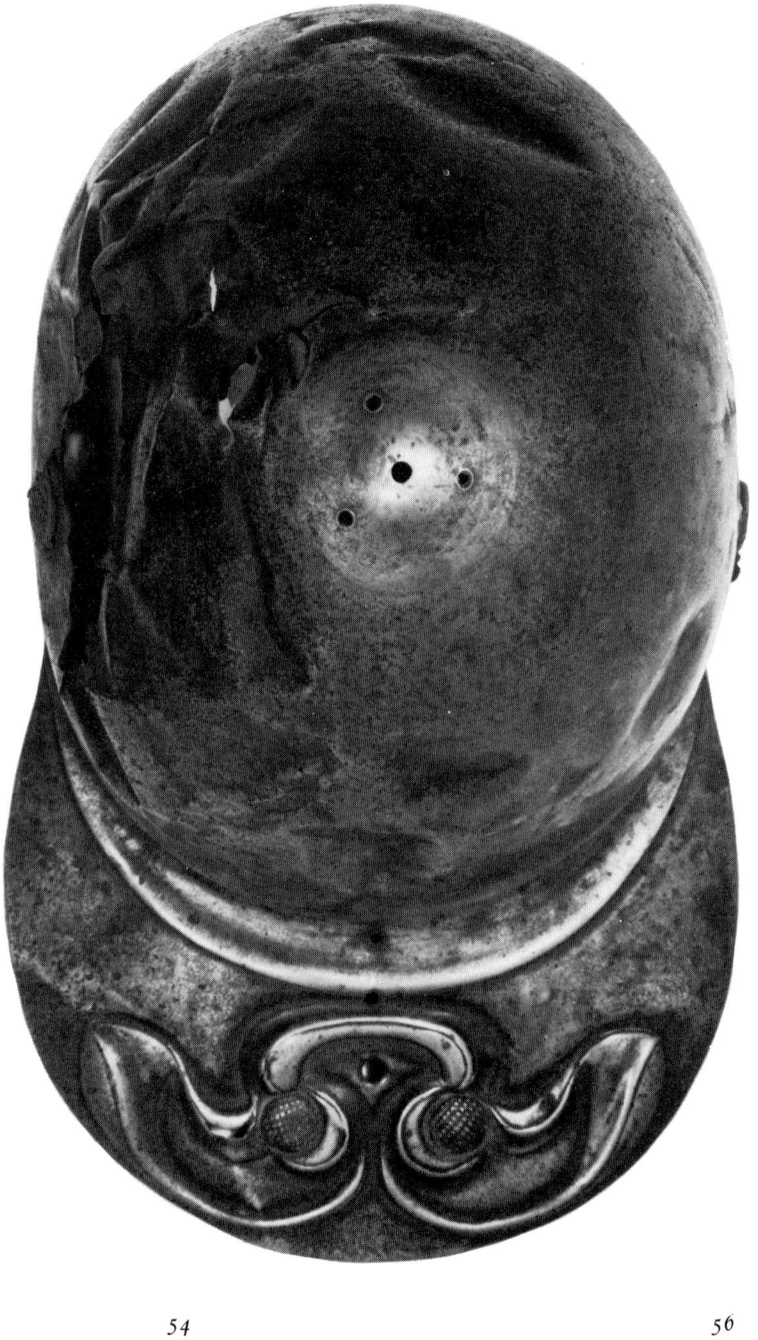

54

56

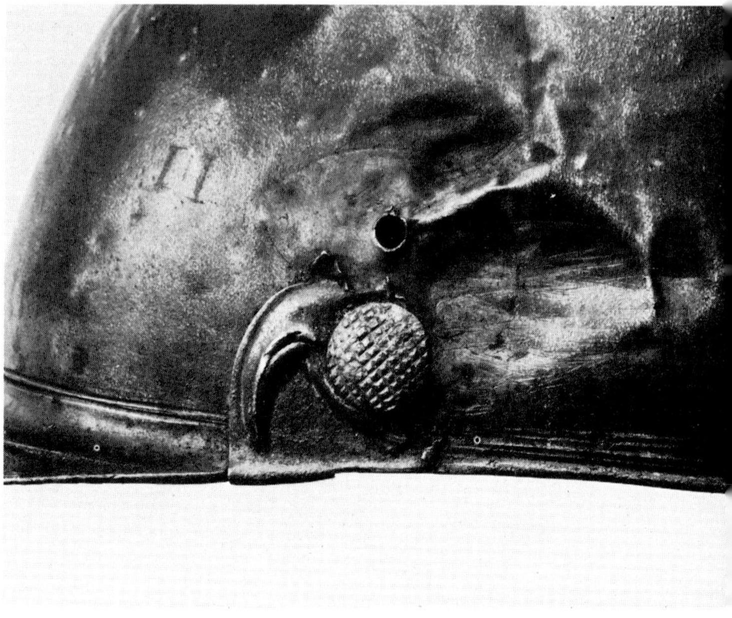

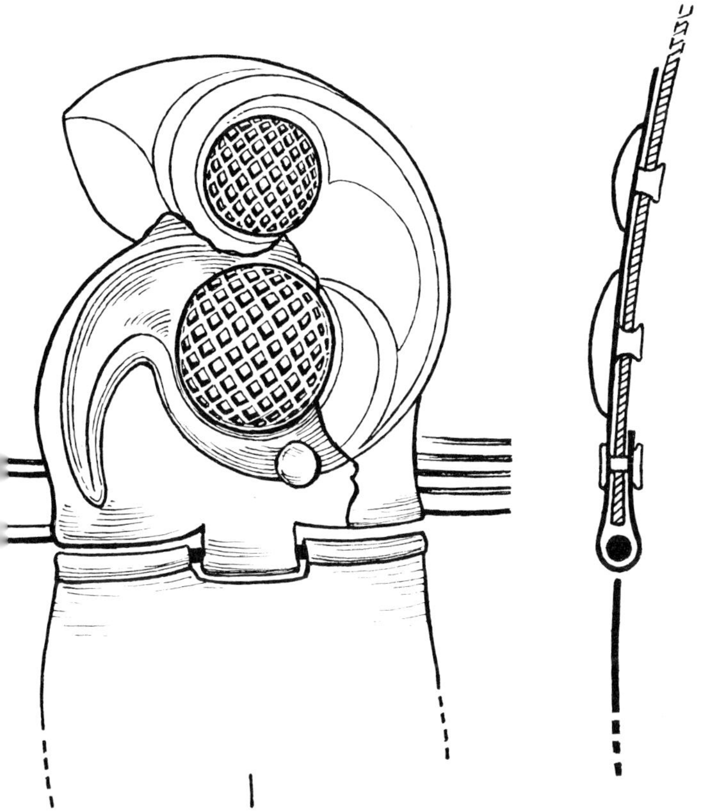

57

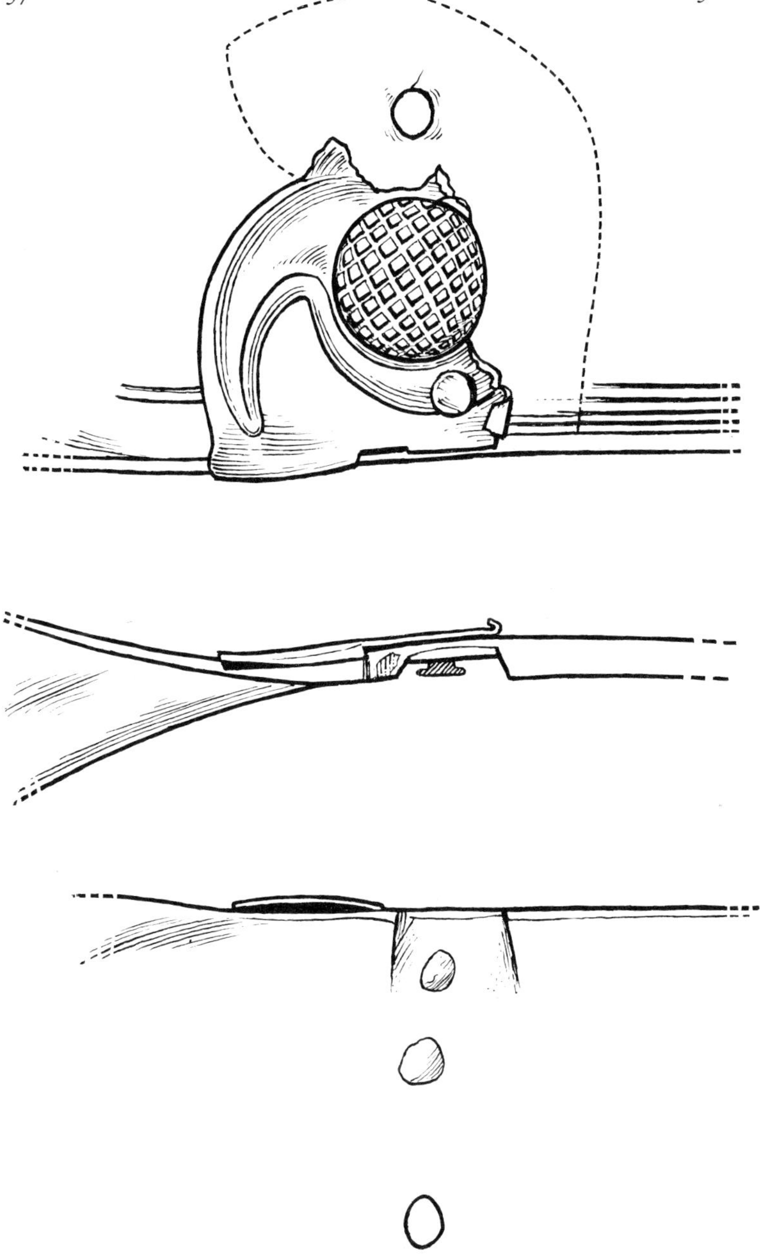

58

Bibliography

J. W. Brailsford, 'Notes on the Battersea Shield and two Iron Age helmets from Britain', *Acts of the IV International Congress of Pre- and Protohistoric Sciences*, Madrid, 1954, p. 759.

Guide to Antiquities of the Early Iron Age in the Department of British and Mediaeval Antiquities, British Museum, London, 1925, p. 107, fig. 65.

Later Prehistoric Antiquities of the British Isles, London, 1953, p. 68, pl. xviii.

CHAPTER FIVE

THE IPSWICH TORCS

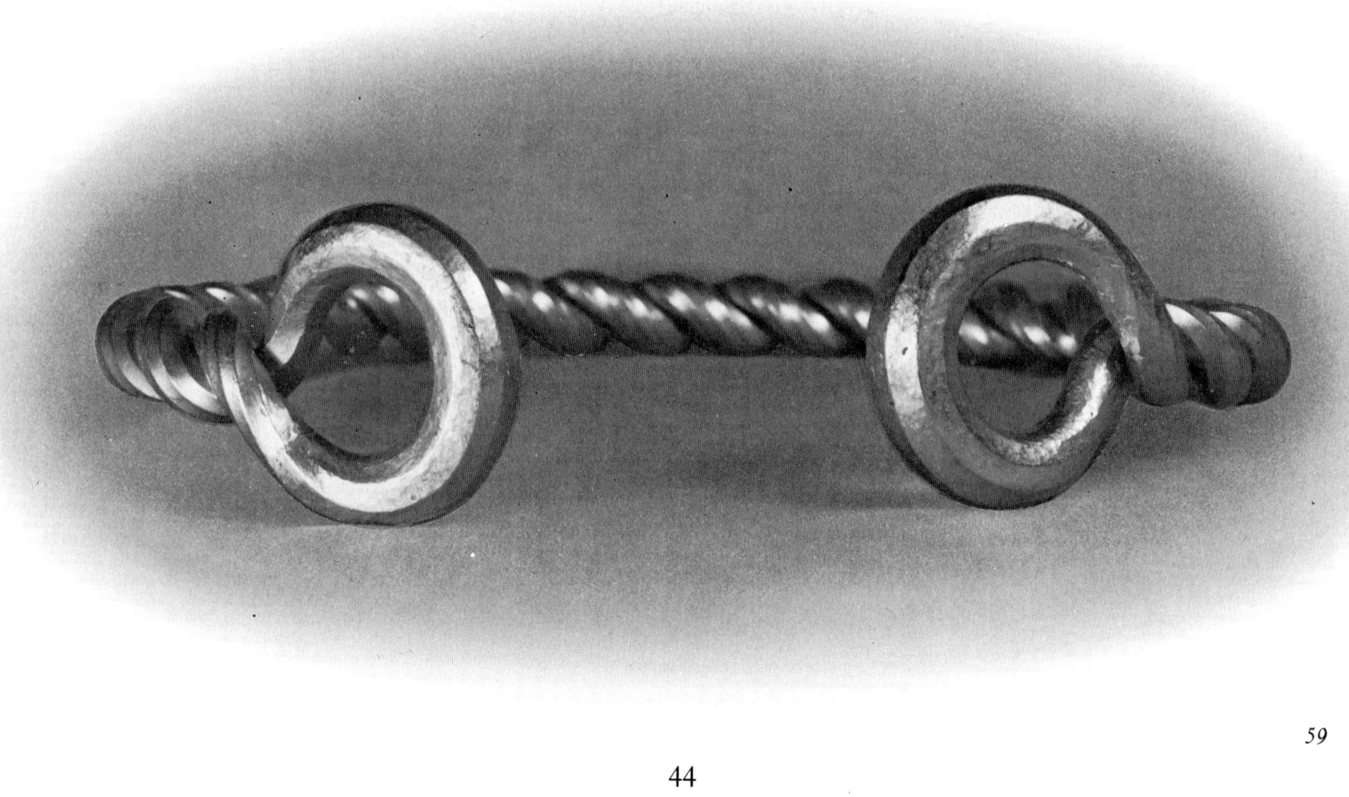

59

IV Five gold torcs were found on the 26th
, 60, 64, October 1968, on the crest of a hill at Belstead
67, 70 on the eastern outskirts of Ipswich. A sixth
75 example, found on the 18th October 1970, must undoubtedly have come from the same hoard although it had been moved a considerable distance during the course of building operations in the area. All the torcs are exceptionally fine examples of Early Celtic craftsmanship and, owing to the unfinished nature of most of the pieces, the group provides technological information which is of quite exceptional interest.

During the course of building operations at Belstead Mr Malcolm Tricker, who was operating a mechanical earth-mover, saw an object gleaming in the loose soil. He pulled it out and found it to be a gold torc. It had a second torc hooked to it. Three more torcs also hooked together were recovered from the same place. After washing the torcs, Mr Tricker, realizing that they were gold, took them straight to the Ipswich Museum. A Treasure Trove Inquest on the first five torcs was duly held on the 18th December 1968. The evidence indicated that the torcs had undoubtedly been deposited with the intention of being recovered and a verdict of Treasure Trove was accordingly returned. The torcs may have been buried by the goldsmith from whose workshop they came or by a marauder who had looted a goldsmith's stock.

After the inquest the British Museum exercised its option on finds of Treasure Trove and acquired the five torcs. They were valued at £45,000 and the full market value was paid to Mr Tricker, the finder, by the Museum. This was the highest price ever paid by the British Museum for Treasure Trove. Generous contributions towards the cost were made by the National Art Collections Fund, the Goldsmiths' Company and the Pilgrim Trust. Electrotypes of the torcs were presented to the Ipswich Museum.

On the 18th October 1970, Mr P. J. Gorham was digging his garden at 50, Holcombe
Crescent, Ipswich, when he found a sixth *75*
gold torc. The find-place was within a hundred yards of the 1968 find and there can be no doubt that the sixth torc originally belonged to the main hoard since soil from the original site had been used to make up Mr Gorham's garden.

The weight of the torcs varies between 858 gm. (No. 3) and 1044 gm. (No. 2), and their diameter is almost uniformly 18·7 cm. except for No. 2, which is 19·6 cm. in diameter. The torcs are made of gold, silver and copper in proportions varying between 77·3 per cent and 88·7 per cent of gold, 10·7 per cent and 18·8 per cent of silver and 0·4 per cent and 4·4 per cent of copper, and, again, No. 2 is the exception. Its composition is: the terminals contain 78·1 per cent gold, 10·1 per cent silver and 11·8 per cent copper, while the wires of the hoop contain 65·9 per cent gold, 27·8 per cent silver and 6·3 per cent copper.

The hoop of torcs Nos. 1–5 is made up of two faceted rods twisted together. No. 1 has
plain ring terminals and is the only example of *59*
this form in the hoard. It is unusually well finished and since other examples of the plain terminal form are known, for instance from Snettisham and Bawsey, this torc may be
regarded as a finished article. The terminals of *62, 63,*
Nos. 2–5 are decorated with ornament of the *65, 66*
Snettisham type (see p. 57). The roundels of *68, 69,*
concentric ridges found on other examples of *72, 73*
Snettisham-type ornament are absent on these Ipswich examples, and it is of interest that the areas of incised 'matting' are also absent. Torcs 2–5 were never finished and the ornament presents a very rough appearance when compared with that on the great torc from Snettisham. Moreover, the areas of 'matting' or hatching which are found on the Snettisham torc, and on other examples of the same kind of ornament, had not yet been applied to the Ipswich torcs Nos. 2–5. On No. 2 especially
the roughness of the ornament and the dis- *61–63*
tinctive character of the surface suggests that the terminals may have hardly been touched since they were cast from wax models.

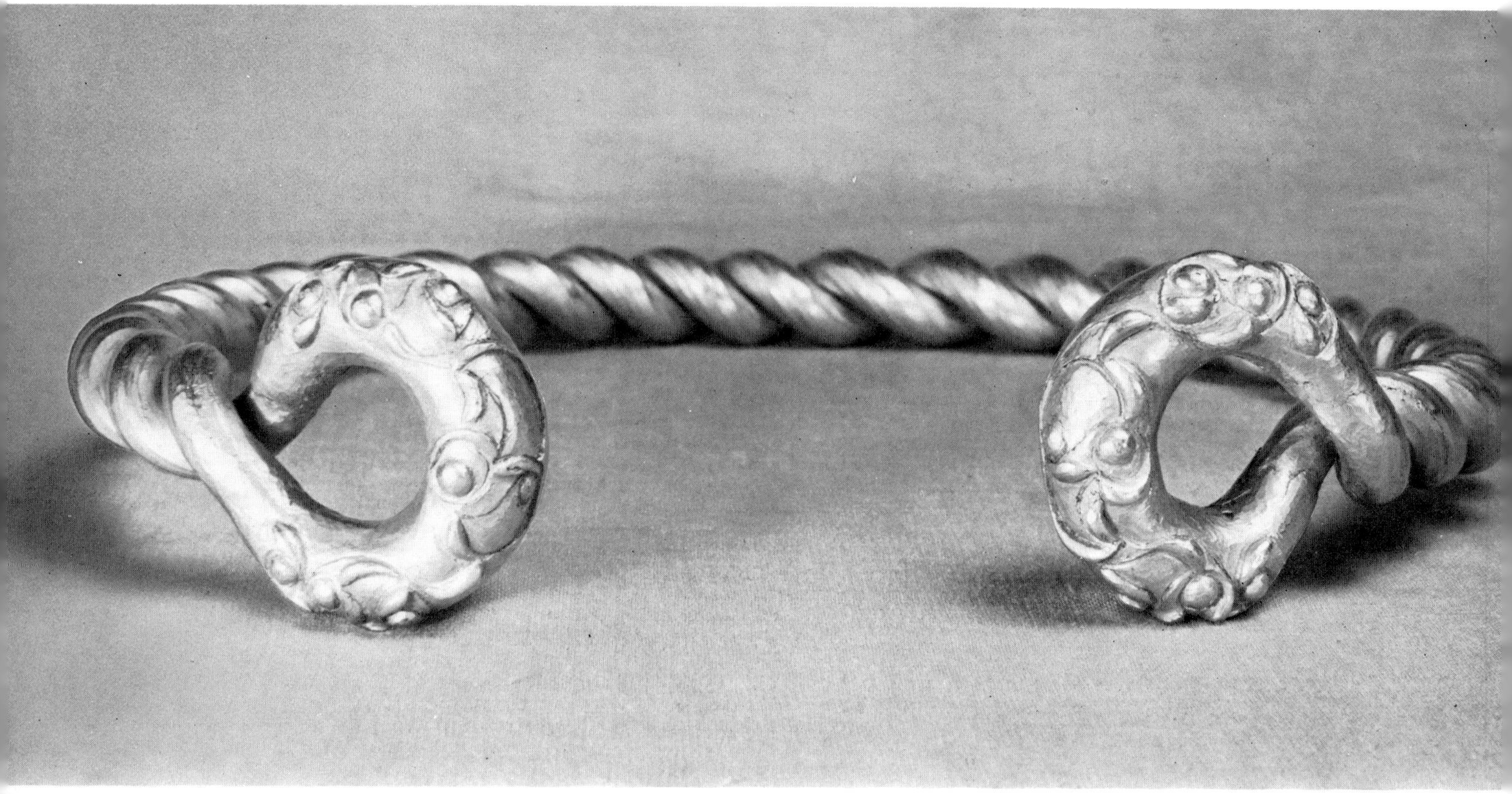

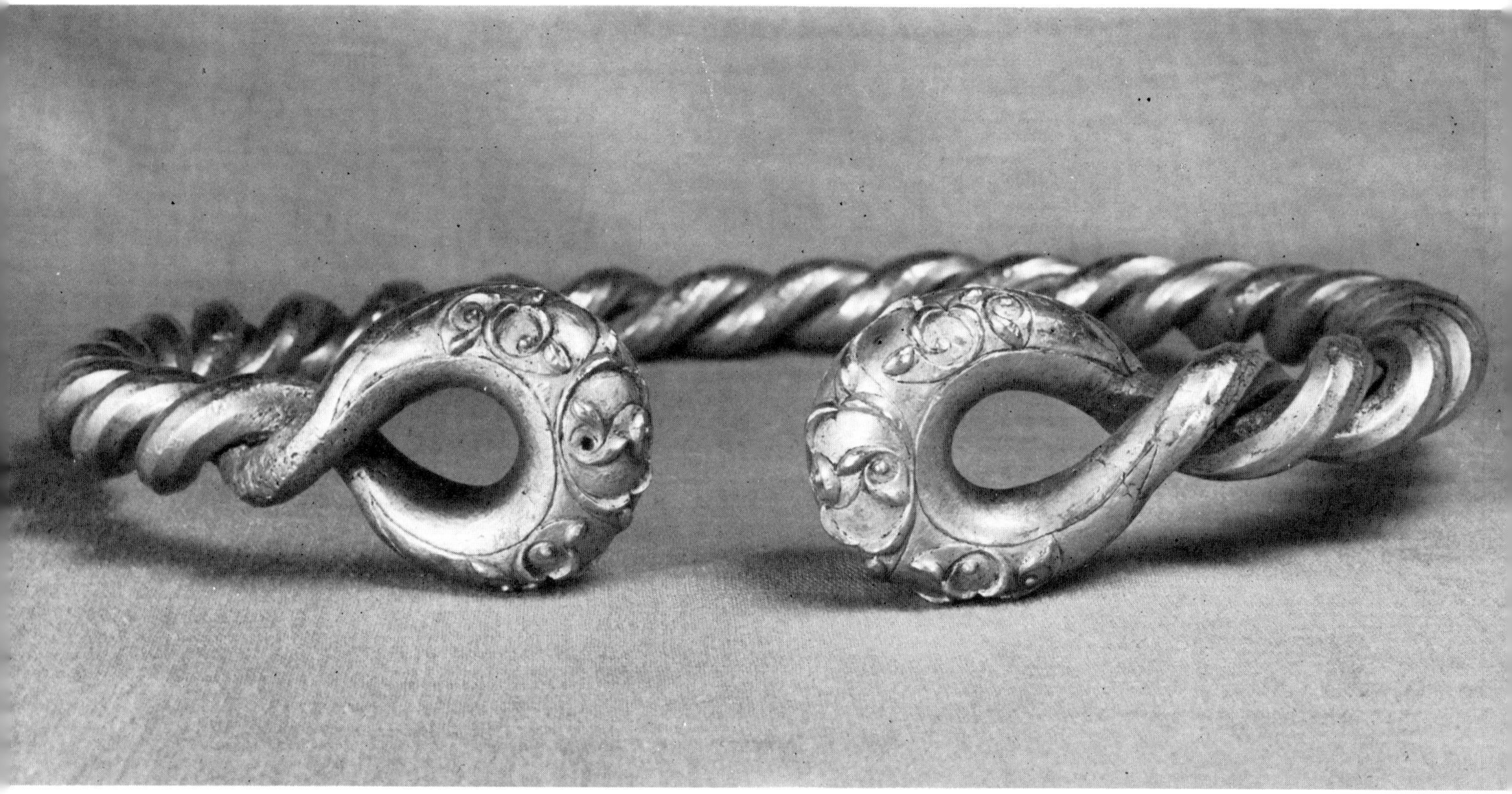

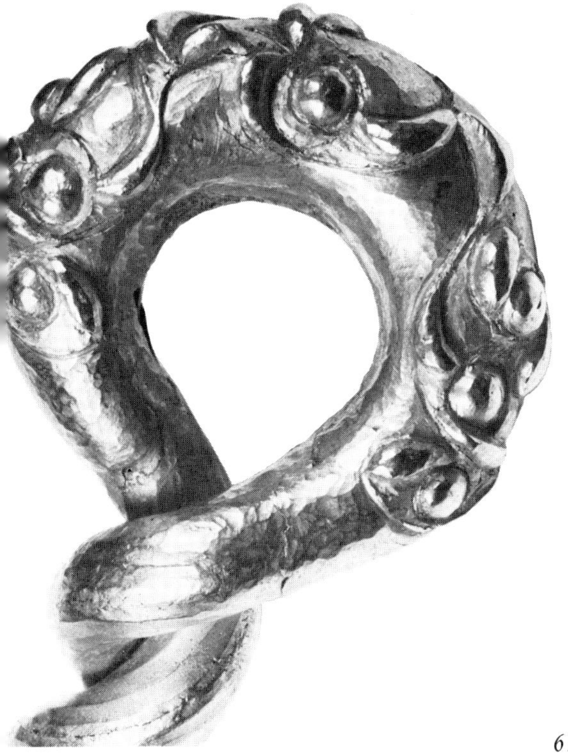

61

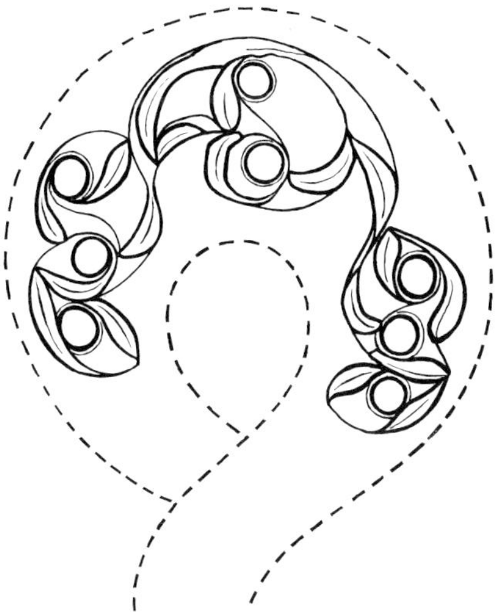

62

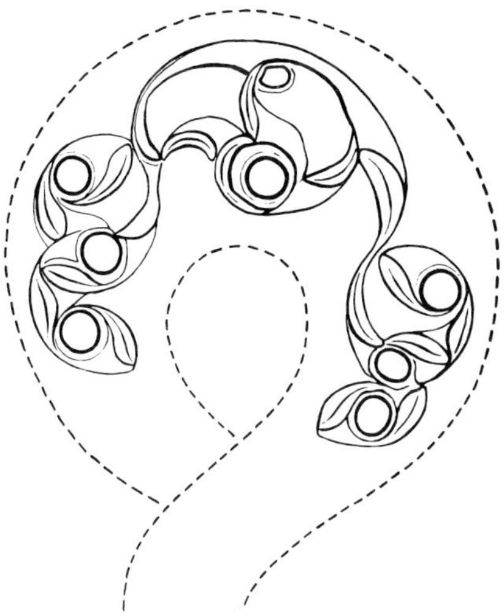

63

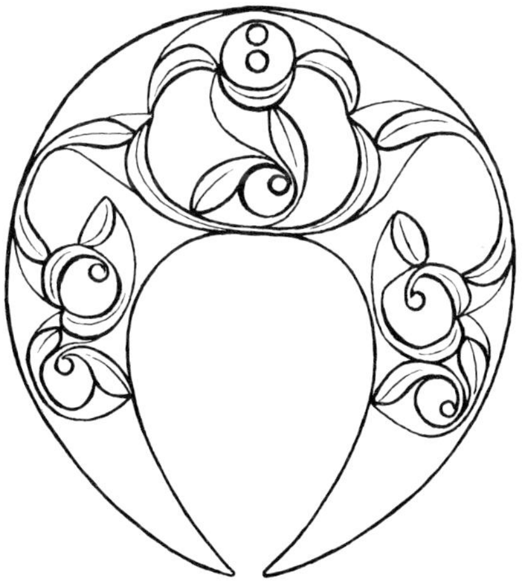

65

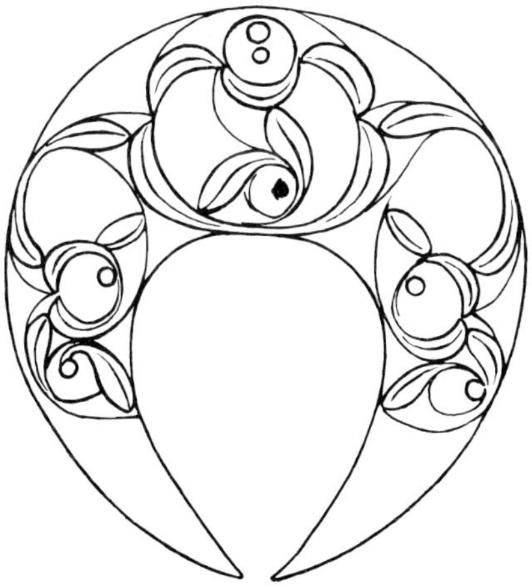

66

60

◄

64

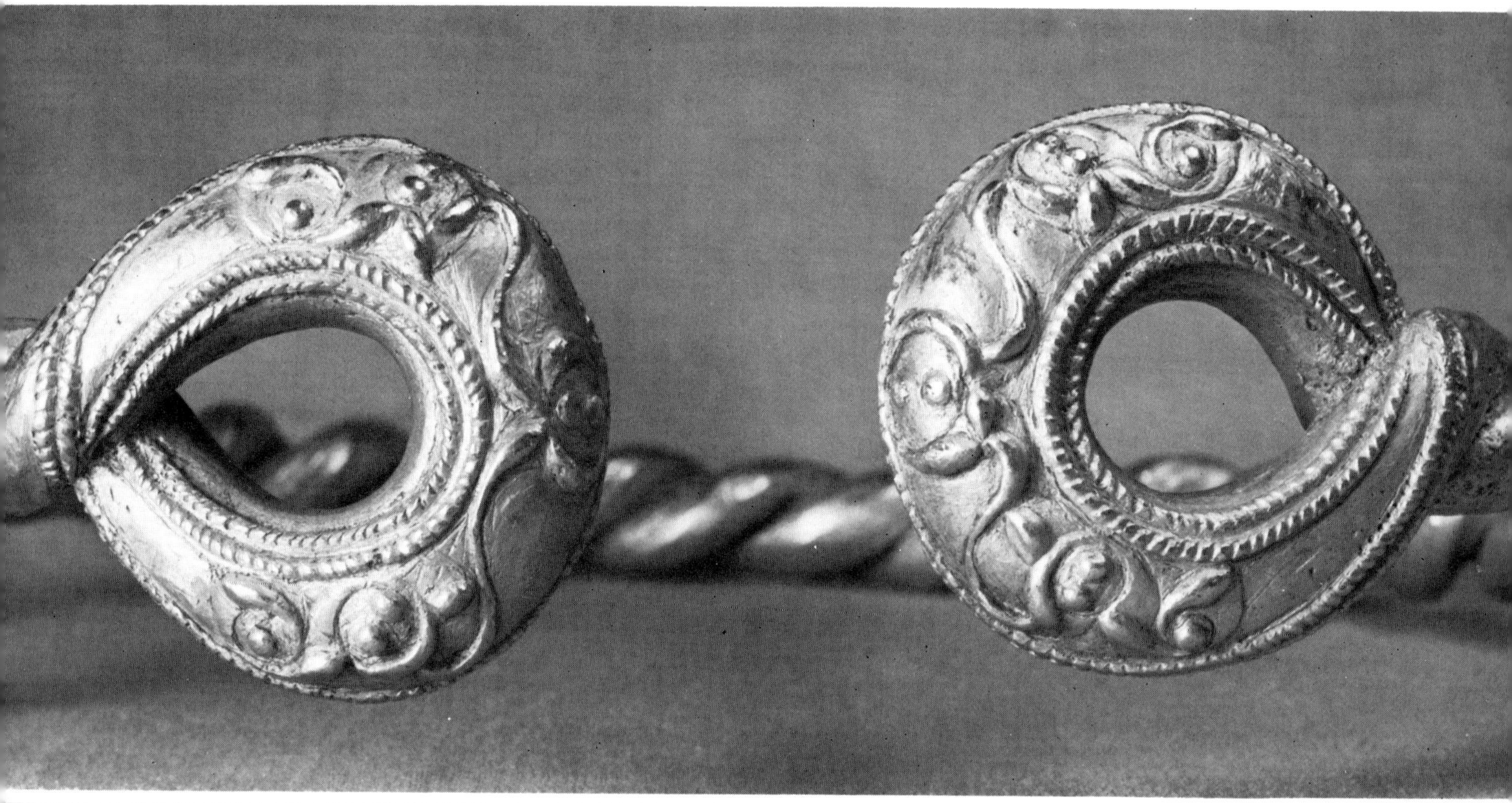

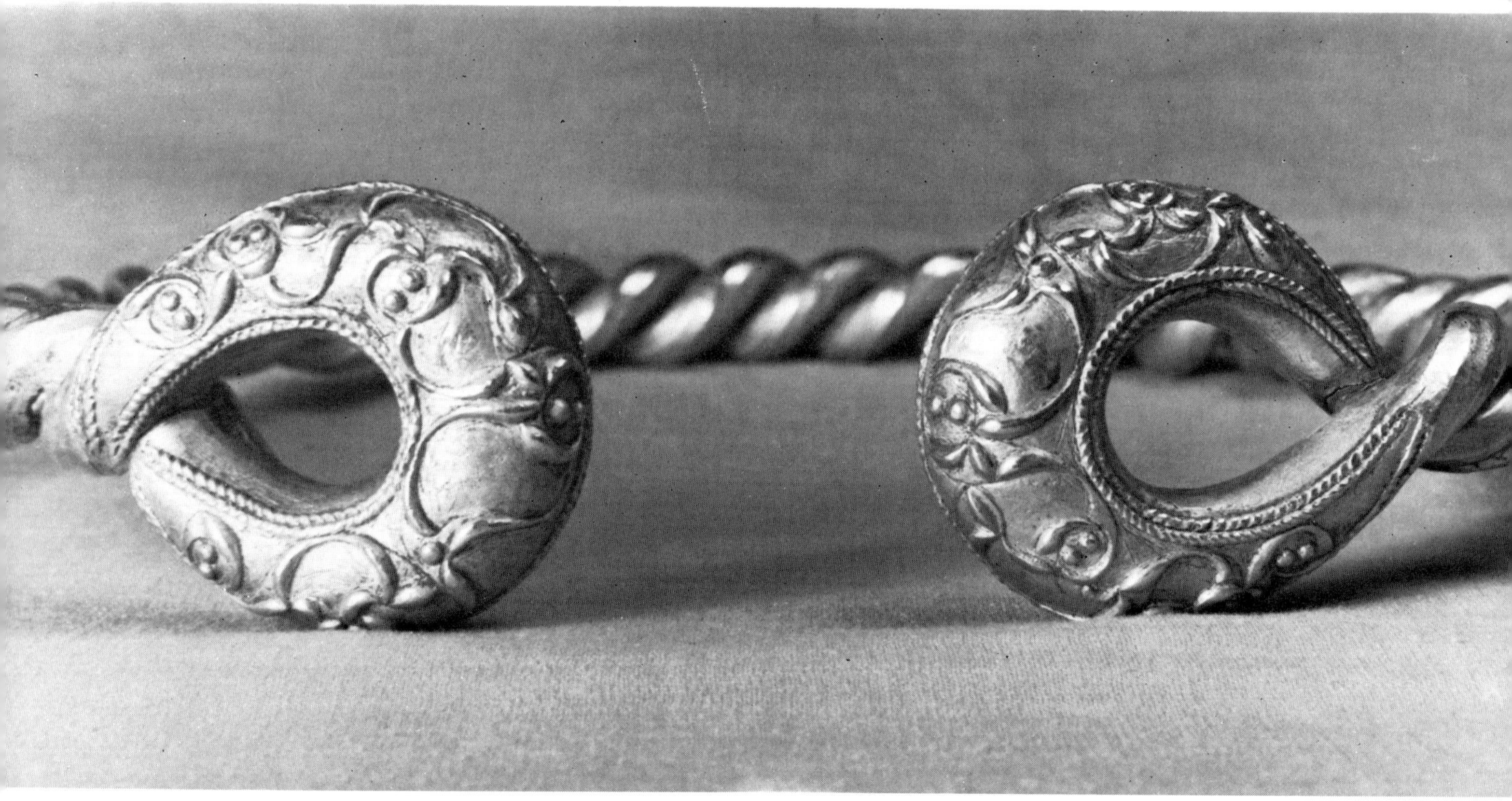

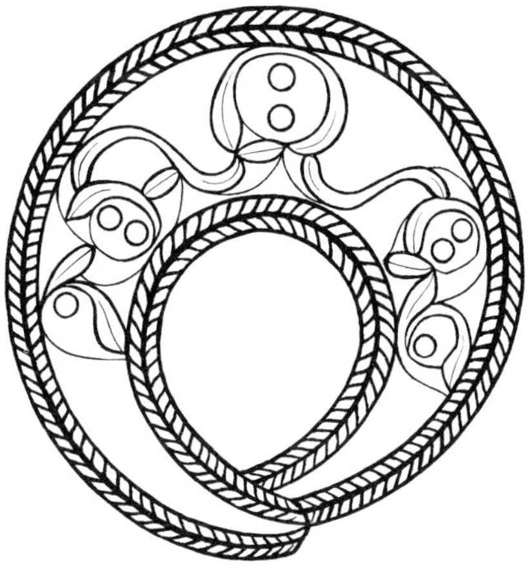

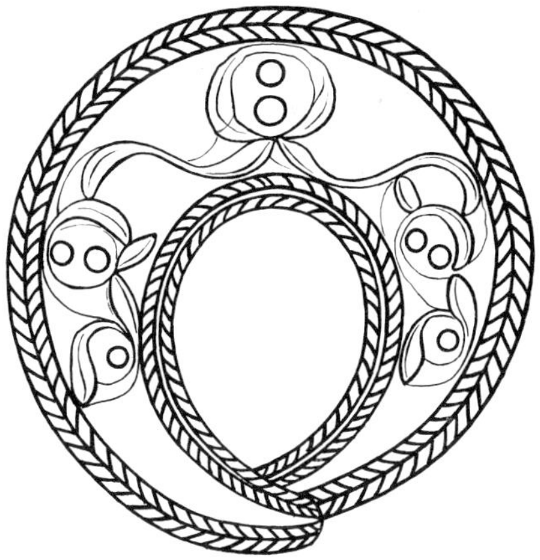

68

69

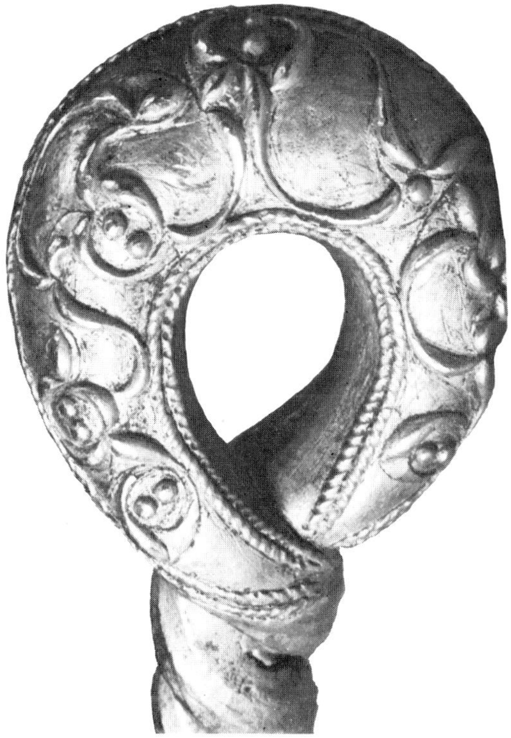

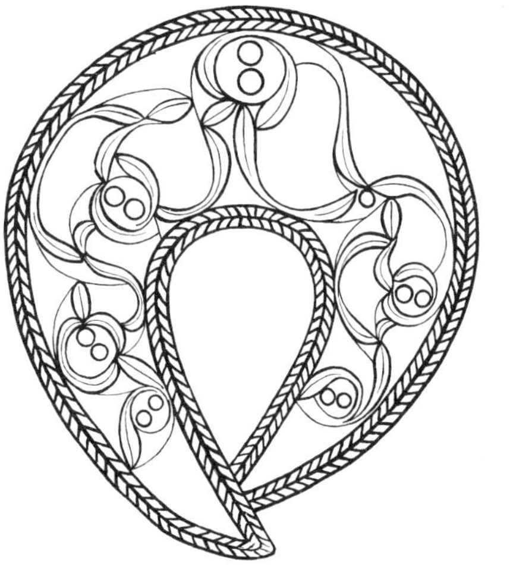

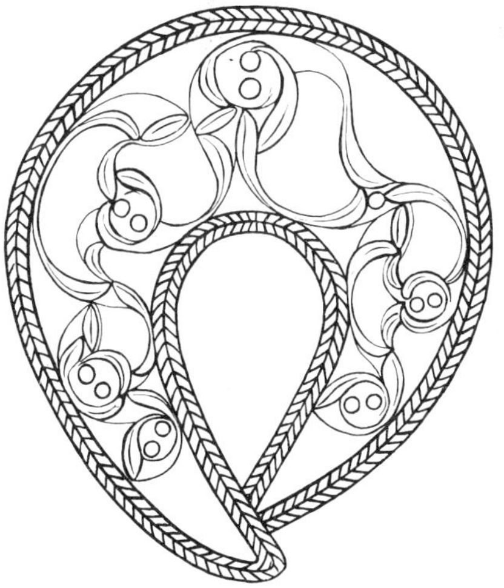

72

73

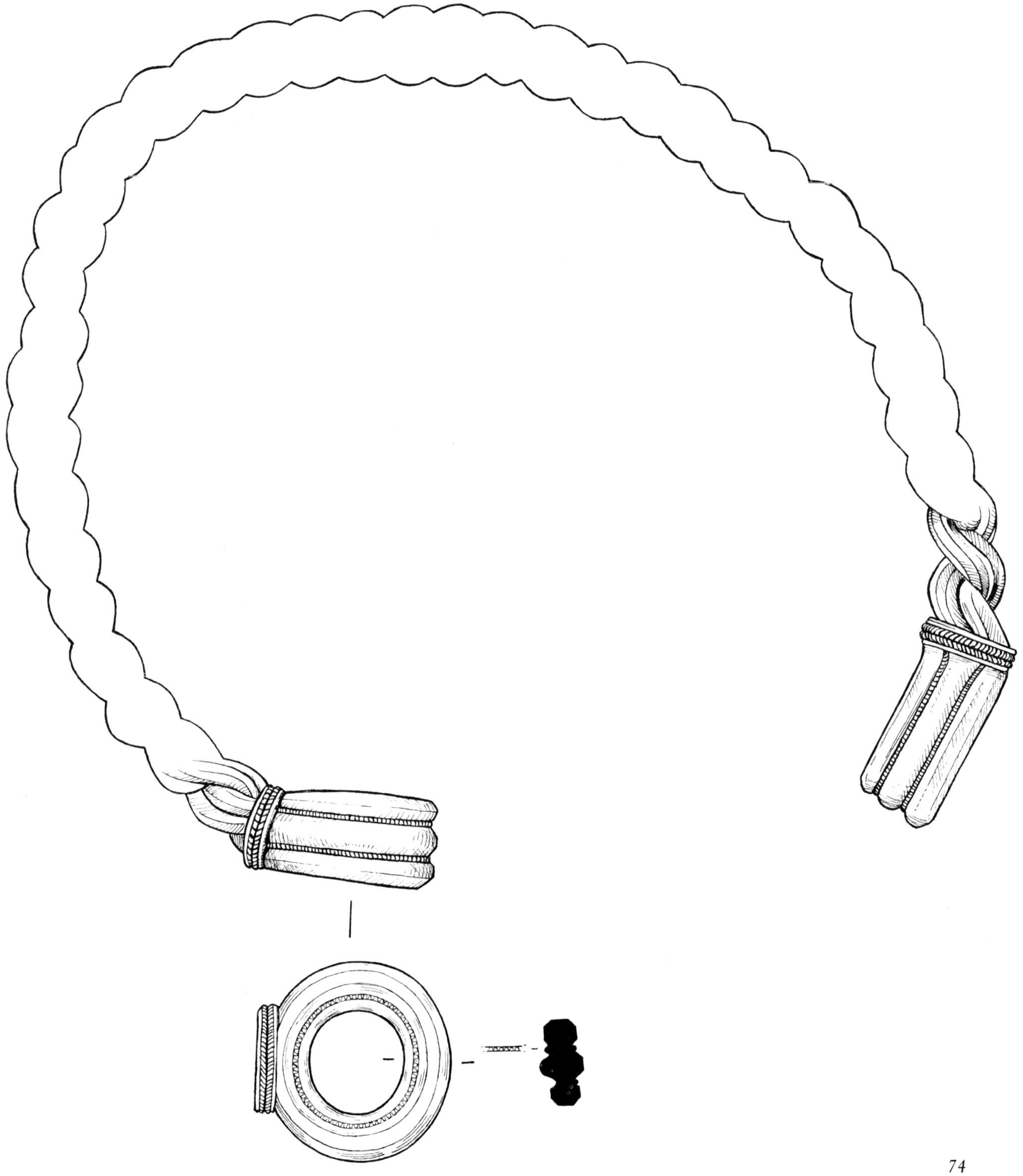

74

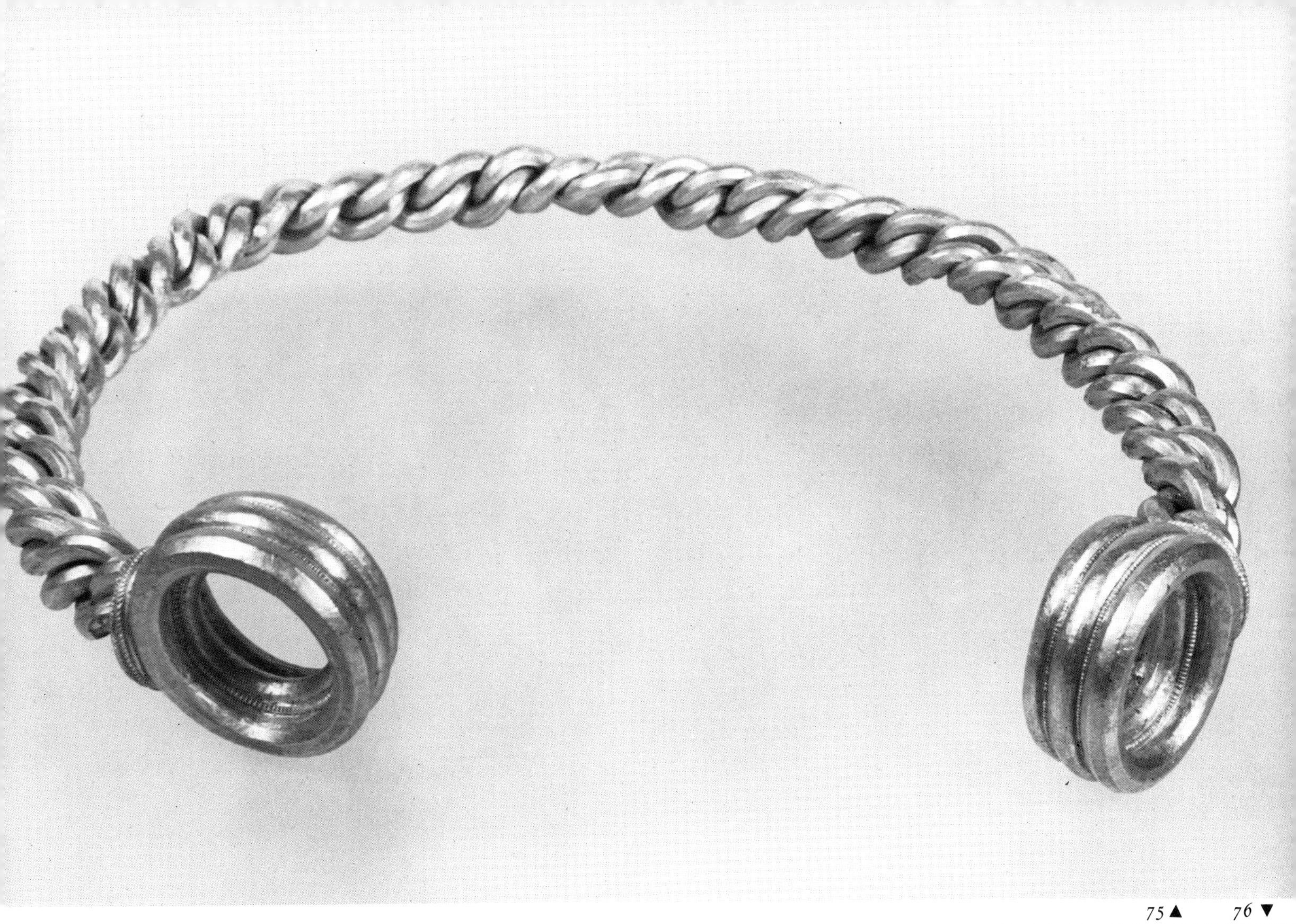

75▲ 76▼

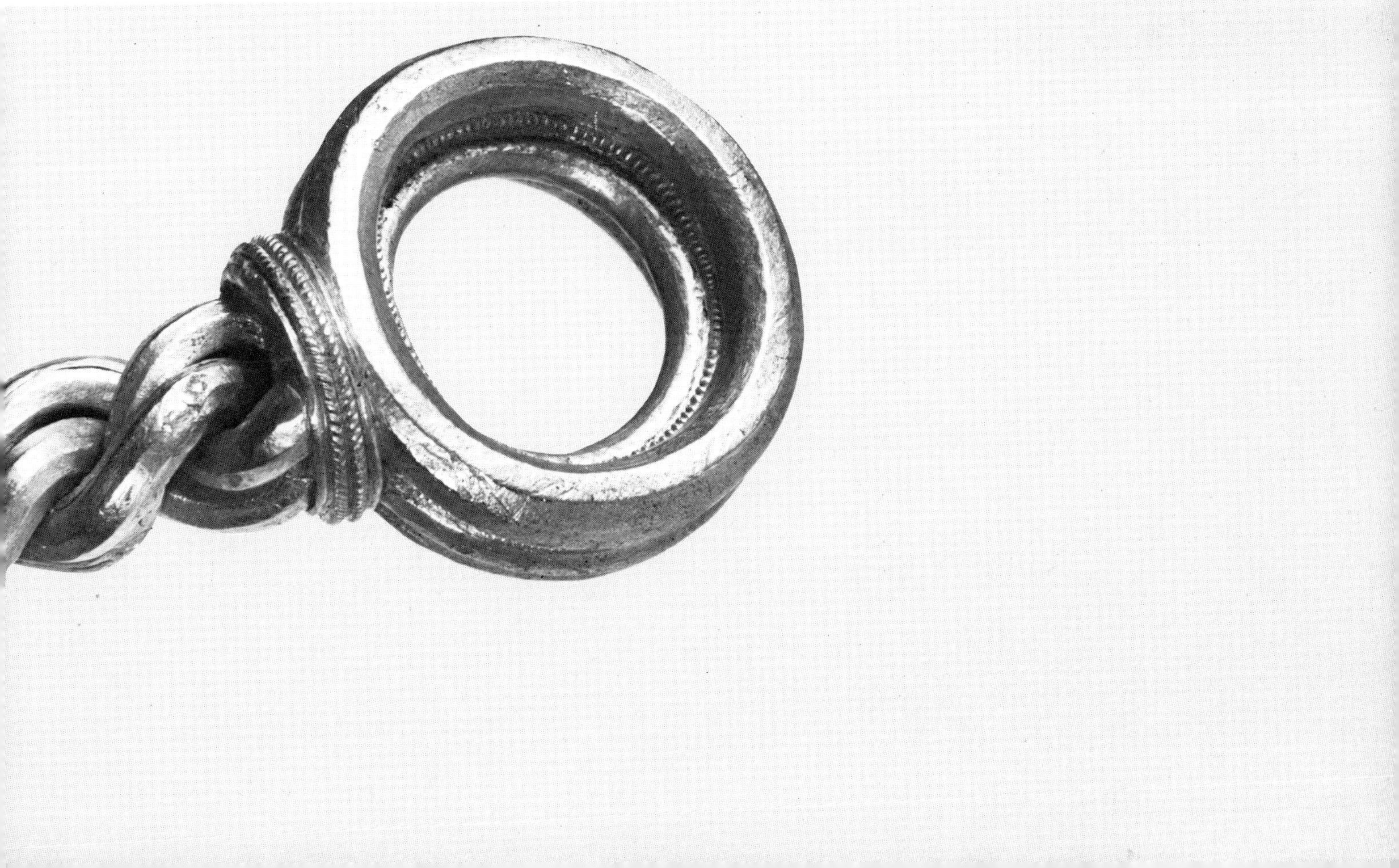

74, 75 The rods making up the hoop of No. 6 are faceted and relatively massive but multiple and intertwined in a far more complex manner than the simple twist of Nos. 1–5. On No. 6 both the form of the terminals and the ornament on them are quite different from those on its companions. The form of the terminals on No. 6 is generically similar to those on the 76
Iron Age torcs from Glascote and Needwood Forest, both in Staffordshire. This feature distinguishes No. 6 from Ipswich torcs Nos. 1–5 which are all at home in East Anglia.

Bibliography

J. W. Brailsford, 'A Hoard of Early Iron Age Gold Torcs from Ipswich', *Proc. Suff. Inst. Arch.* 31, pt. 2, (1968), 158f.

J. W. Brailsford and J. E. Stapley, 'The Ipswich Torcs', *Proc. Prehist. Soc.* 1972, pp. 219ff.

E. Owles, 'The Ipswich Gold Torcs', *Antiquity* 43 (1969), p. 208.

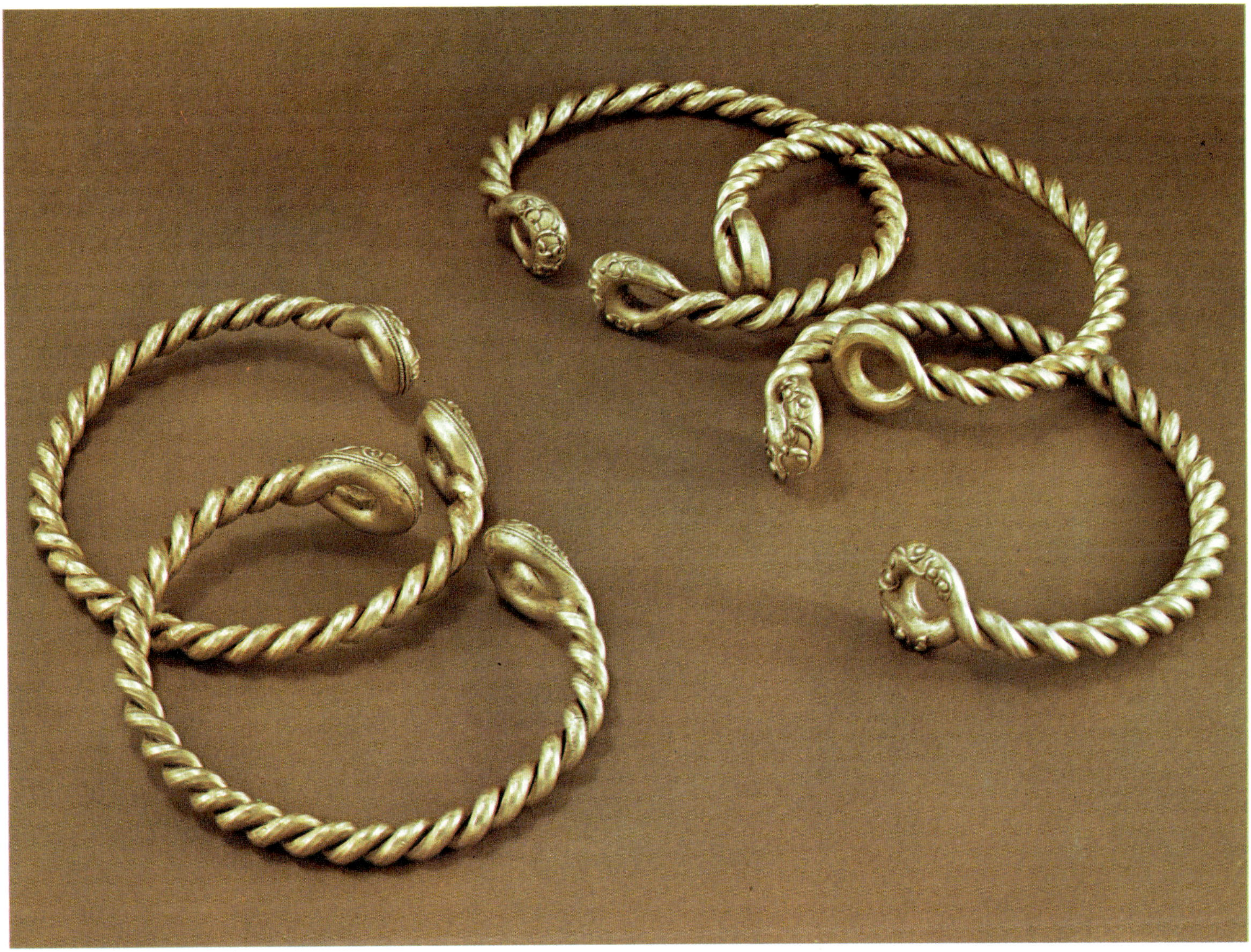

IV

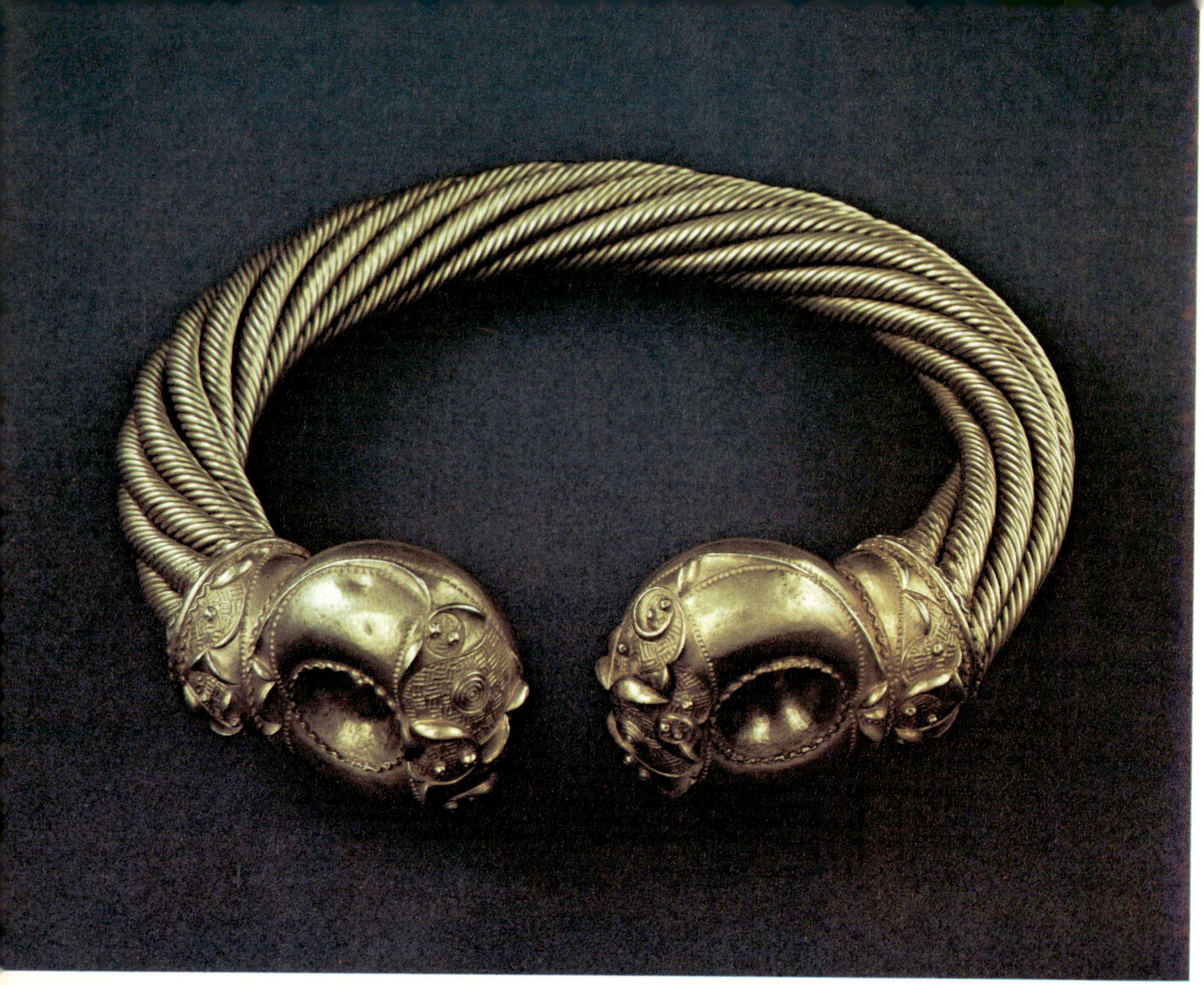

V

VI

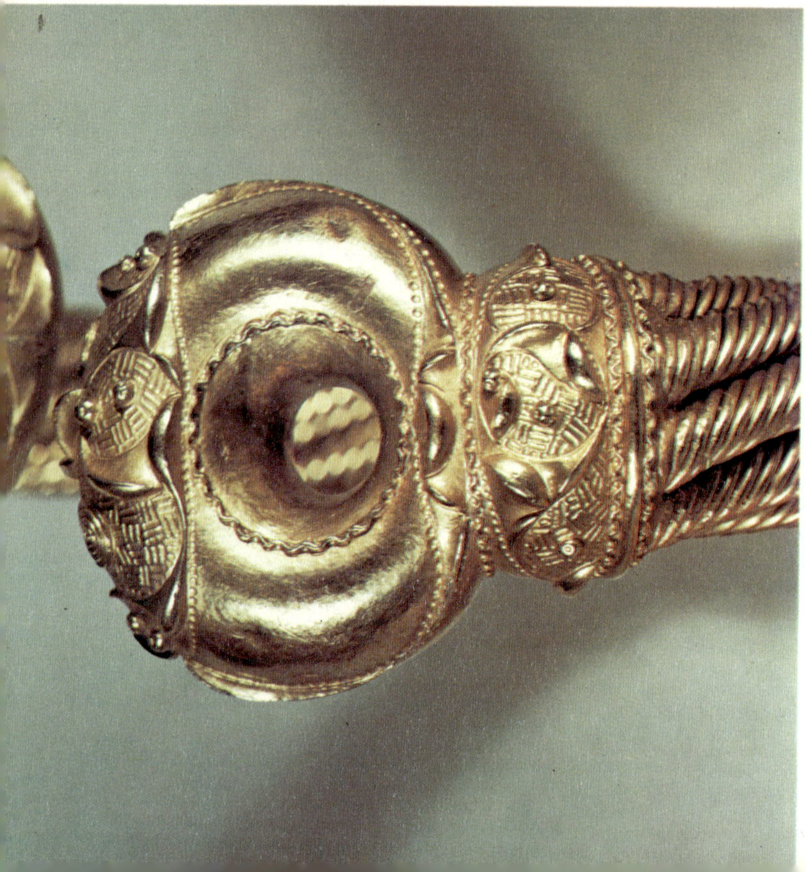

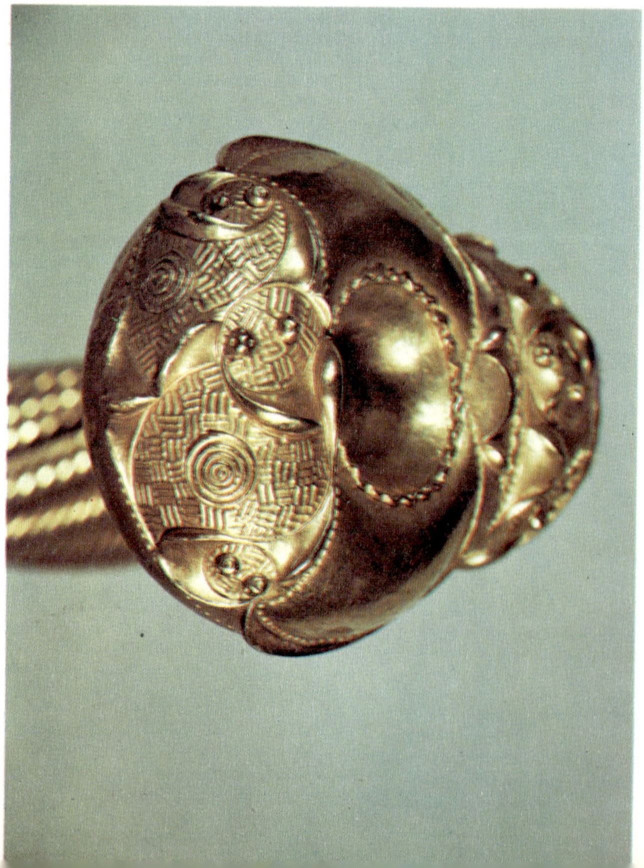

CHAPTER SIX

THE SNETTISHAM TORC AND BRACELET

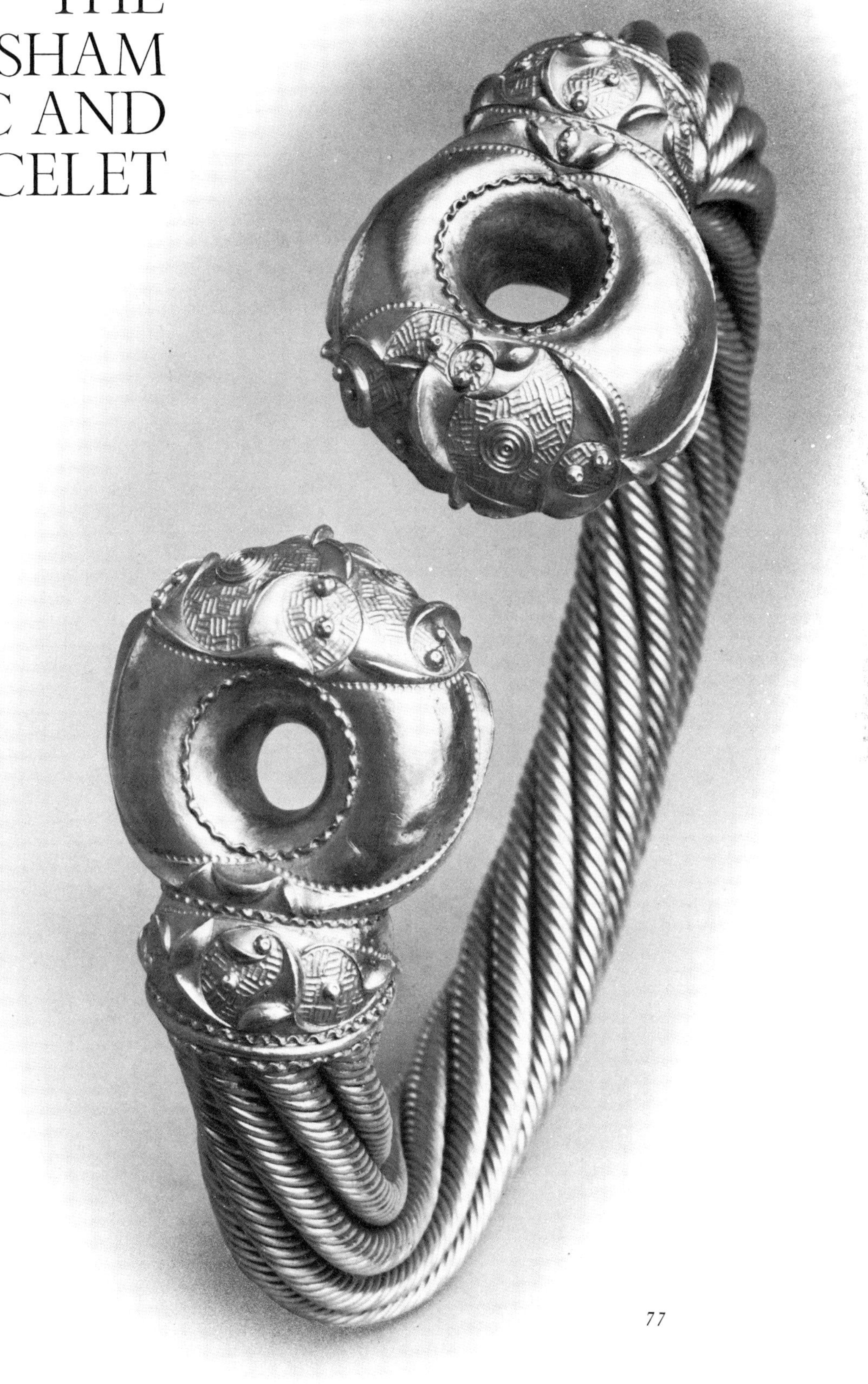

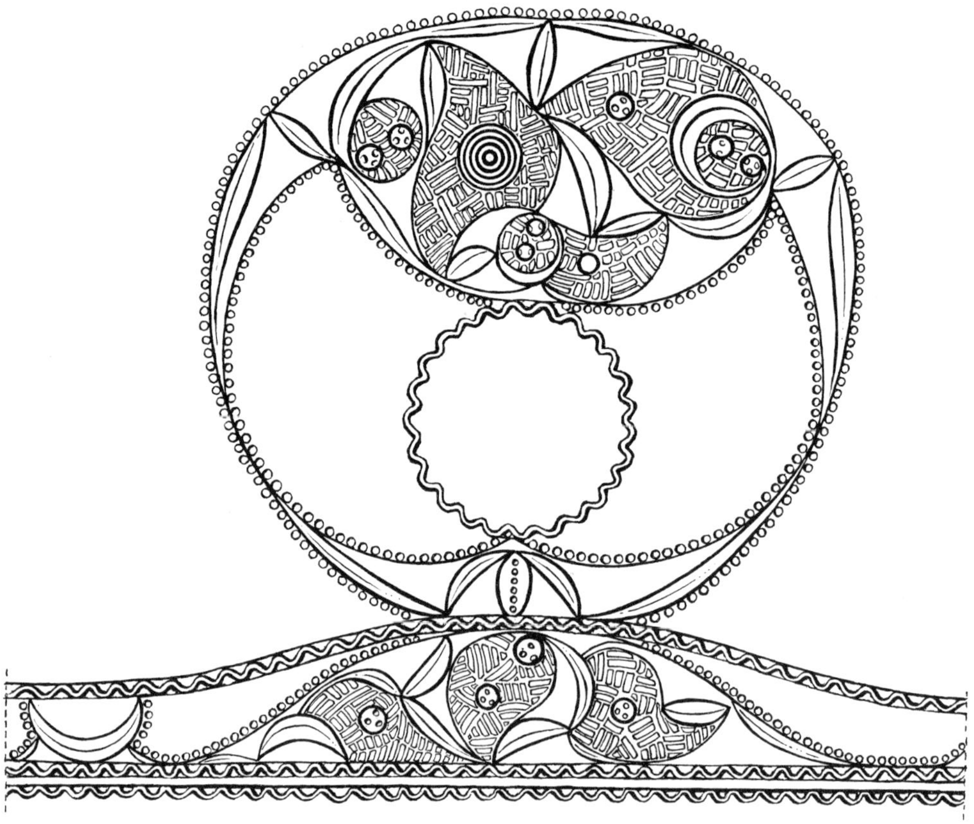

78

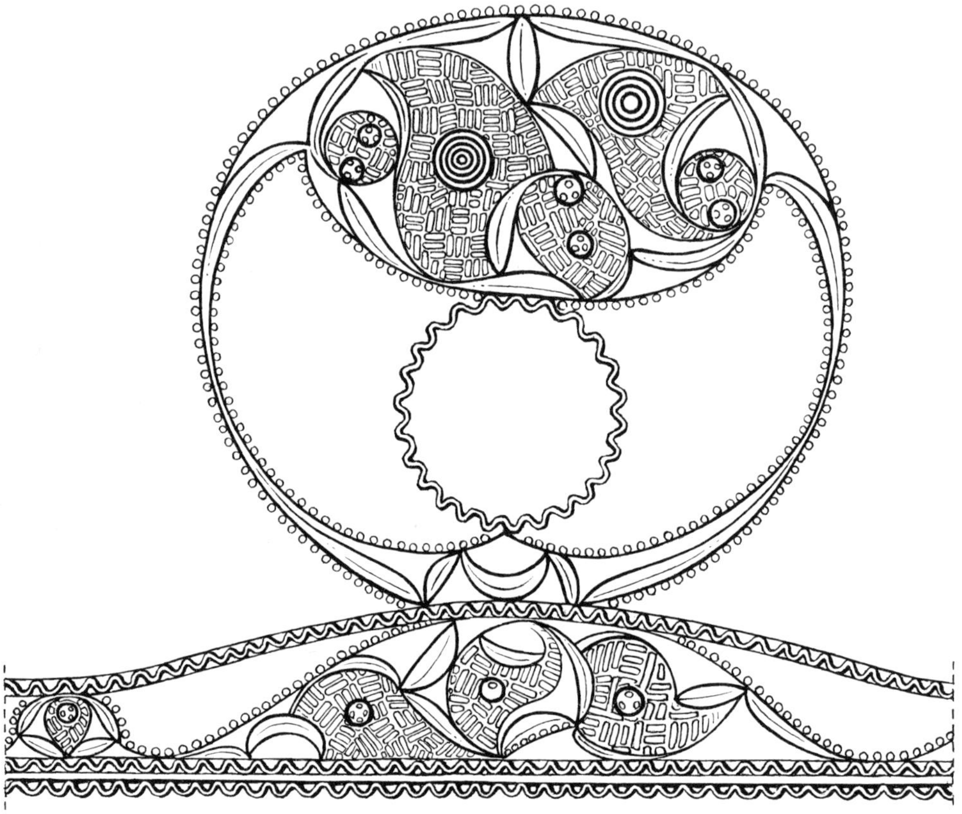

79

77, V The great gold alloy torc from Snettisham,
Norfolk, was ploughed up in 1950. It was
88, 89 associated with a bracelet decorated with the
same kind of ornament as that on the torc, and
also with a damaged gold alloy torc of the so-
called 'buffer' type. This group is one of a
number of such finds which have been made
on Ken Hill at Snettisham, and represents the
stock-in-trade of a metalsmith, as is shown by
the fact that they contain not only finished
products but also, besides coins, damaged
objects and scrap metal. Apparently all the
items were buried for safety in some time of
emergency and the owner was, in the event,
prevented from recovering them.

The group including the great torc, and
another plain ring terminal torc which was
found shortly before, were acquired by the
British Museum as Treasure Trove, and an
ex gratia award of £1850 was paid to the finder.
The other finds from the site, and replicas of
those which came to the British Museum, are
now in the Castle Museum at Norwich.

The 1950 find was preceded by a discovery
in 1948 which included tubular gold torcs
of a most unusual form. The finder of the
tubular torcs believed them to be part of a
brass bedstead and they were left in the hedge-
row in full view of passers by, along a busy
main road, for several days before being
brought to the notice of local archaeologists.

The great Snettisham torc is about 20 cm.
in diameter and the hoop consists of eight
strands, each composed of eight twisted wires
80–84 with the ends soldered into the sockets of the
hollow ring terminals. It weighs 1085 gm. and
its composition is approximately 58 per cent
gold, 38 per cent silver and 3 per cent copper.
The bracelet was originally 8·2 cm. in diameter,
and is hollow, with a groove round the decor-
ated outer edge and a soldered joint running
round the inside. It weighs 111 gm. and the
composition of this is approximately 96 per
cent gold and 4 per cent silver, an exceedingly
high percentage of gold. The buffer terminal
torc is incomplete and its composition is
approximately 80 per cent gold, 17 per cent
silver and 3 per cent copper.

The ornament on the great Snettisham torc
and bracelet, which may be called 'Snettis-
ham-type' ornament, is distinctive of Early
Iron Age art of the first century BC in Britain,
and a brief survey of it may be quoted from a
recent paper on the Ipswich torcs, p. 45, No. 2.
'This type of ornament comprises designs
characteristically made up of curved ridges,
areas of "matting" (or hatching) and small *VI, VII*
spherical bosses. On the Snettisham torc each
of the small bosses bears three fine punched *85, 86*
marks. Snettisham-type ornament occurs
characteristically on ring terminal torcs such
as those from Ipswich, and on the well-known *59–73*
multi-strand ring terminal torc from Snettis- *77*
ham, and on the terminals from similar torcs
which have been found at Sedgeford, and at
Cairnmuir in Peeblesshire. On both these
examples the arrangement of three fine punch
marks recurs. Other examples of the Snettis-
ham class of ornament occur on objects of
other types, for instance the "buffer" terminal
of a torc from Clevedon in Somerset, a fine
gold bracelet from Snettisham, and even on the *87–90*
remarkable horned helmet from the River *36, 37, 39*
Thames at Waterloo Bridge. It has been
pointed out how on the Snettisham torc, the
Cairnmuir terminal and the Sedgeford torc,
the small spherical bosses are further distin-
guished by the presence of three fine punch
marks. This correspondence in the finest detail
surely indicates that these three pieces at least
are from the same workshop. This conclusion
is not unexpected as regards the Snettisham
and Sedgeford torcs, which were found only
two miles apart, but it is surprising to find the
same correspondence in minute detail on the
Cairnmuir terminal which comes from the
other end of the country. Although all
examples contain the same elements, the layout
of the Snettisham class ornament might be *78, 79*
adapted to the form of the object which it
decorated. Thus, the compact layout of the
ornament on the Snettisham torc is very differ-
ent from the drawn-out design on the Thames *51, 52*
helmet.

'Attention has been drawn to resemblances between the ornament on the Ipswich torcs and that on the Llyn Cerrig crescentic plaque, the Torrs pony cap and the series of Iron Age bronze mirrors. It would, however, hardly be possible to date the Ipswich torcs on stylistic evidence were it not that a firm date for one point during the lifetime of the Snettisham class of ornament is provided by the great torc from Snettisham itself. One of the hollow terminals of this contained a coin of the Atrebates of Allen's type Gallo–Belgic Dc. This coin may have been minted either in Gaul or in Britain, and a worn specimen of the type was found on Jersey in the Le Catillon hoard, which was deposited between 56–51 BC. It therefore appears that the Gallo–Belgic Dc coinage was current during the second quarter of the first century BC and the great torc from Snettisham will be of this date.'

The date of deposition of the Snettisham torc and the objects associated with it cannot be determined with any certainty, but since it can be argued from the evidence of the coins that the Snettisham treasure as a whole originated between South Suffolk and the Thames Basin, the burial of the Snettisham treasure may be associated with the overthrow and flight of Addedomarus, king of the tribe of the Trinovantes of Essex, following his defeat by Tasciovanus, king of the Catuvellauni of Hertfordshire, in 10 BC.

As regards the use of torcs such as those from Snettisham and Ipswich, it must be borne in mind that such objects must have been exceedingly precious and would only have been worn by people of the highest rank, and then perhaps only on ceremonial occasions. One might perhaps draw a comparison between torcs of this kind and the modern English crown jewels. Or it may have been the case that these torcs were made only as an ornament for an idol, or as votive objects to be deposited in a shrine or sacred site.

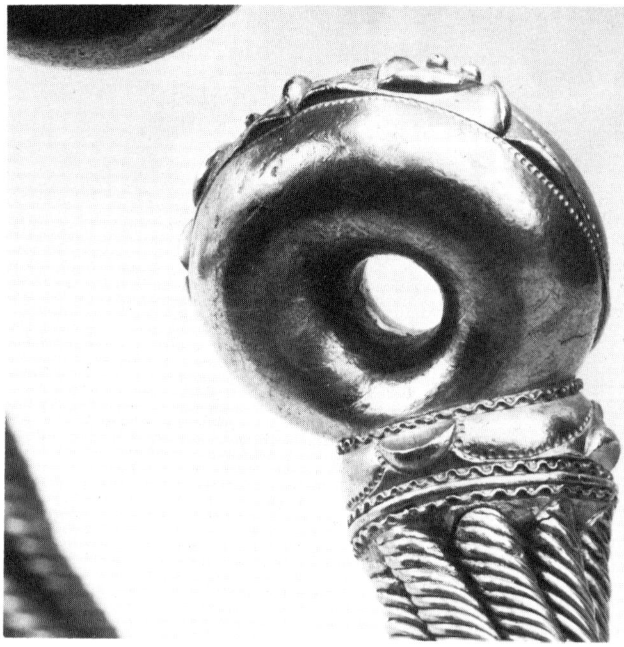

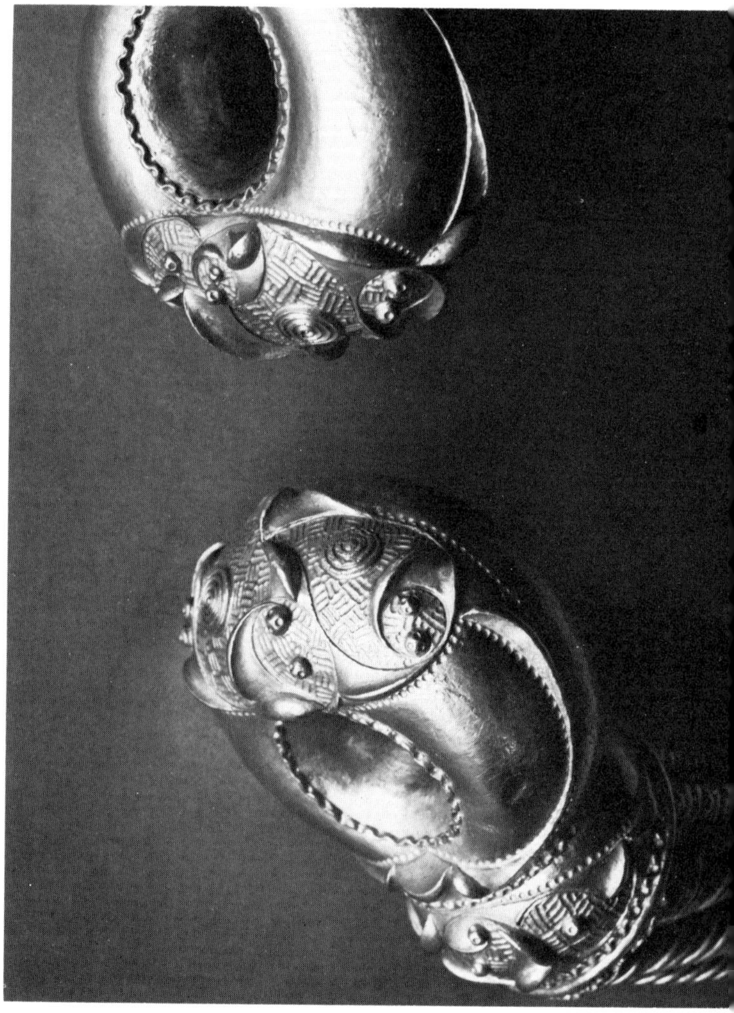

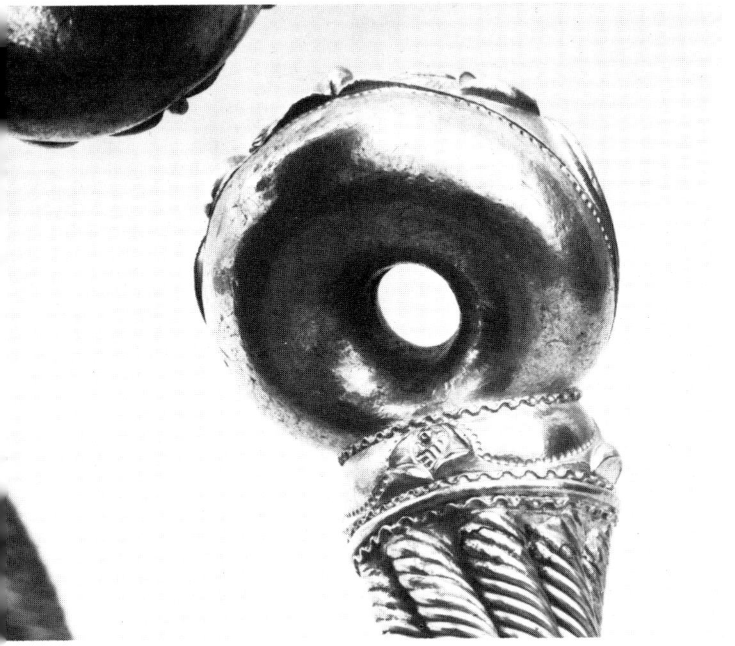

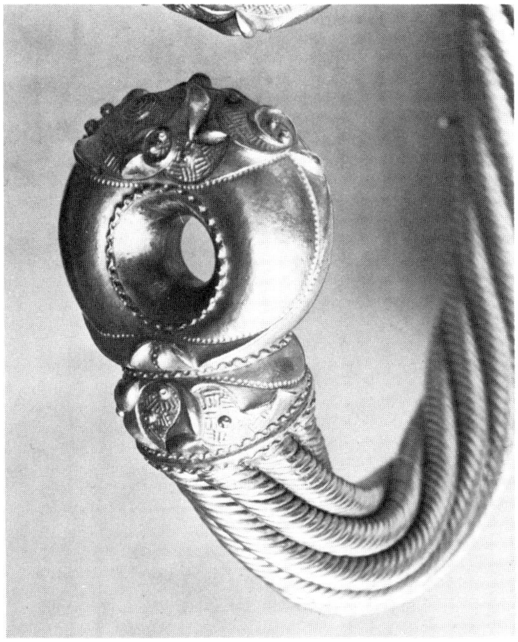

80 81 82

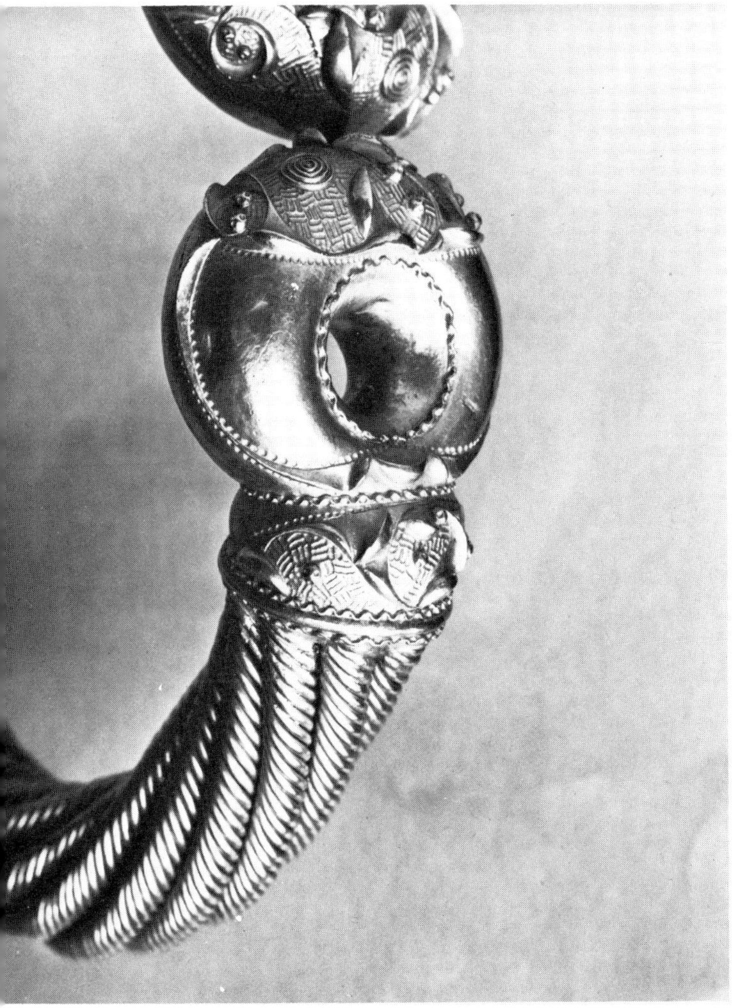

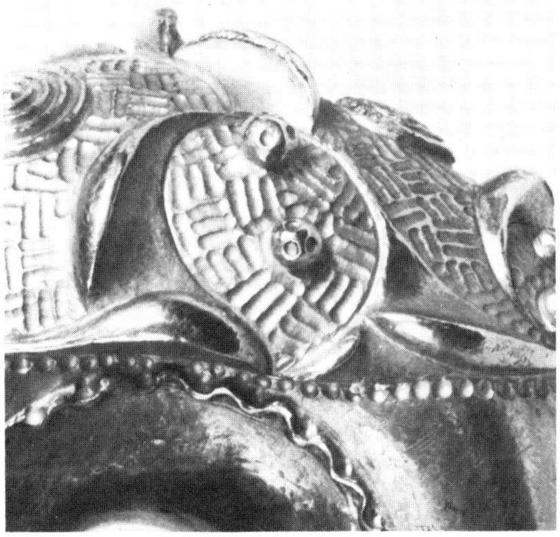

85

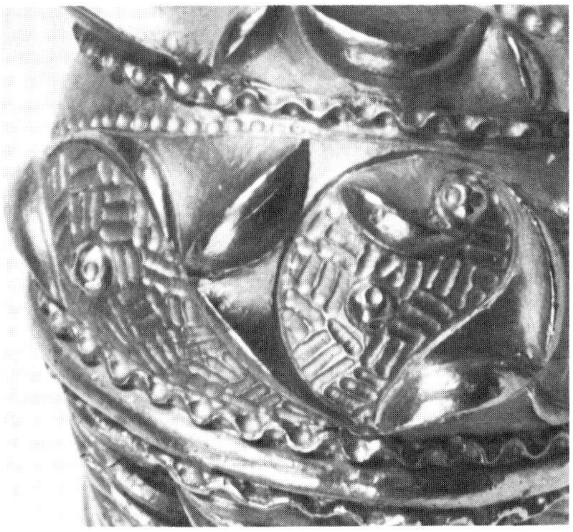

83 84 86

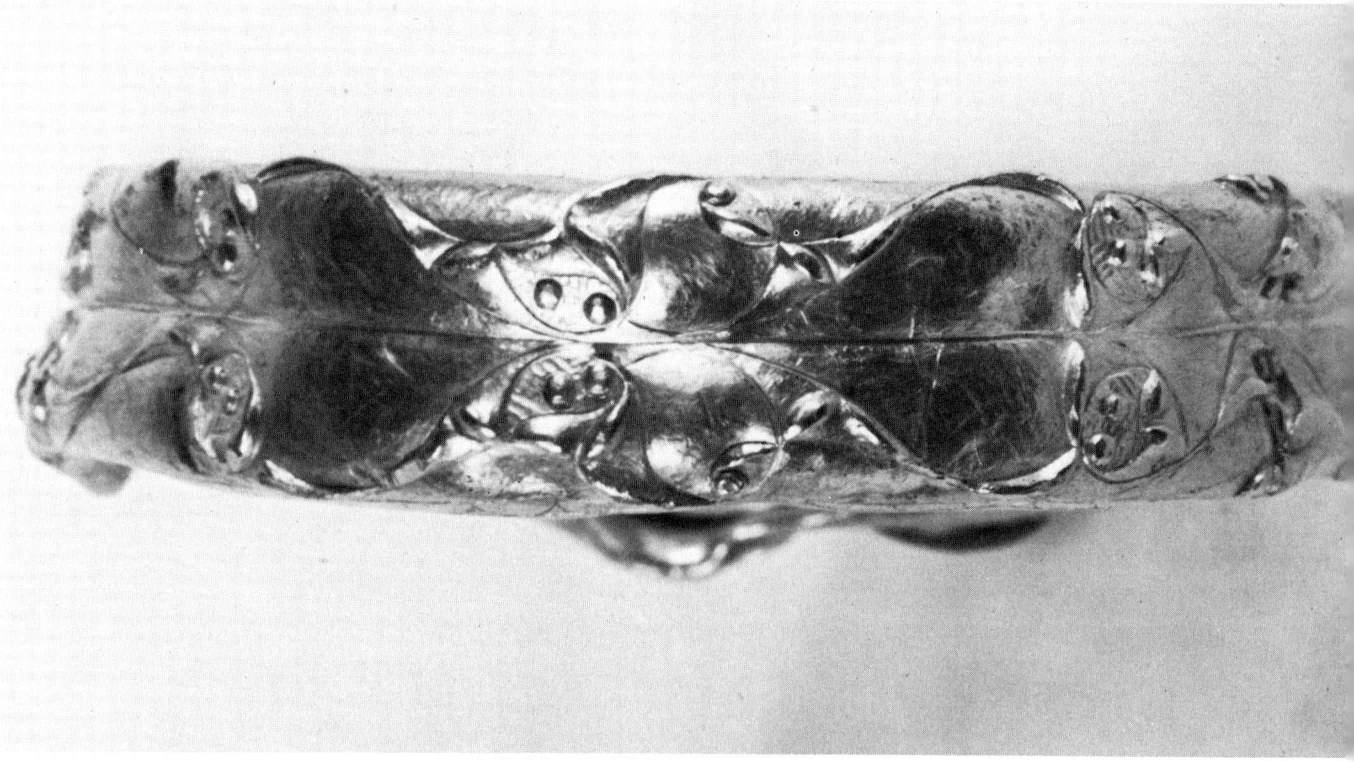

87

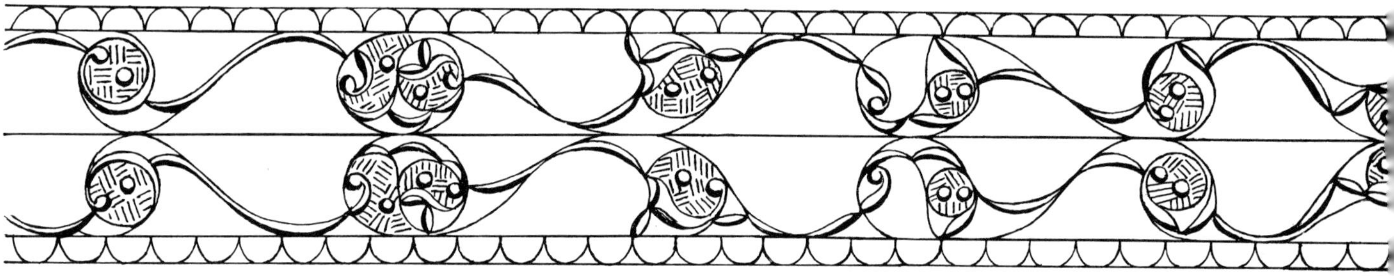

90

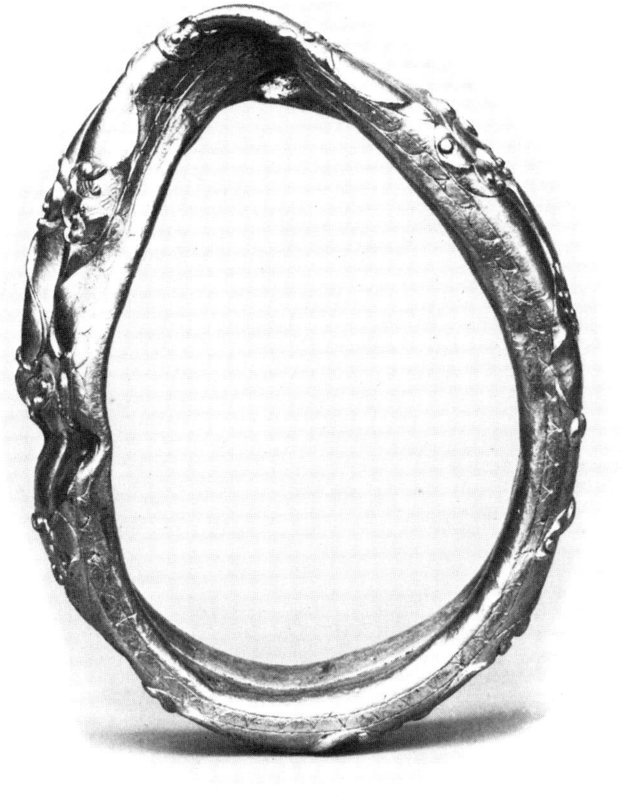

88

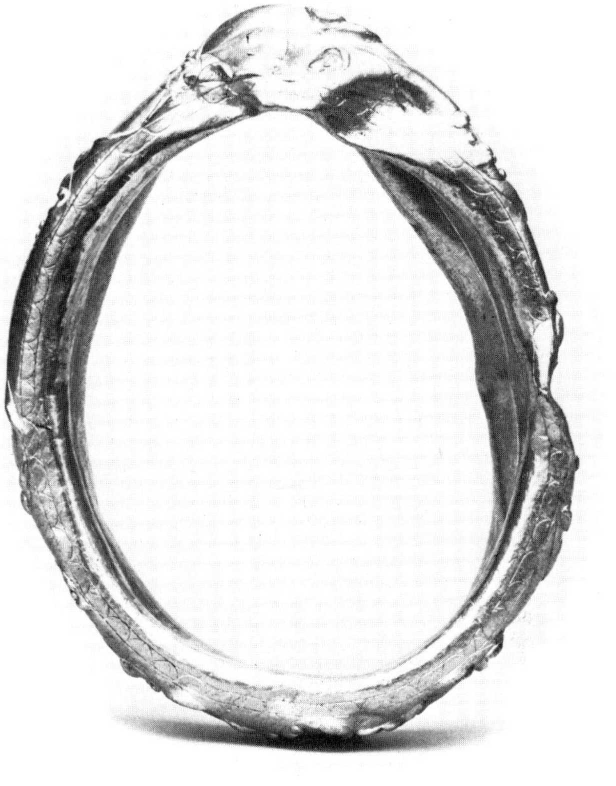

89

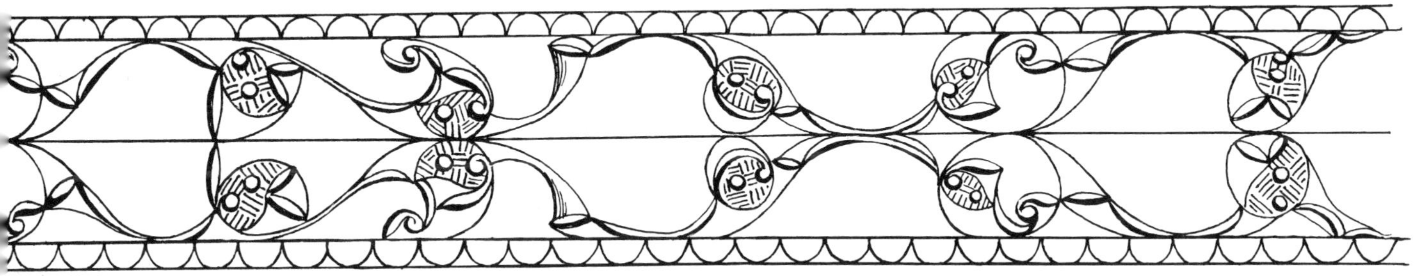

Bibliography

Later Prehistoric Antiquities of the British Isles, London, 1953, pp. 66, 68, frontispiece and pl. xvii.

R. Rainbird Clarke, 'The Early Iron Age Treasure from Snettisham, Norfolk', *Proc. Prehist. Soc.* 1954, pp. 27ff.

C. Fox, *Pattern and Purpose*, Cardiff, 1958, pp. 45, 48, figs. 33–4.

J. V. S. Megaw, *Art of the European Iron Age*, Bath, 1970, no. 291.

CHAPTER SEVEN

BRONZE MIRRORS

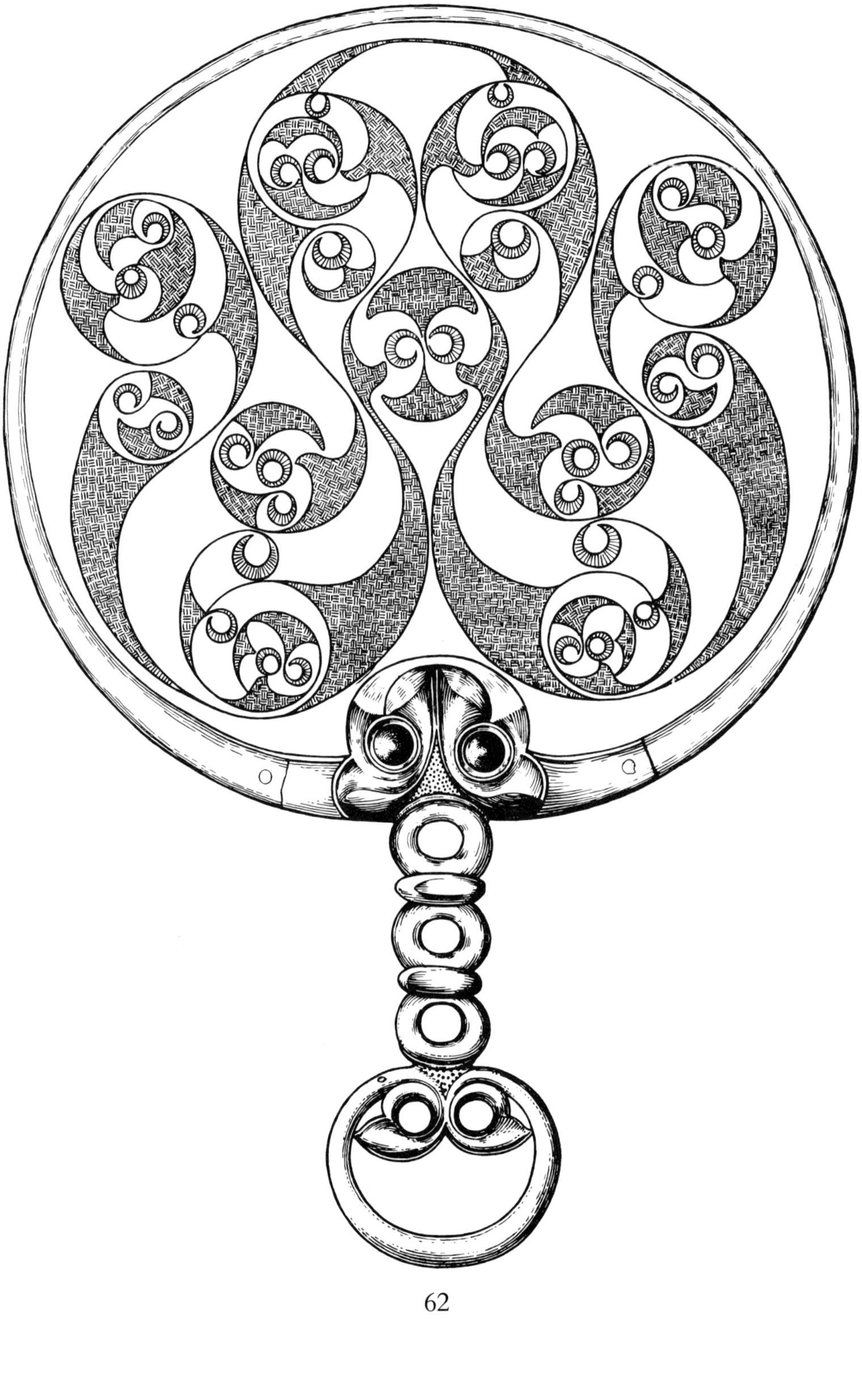

62

The collection contains two fine examples of the decorated bronze mirrors which are among the most notable products of British craftsmen during the Early Iron Age. Both belong to what has been defined as the 'Western Mirror School'. Characteristics of the school are: (*a*) the large size of the mirrors, which were probably designed for suspension; (*b*) handles of multiple-loop type; (*c*) ornament engraved or chased in regular 'basketry' and hatching; (*d*) designs of fold-over symmetry, some set out with compasses, and (*e*) crescent-rings and 'peltae' are prevalent motifs of the design.

These mirrors were made in the first half of the first century AD. With the exception of the
95, VIII example from Desborough, Northamptonshire, and an exported mirror found at Nijmegen in the Netherlands, they have only been found in the English West Country. Similar ornament to that on the 'Western Mirror School' occurs on a harness mount from the Polden hoard from Somerset, which is also in the Department of Prehistoric and Romano-British Antiquities. This hoard was found about 1800 somewhere on the Polden Hills and was made up of horse gear – bits, terrets, strap-links, fittings which have been interpreted as fastenings for a horse-cloth or caparison, together with three shield bosses, brooches and some other items. The hoard was probably concealed *c.* AD 50, perhaps at the time of the Roman advance into the Mendips.

Surprisingly, the motifs found on the South-western mirrors also appear on a crescentic plaque from Balmaclellan, Kirkcudbrightshire.

THE HOLCOMBE MIRROR

This mirror was found in an Iron Age pit underlying a Roman villa, at Holcombe, near Uplyme, Devon, in 1970. It appeared that the pit had been deliberately filled in one operation and that the mirror had been deliberately buried in it for concealment. The mirror measures 37·2 cm. long from rim to handle end, and 26 cm. wide. The mirror-plate is only *92*
1 mm. thick and is framed by a rim of cylindrical section. The handle is a variant of the *94*
multiple-loop type and is notable for the pair of trumpet scrolls set back to back in the terminal ring with a triangle of punched stippling above, and also for the elaborate ornamentation of the moulding where the handle joins the mirror itself. When inverted, this moulding, at first sight merely a stylized design, is seen, in characteristic Celtic fashion, to emerge as a fantastic face, whether owl or *94*
cat, the eyes of which are formed by two studs of red glass. The punched stippling, incidentally, although not known on other mirrors, does occur on pieces in the Polden Hill hoard and so may be regarded as at home in the South-west. If it is accepted that its designers intended the Holcombe mirror to be seen with the handle uppermost it follows that such mirrors, whether or not they were used in this position, were at least so suspended when not in use. This conclusion is supported by the wear on the inside of the terminal ring of the Desborough mirror.

The engraved design on the back of the *91, 93*
mirror was probably set out with a pair of compasses; the outline was then engraved and the filling of the pattern completed by chasing. The design is basically a symmetrical lyre *91*
pattern about the vertical axis, inverted unless the handle is placed uppermost. In spite of the intricacy of the design it consists of very few motifs, simply small crescents or crescent-rings and peltae. The peltae are filled in with 'basketry' made up of alternating panels of three horizontal and three vertical strokes, and the crescents are filled with a series of radial lines.

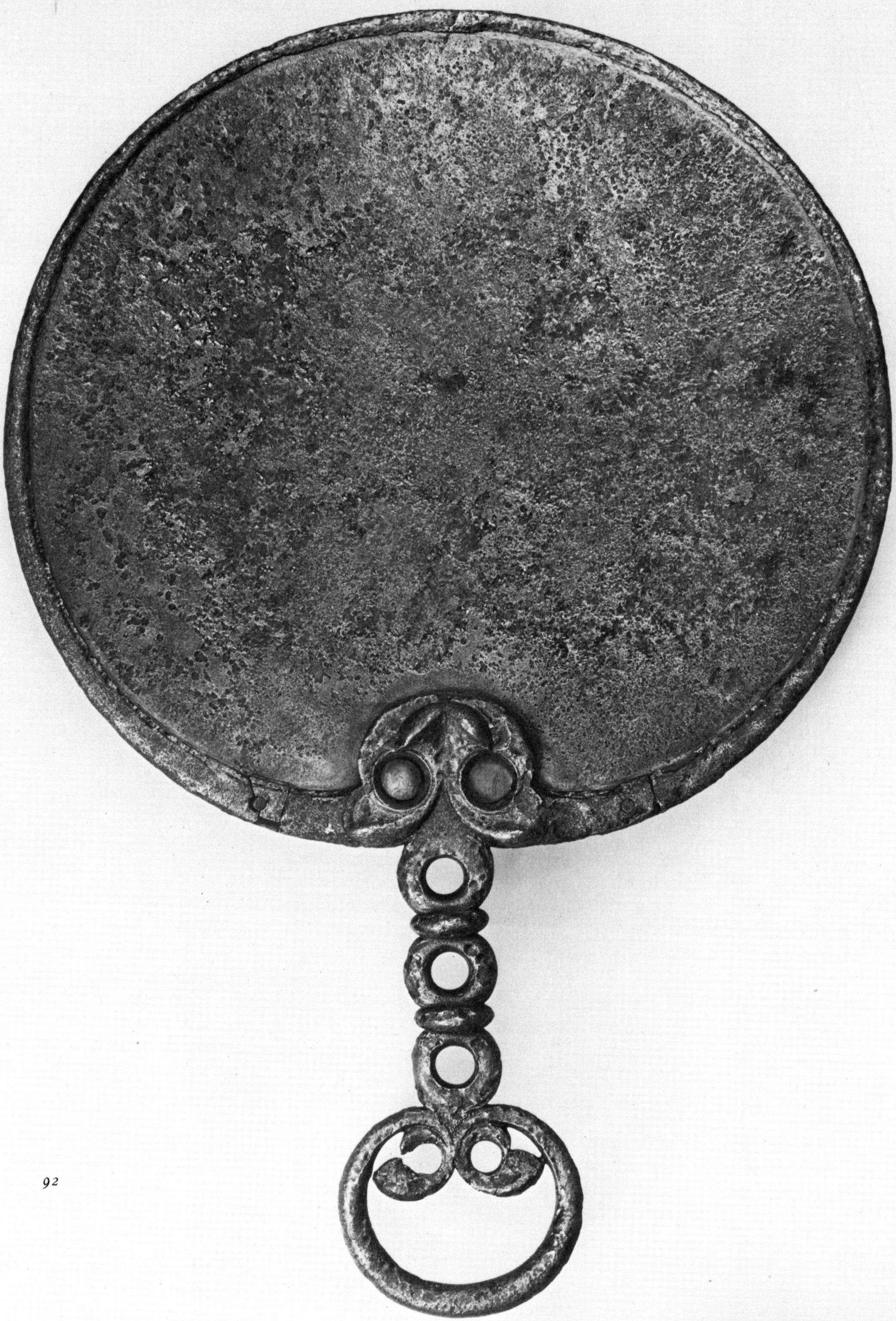

92

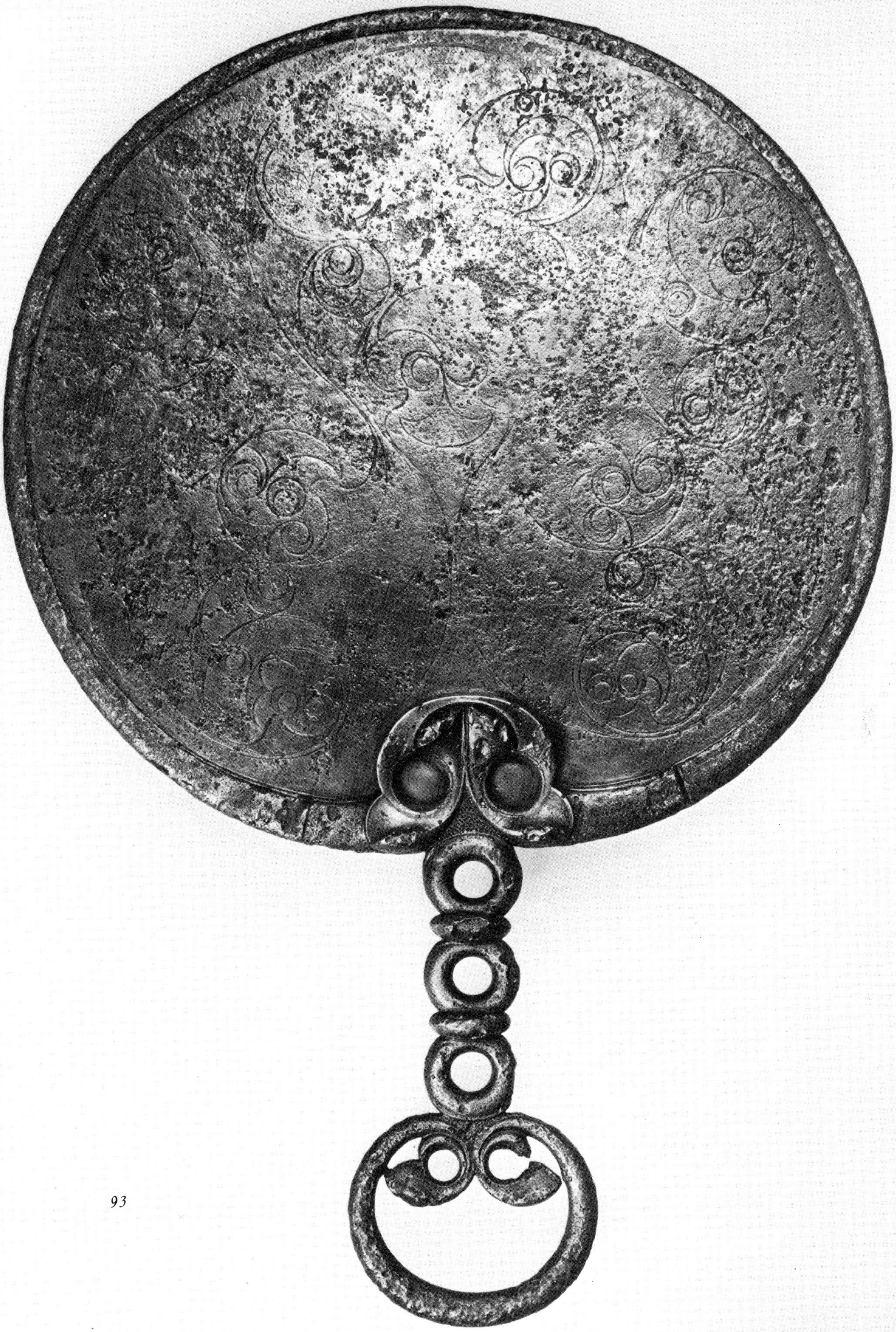

93

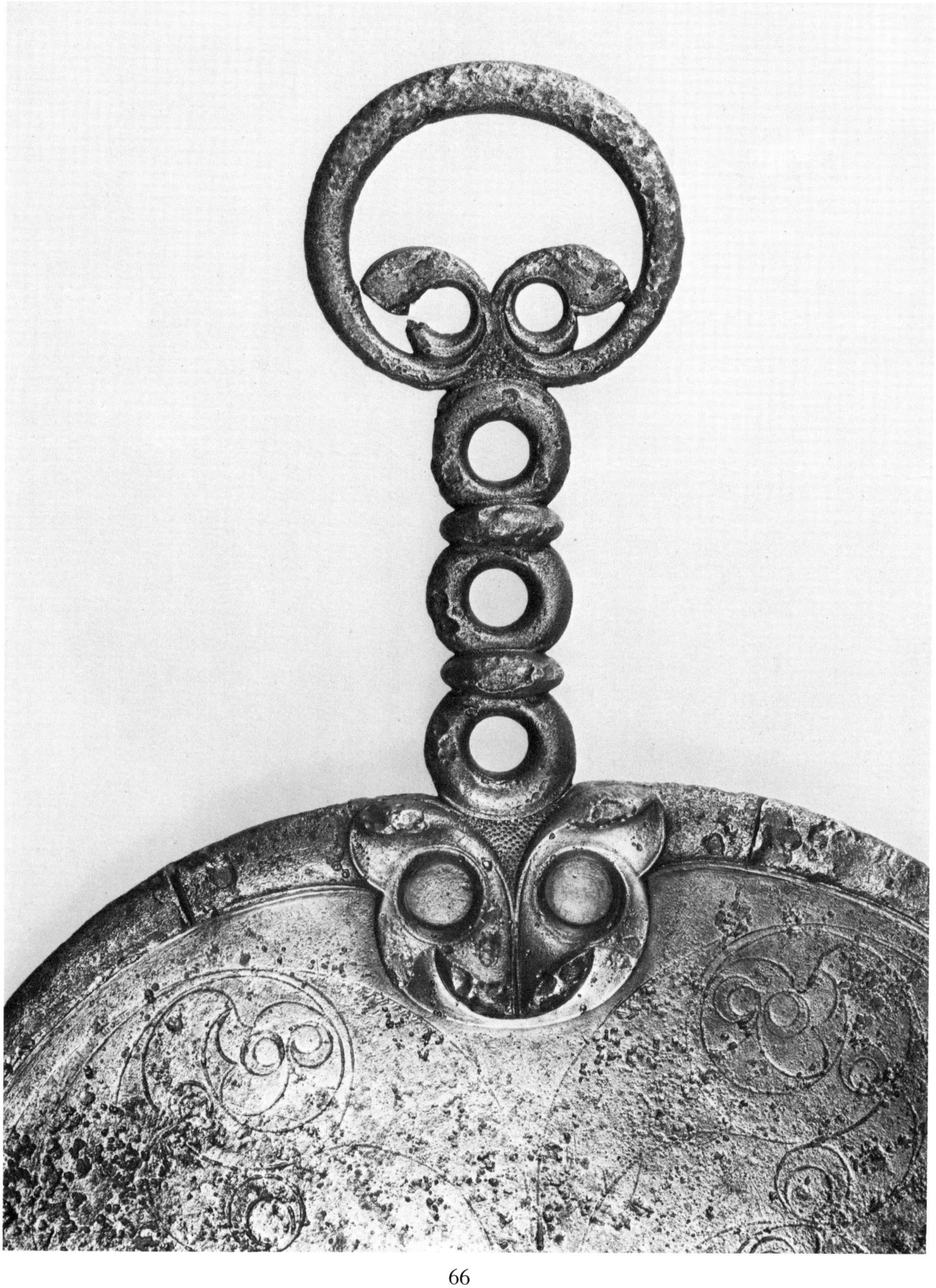

94

95

THE DESBOROUGH MIRROR

This mirror was found on the outskirts of
VIII Desborough during digging operations for ironstone in 1908. It is not recorded as having been associated with any objects of archaeological significance but it had probably been deposited in a grave, as was the case of the mirrors from Birdlip, Gloucestershire, and Colchester, Essex. The Desborough mirror is kidney-shaped and measures 26 cm. wide and 35 cm. high. It is closely similar to the Holcombe mirror, the design, basically a 95
lyre-pattern, having a fold-over symmetry and being made up of the same motifs as is the case with the Holcombe mirror and other examples of the 'Western Mirror School'.

Bibliography

Guide to Antiquities of the Early Iron Age in the Department of British and Mediaeval Antiquities, British Museum, London, 1925, p. 122, pl. x, fig. 133 (Desborough Mirror).

Later Prehistoric Antiquities of the British Isles, London, 1953, p. 66, pl. xvi (Desborough Mirror).

A. Fox, 'The Holcombe Mirror', *Antiquity* 46 (1972), pp. 293ff.

A. Fox and S. Pollard, 'A Decorated Bronze Mirror from an Iron Age Settlement at Holcombe near Uplyme, Devon', *Antiquaries Journal* 53, pt. 1 (1973), pp. 16ff.

C. Fox, 'A Shield Boss of the Early Iron Age from Anglesey', *Archaeological Cambrensis* 98 (1945), pp. 199ff. (development of mirror ornament).

C. Fox, 'Celtic Mirror Handles in Britain', *Archaeologia Cambrensis* 100 (1948), pp. 24ff.

R. A. Smith, 'On a Late Celtic Mirror found at Desborough, Northants, and other mirrors of the period', *Archaeologia* 61, pt. 2 (1908), pp. 329ff.

T. G. E. Powell, *Prehistoric Art*, London, 1966, p. 243 and illus. 243 (for the Desborough Mirror).

CHAPTER EIGHT

MASSIVE BRONZE ARMLETS

There are two pairs of armlets in the Department belonging to a group of some fifteen similar finds which, with one exception from Ireland, are all from Scotland. It would seem probable that the armlets were made from wax models which were moulded flat and then bent round, when they could be reproduced in bronze by the *cire-perdue* or 'lost wax' method. However, some at least of the armlets appear to have been cast flat and subsequently curved by a process of annealing and hammering. Much consolidation has been carried out on most of the armlets after casting.

Although it is hardly possible to date massive bronze armlets of the Castle Newe and Drummond Castle type at all closely, the group has been ascribed to between 50–150 AD.

THE CASTLE NEWE ARMLETS

IX This pair of armlets was found in the entrance of a souterrain or subterranean chamber at Castle Newe, Aberdeenshire. They are of the so-called 'oval' type, i.e. each armlet is formed of three ribs, the outer two of which continue round the ends to form ring terminals. Their diameter is 14·5 cm.

No. 1 (Registration No. 1946,4–2,2)

100 The ribs are decorated with transverse lenticular ridges. Each space between these ridges is filled by a pair of slender ridges separated to the width of the rib at each end but converging and touching in the centre. Between the main ribs there lies a pair of 'cable-pattern' narrow *97*
ridges. The armlet appears to have been cast by the *cire-perdue* method, since the inside has a finish suggesting the moulding of a wax model. A circular medallion of red and yellow *99*
glass in a chequer pattern is set in the centre of *IX*
one terminal. The glass itself is held in a frame of what appears to be sheet-bronze with two concentric ribs. The surface is partly broken away revealing what seems to be a clay core and the frame and glass inset are held in position by a mass of dark material on the back, *101*
which overlies the edge of the circular hole containing the glass inset and its mount. Slots at the top and the bottom of the terminal probably indicate the position where wires securing the inset and its mount in position were looped over the edges of the terminal.

No. 2 (Registration No. 1946,4–2,1)

The armlet is of the same design as No. 1 and *104*
no doubt originally contained two glass in- *105*
sets in its terminals, but these have now disappeared. Small holes have been drilled into the inner edges of the spaces in the terminals and these, presumably, originally held pegs or wire securing mounts and medallions similar to those on No. 1.

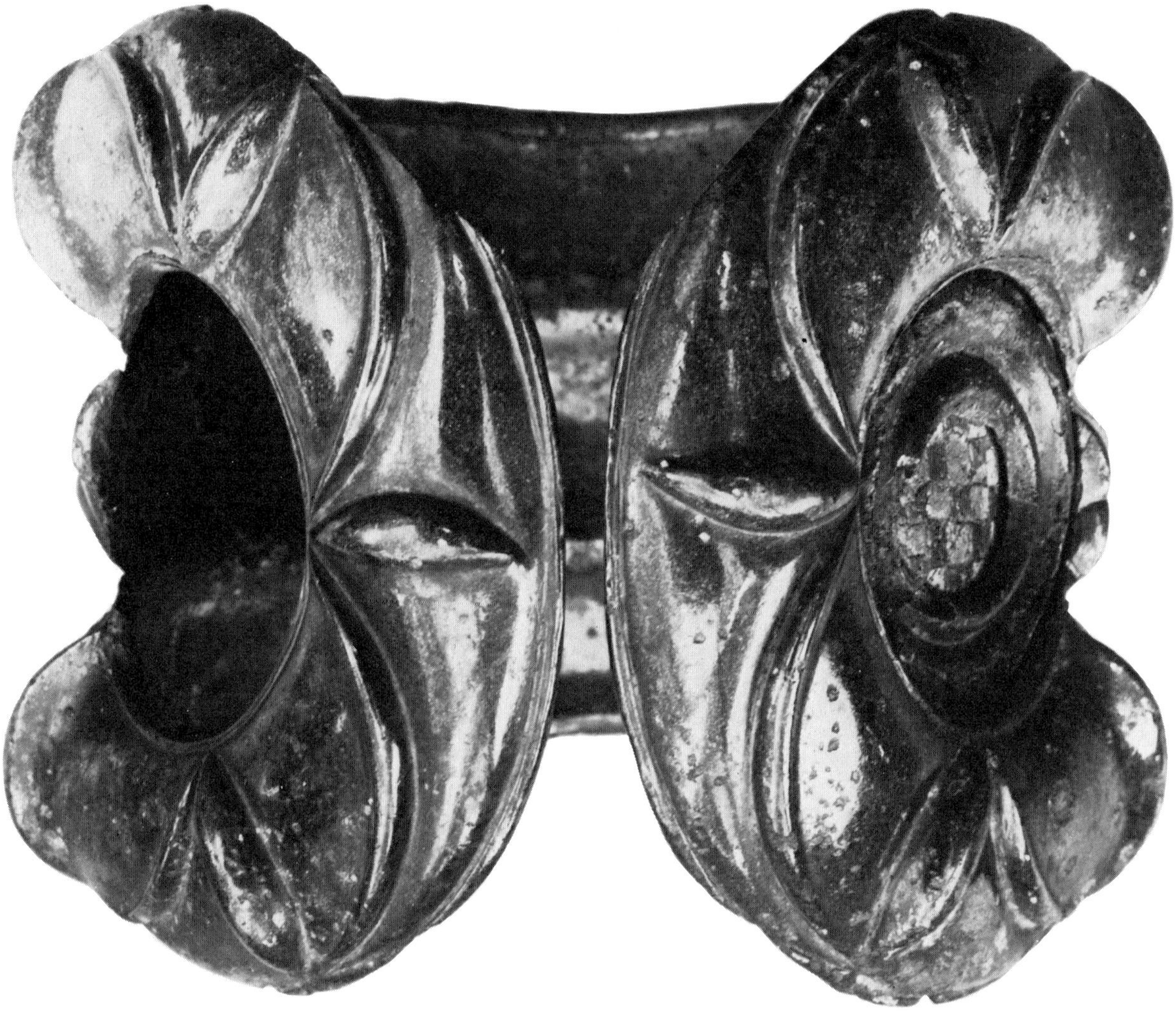

96

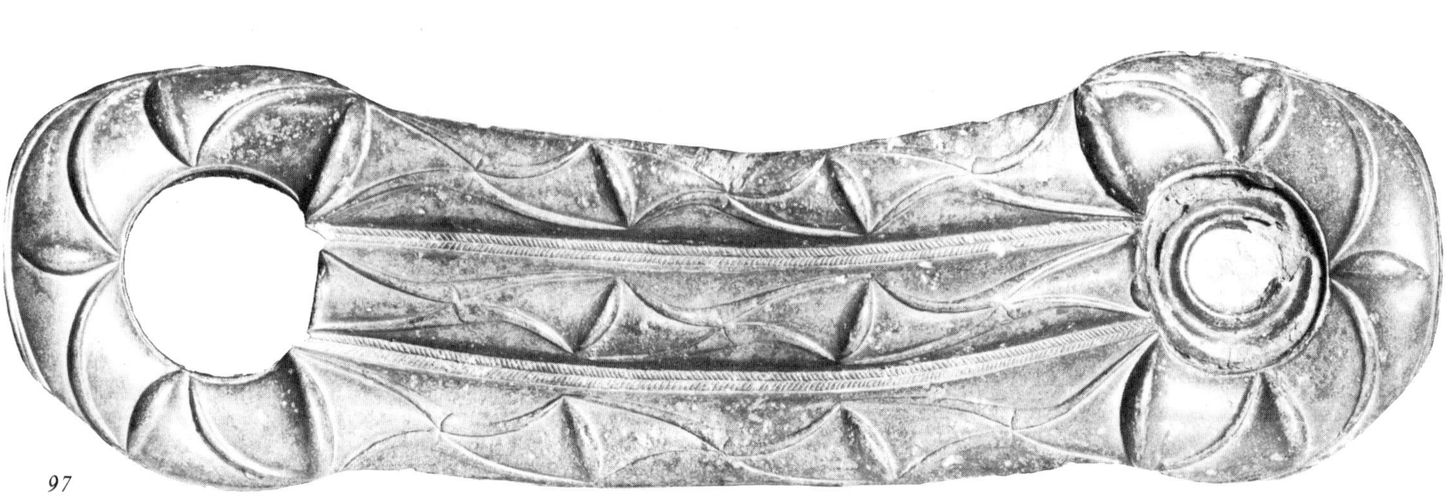

97

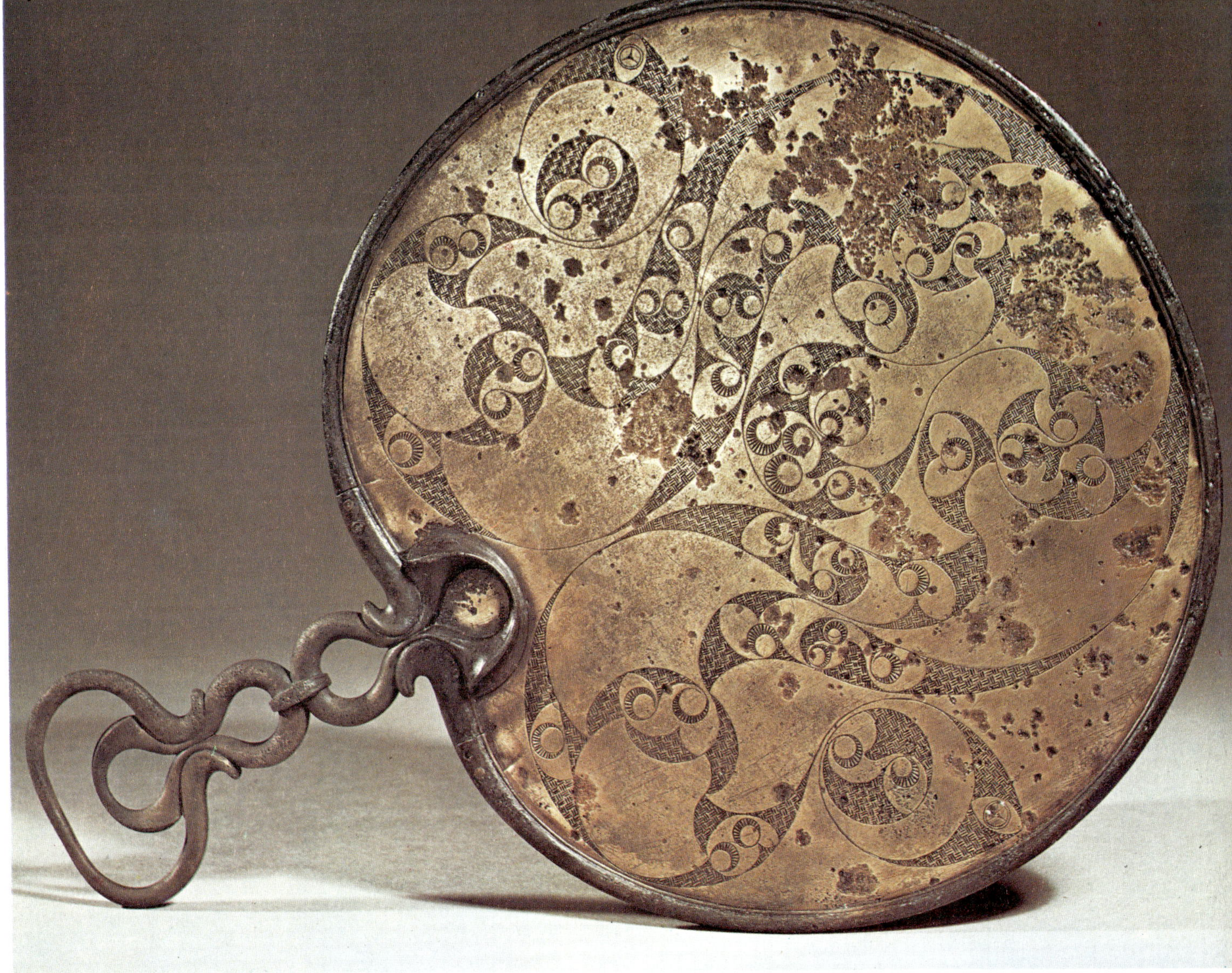

VIII

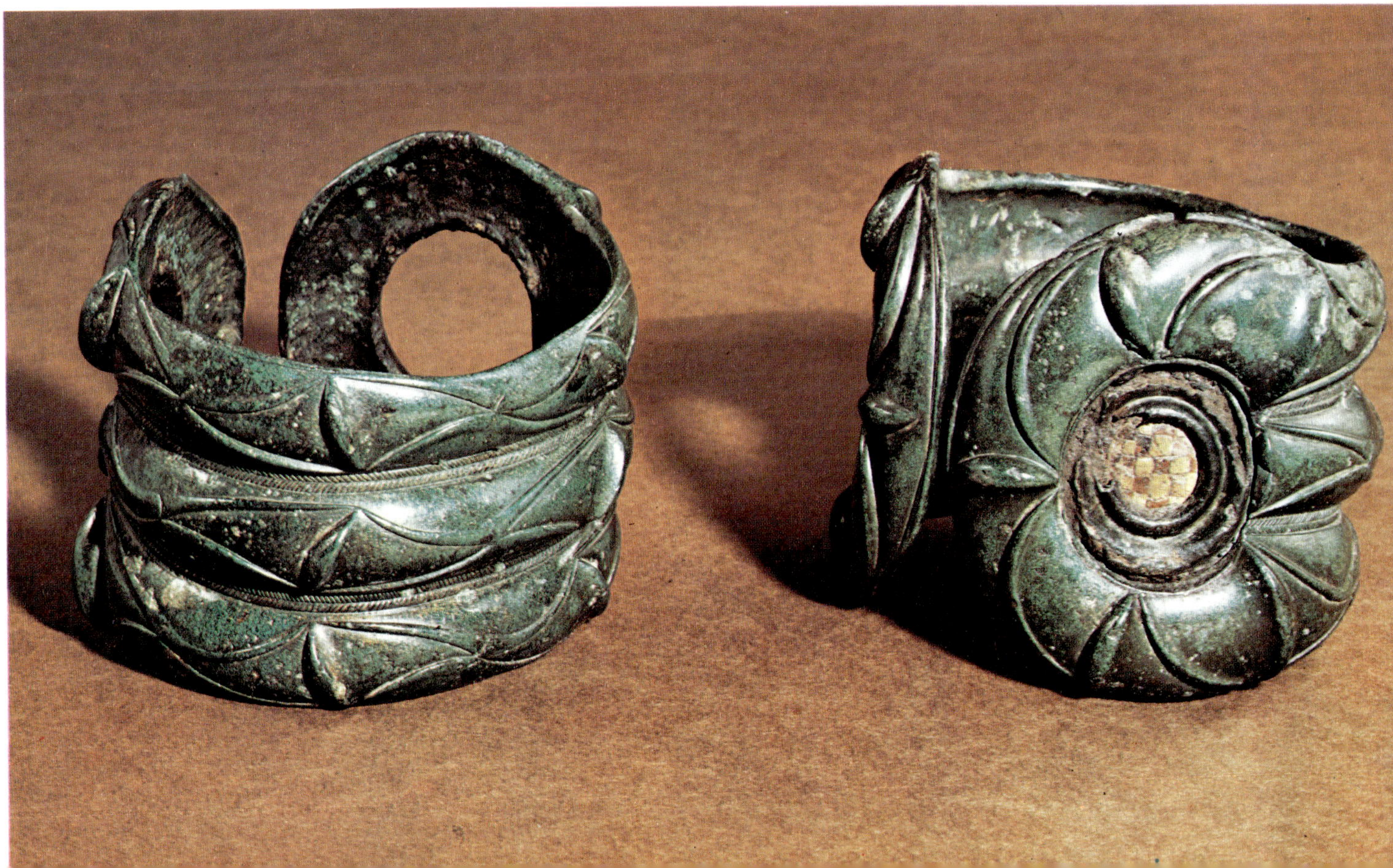

IX

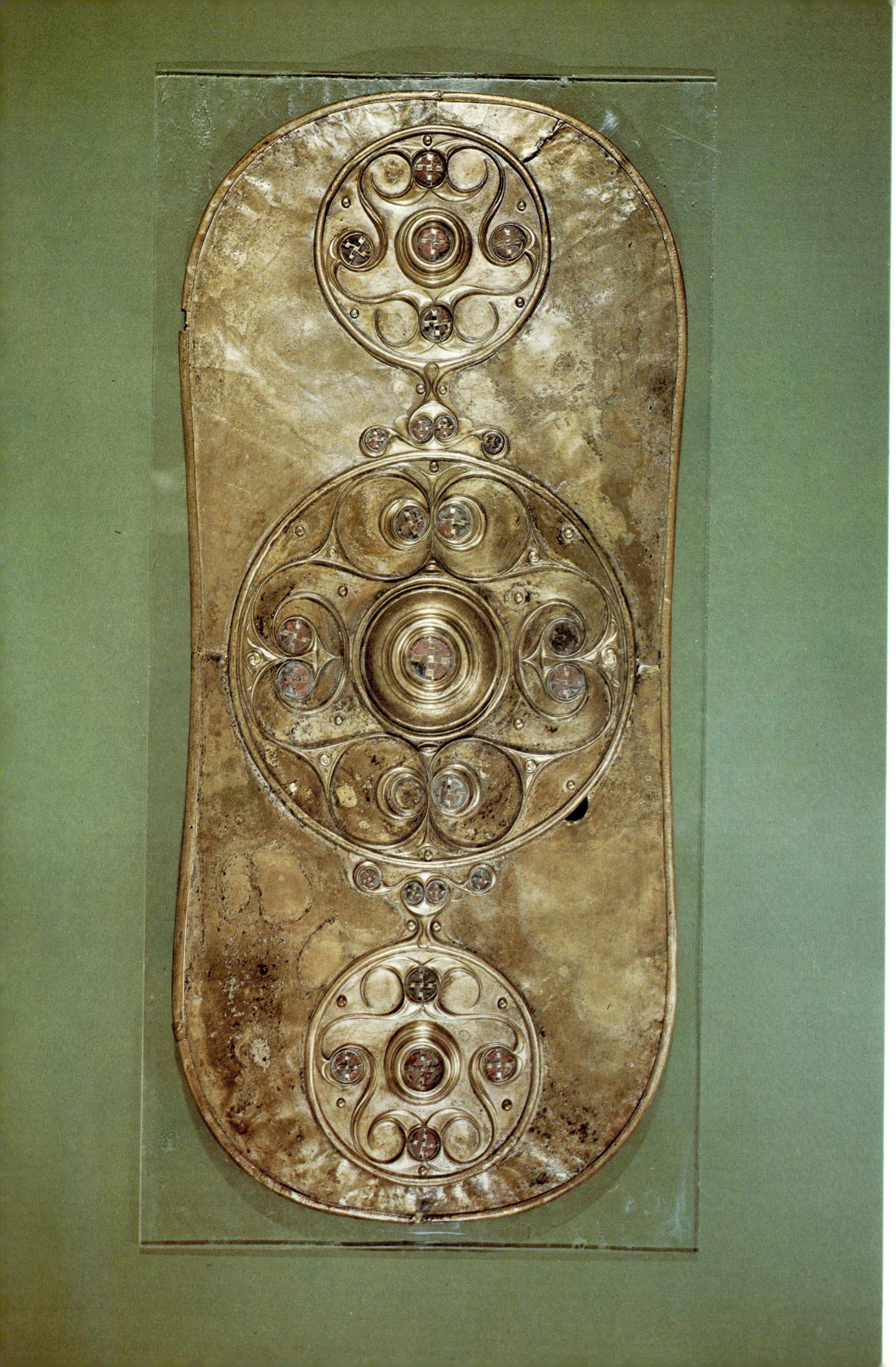

X

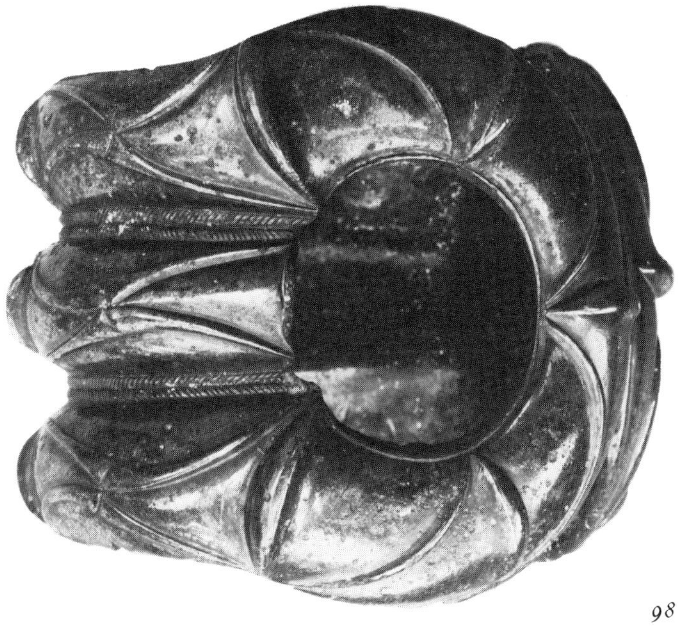

98

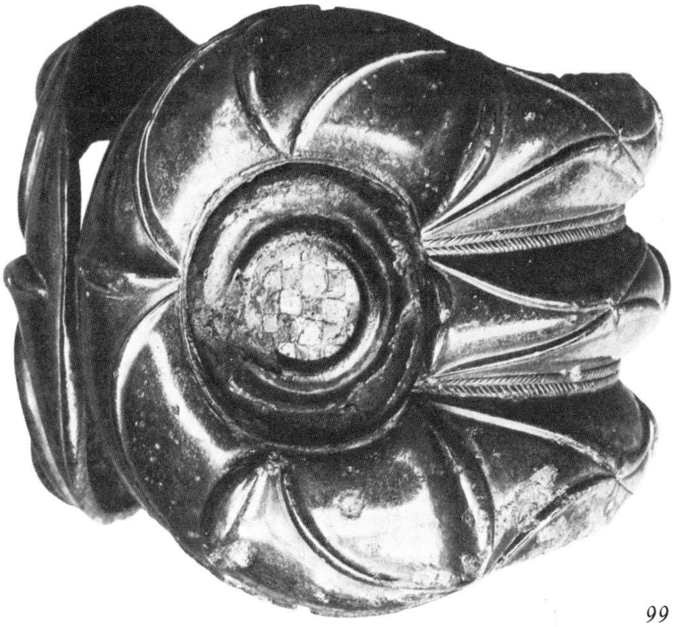

99

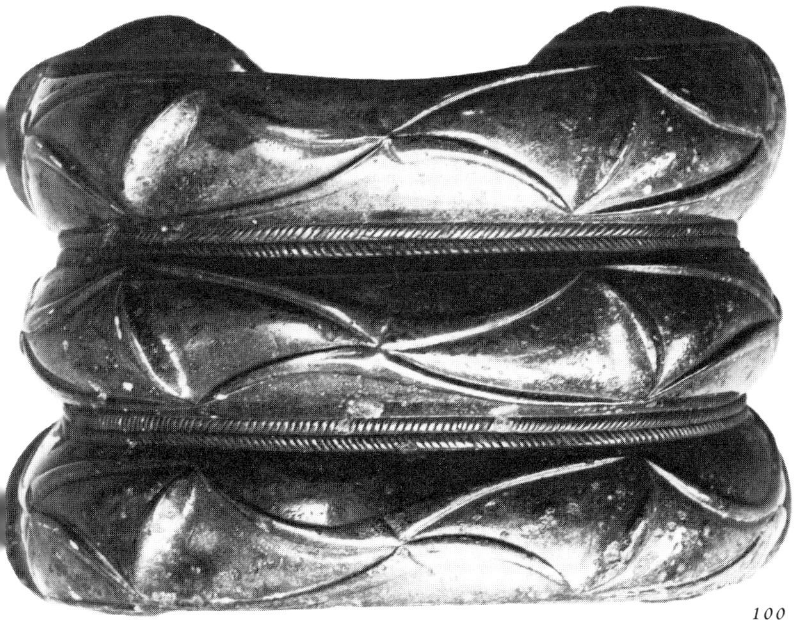

100

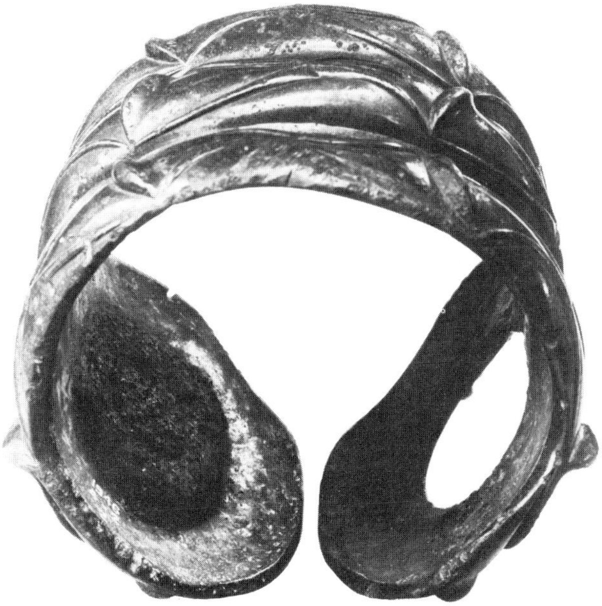

101

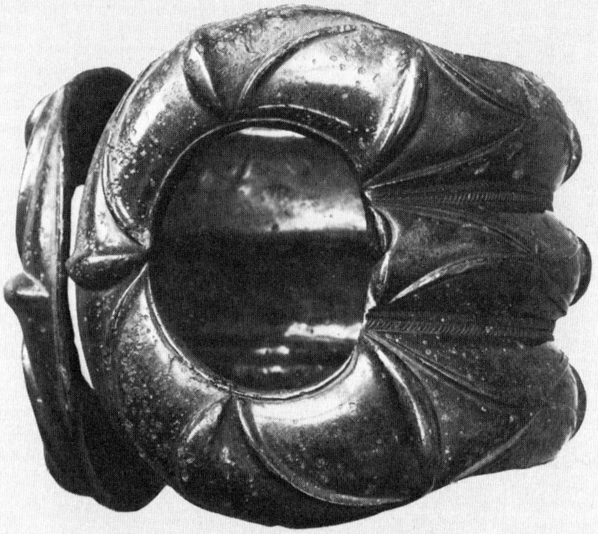
102

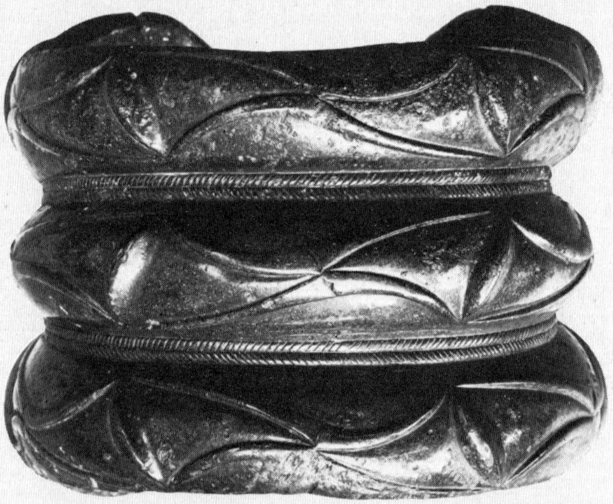
103

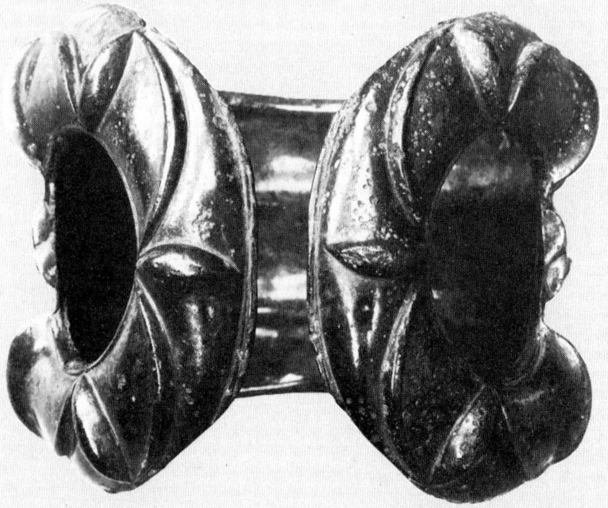
104

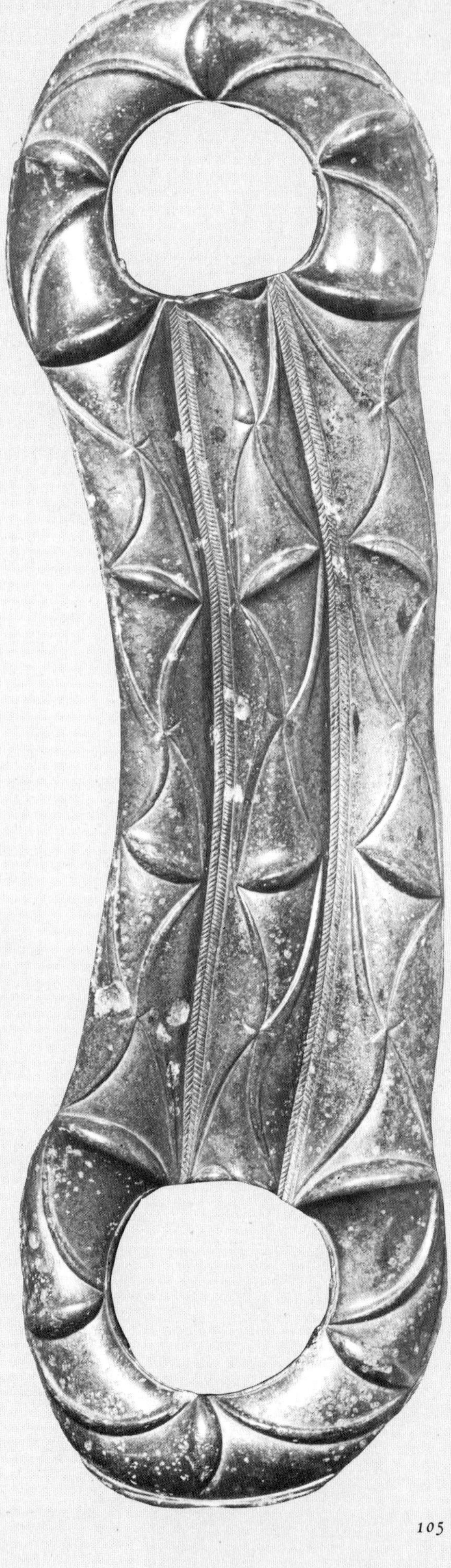
105

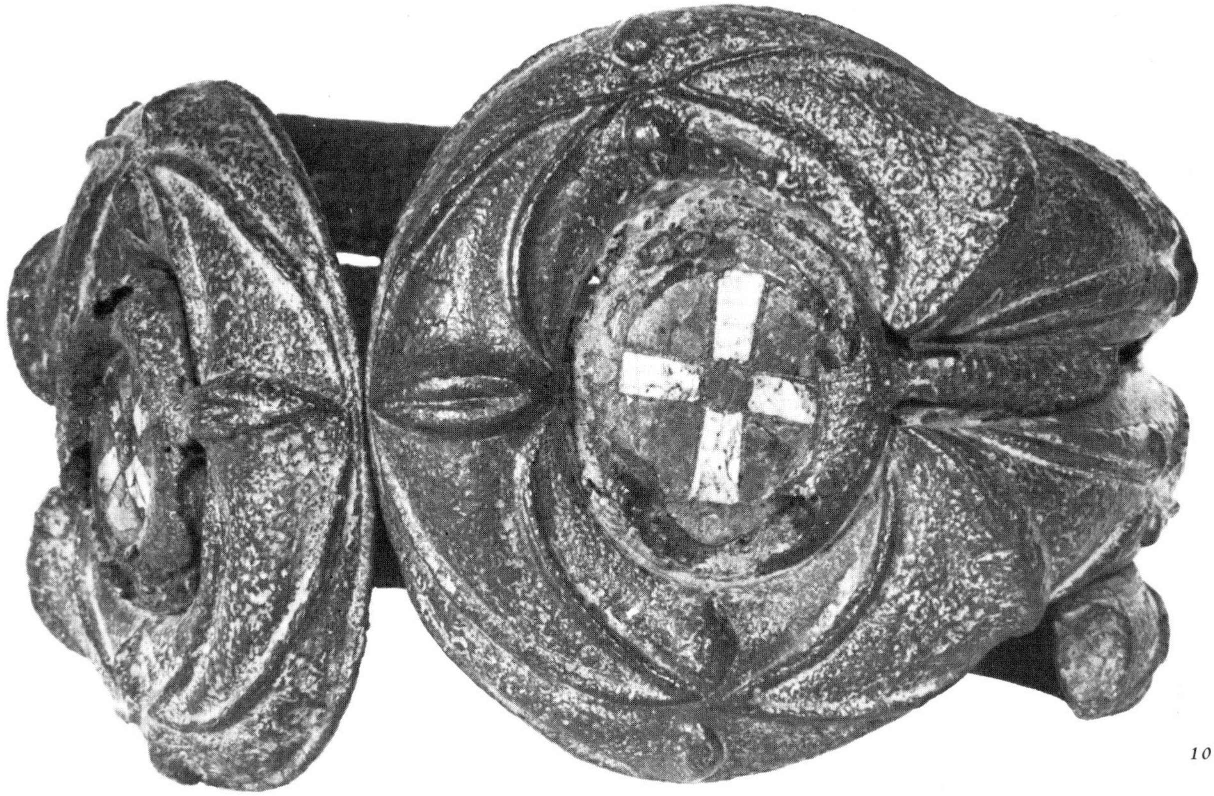

106

THE DRUMMOND CASTLE ARMLETS

This pair of armlets was found in 1837 on the farm of Pitkelloney, near Drummond Castle, and are 14·4 cm. in diameter.

No. 1 (Registration No. 38,7–14,3a)

106 This armlet is of the so-called 'spiral' type, being formed of a spiral of half-round bronze bar. The coils are not joined along their edges except by secondary blobs of metal which have been run in.

114 The lower bar starts a little way in from one terminal, continues to form the margin of the
106–114 opposite terminal and then runs back round the first terminal and back again to end just before the second terminal. The convex outsides of the bars are decorated with transverse lenticular mouldings. Between these are either, (*a*) diagonal ridges flanked by raised semicircles with the curve inwards or, (*b*) crossed-ridges with a pair of small lenticular bosses flanking the junction. The terminals are decorated with a variant of (*b*) above with lipped lenticular mouldings at the end. In the centre of each terminal is a medallion of red glass with a yellow cross. The medallions are set in circular mounts formed of sheet-bronze tubes, and these have extensions between the bars at the front of the armlet. At the back of the medallions is a layer of rust-like encrustation. 112, 113
Each mount is held by a hook fastened over a thin rod lying across the inside of the main bars of the armlet. Inside the main bars are two rough patches of added metal.

No. 2 (Registration No. 38,7–14,3 b)

The general structure is the same as No. 1 115–122
except for a convex moulding with fine transverse ribs which lies between and on the outside of two of the main ribs. This moulding appears to be a separate piece of metal and is hooked over the end of one of the main bars. The ornament is closely similar but not quite identical to that on No. 1. The terminals contain similar glass medallions and mounts but the pattern on the medallions is different, based on a quatrefoil design. The backs of the 121
medallions and the attachment of their mounts 123
are the same as on No. 1.

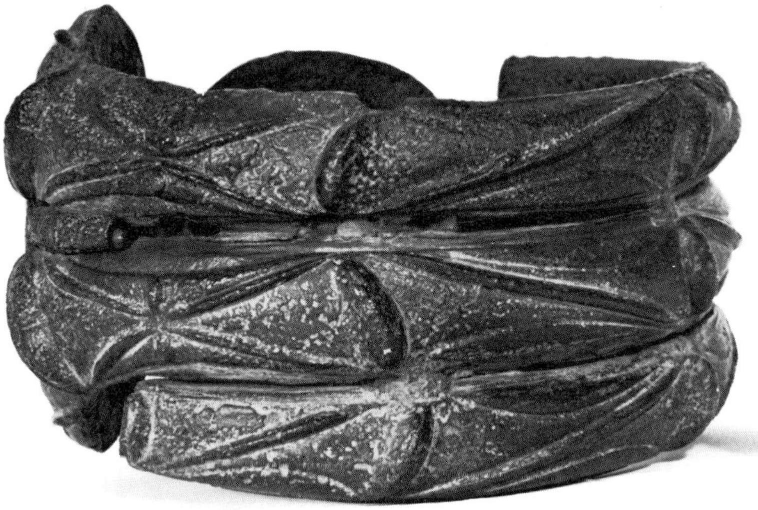

107

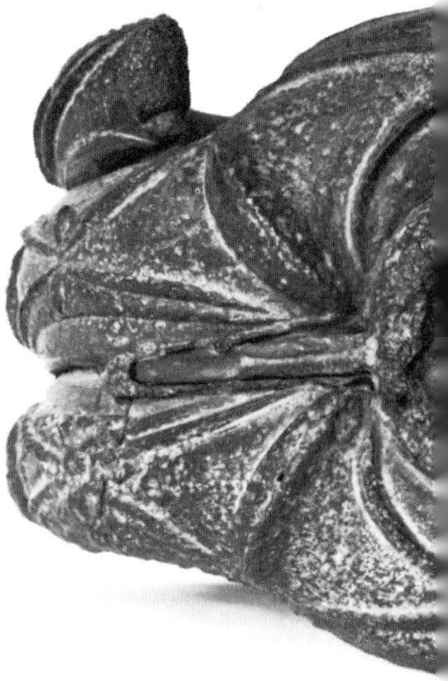

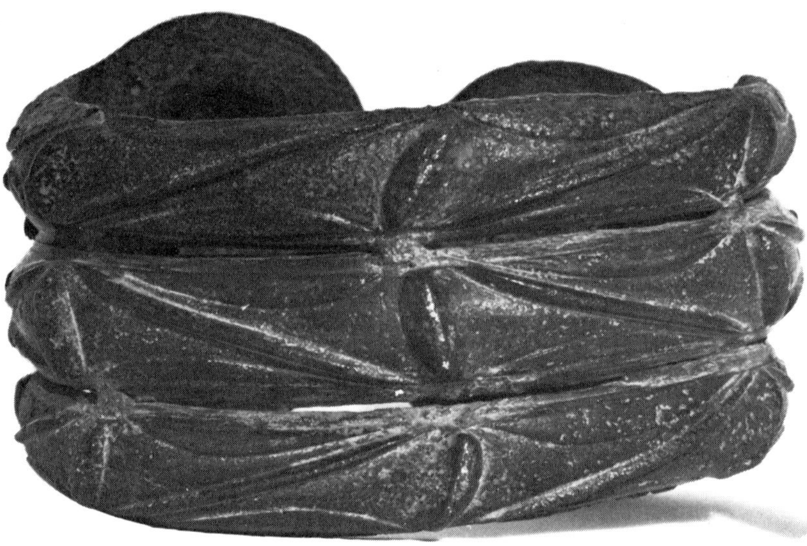

108

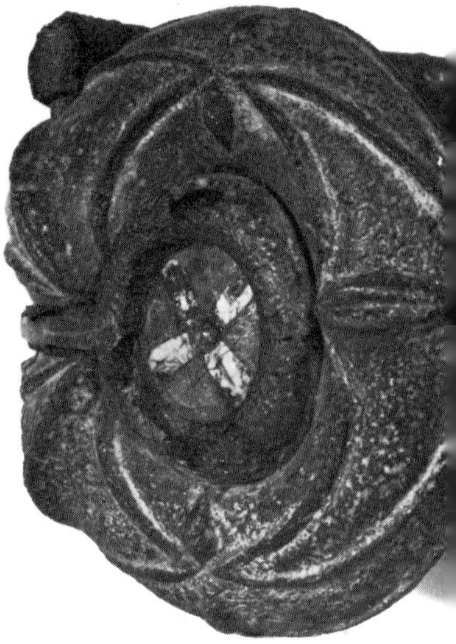

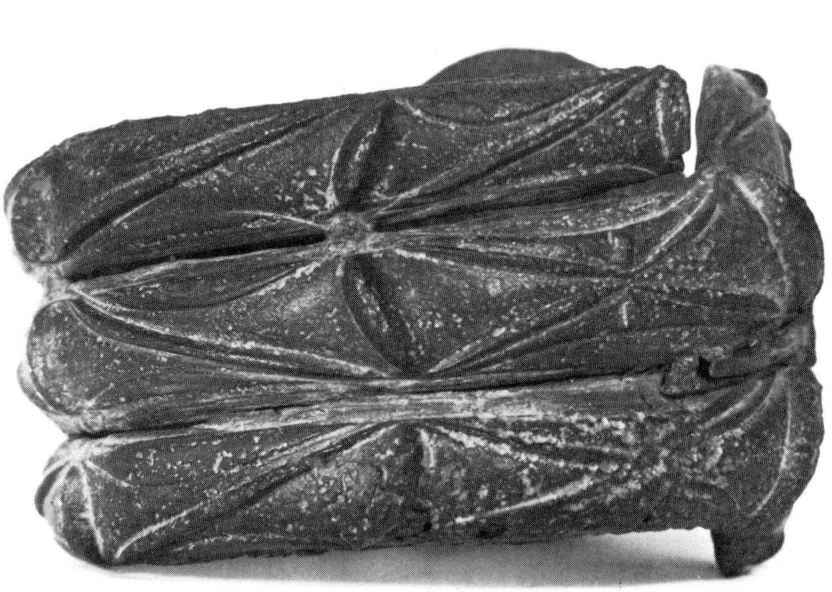

109

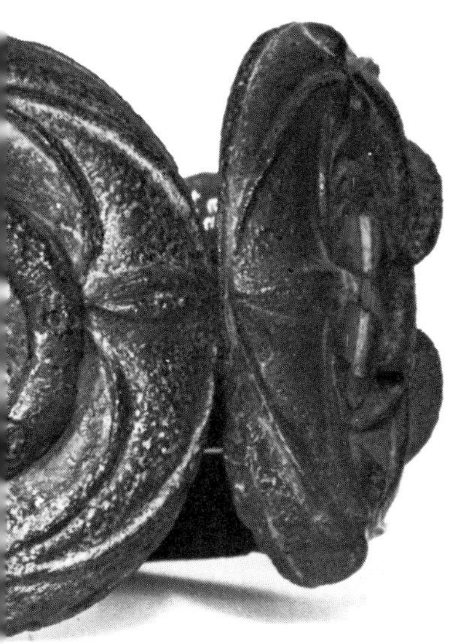

110

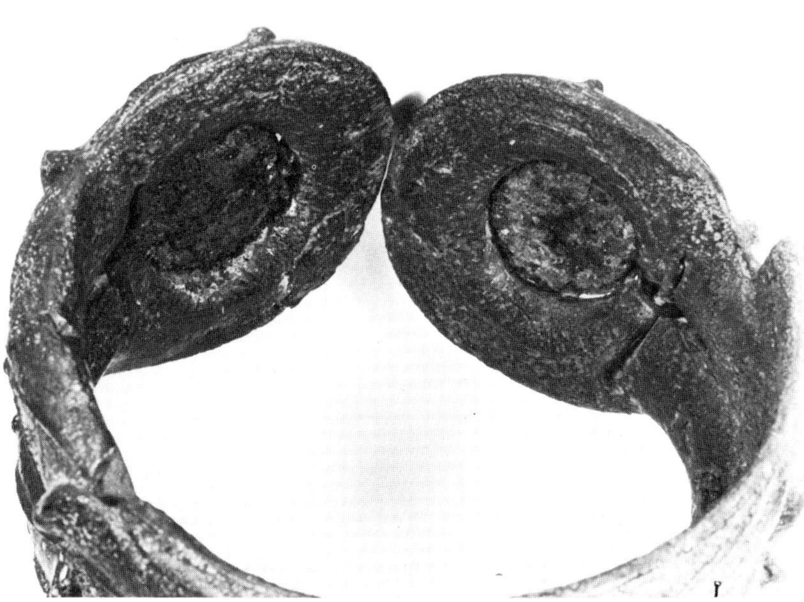

112

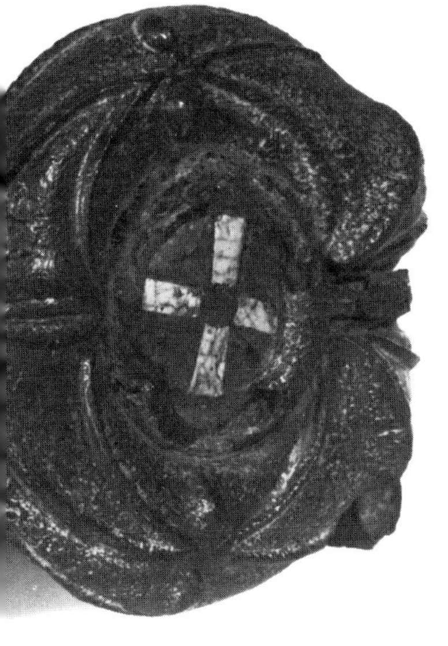

111

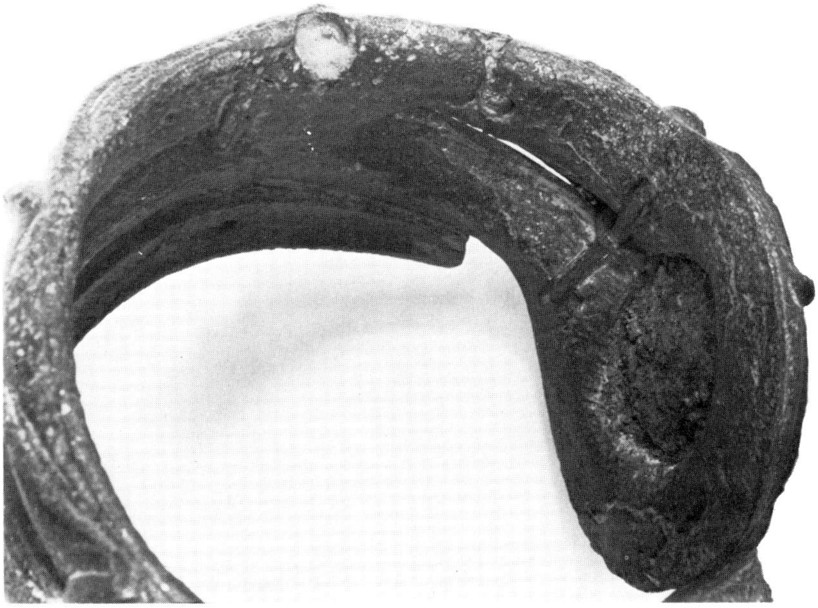

113

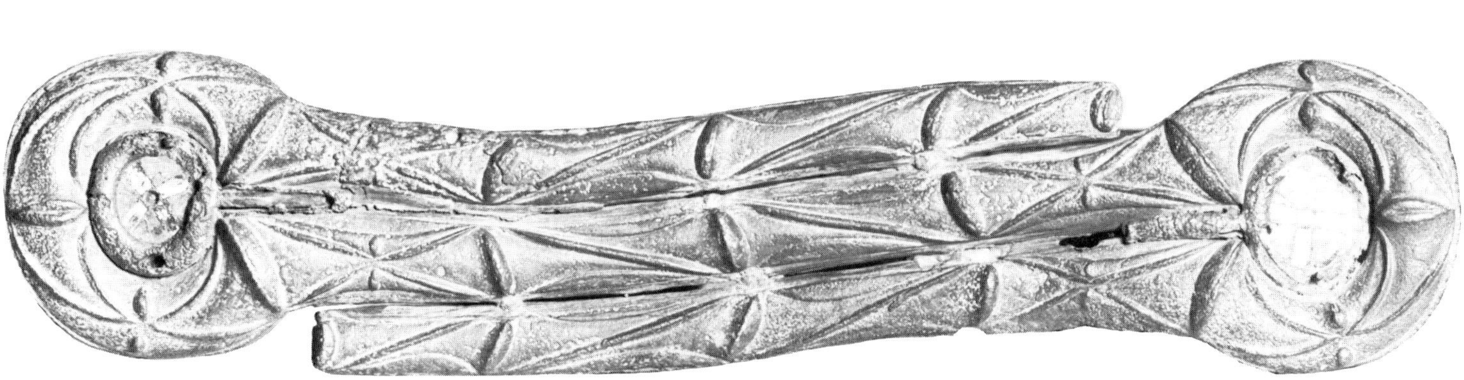

114

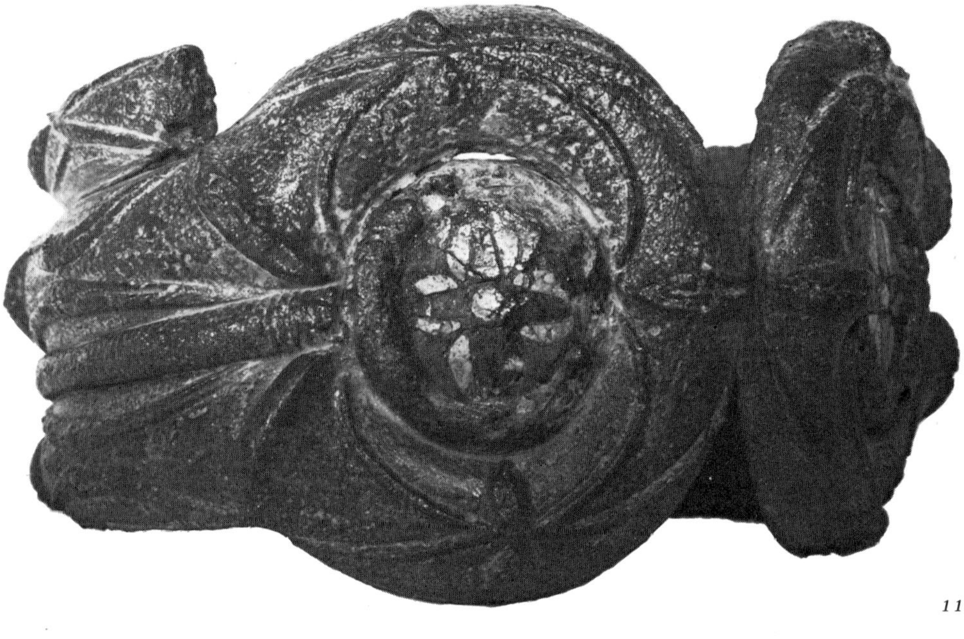

115

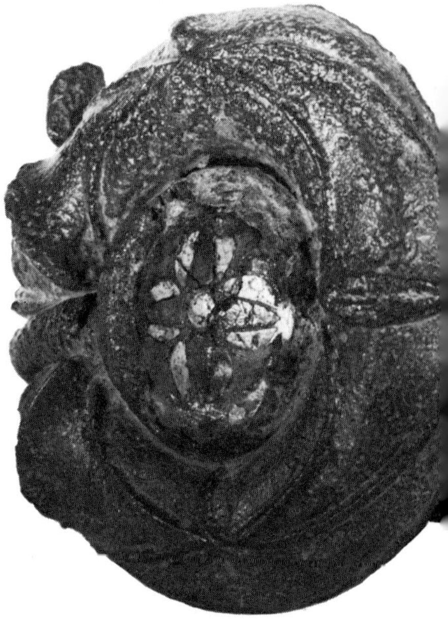

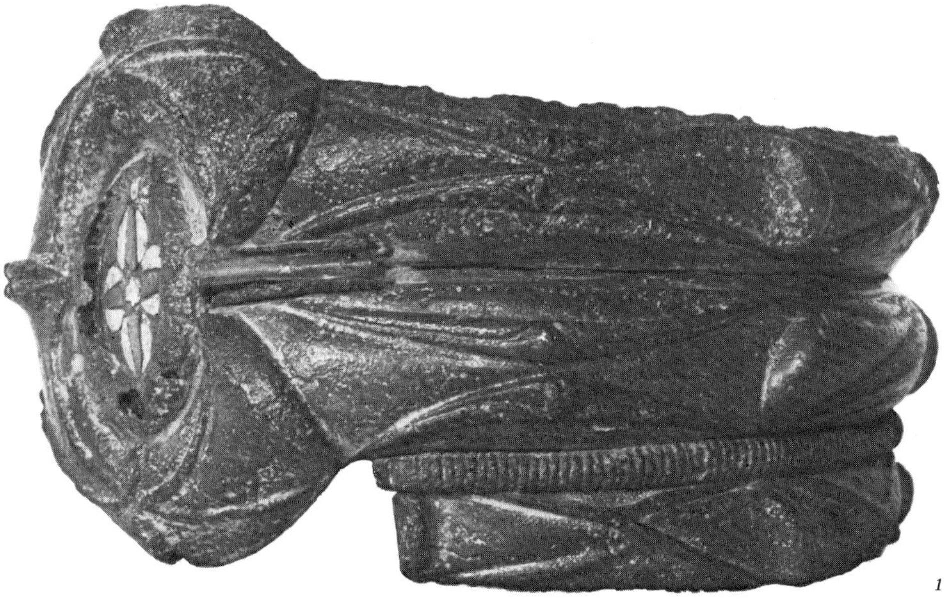

118

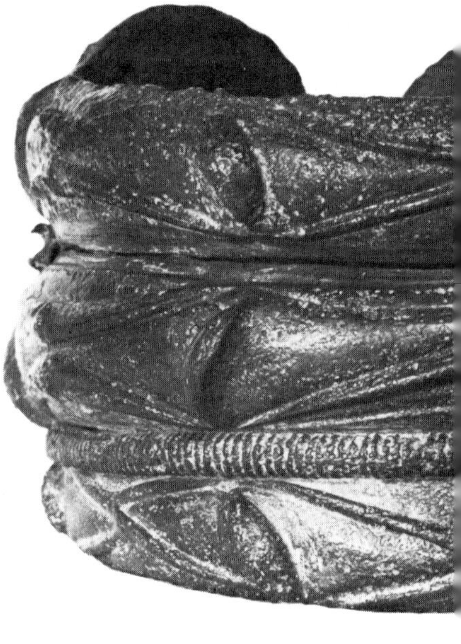

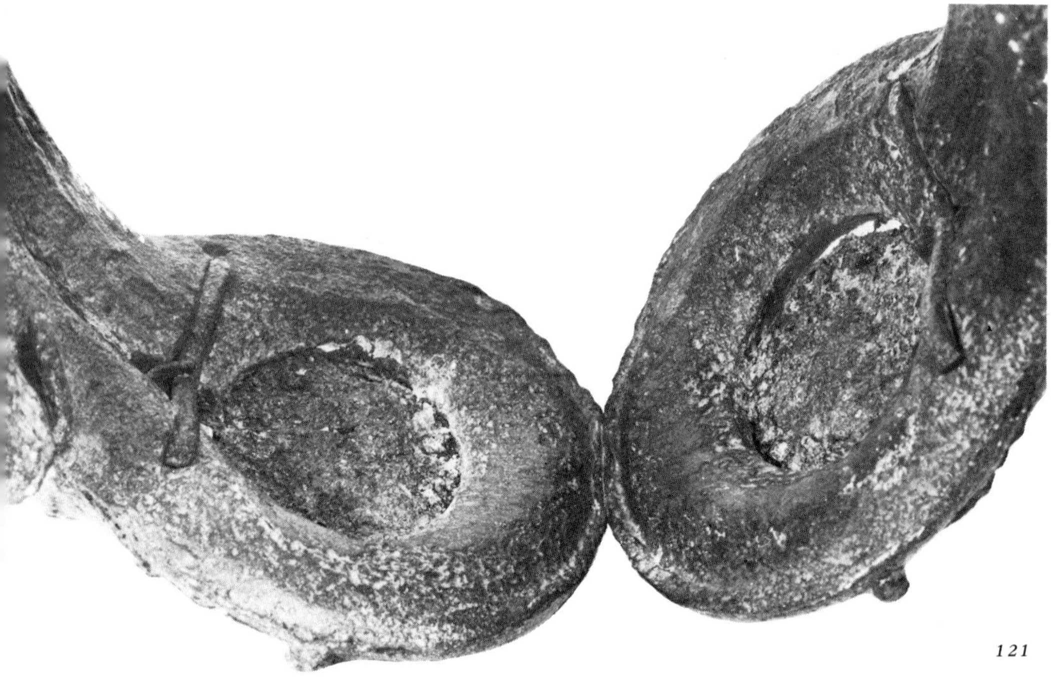

121

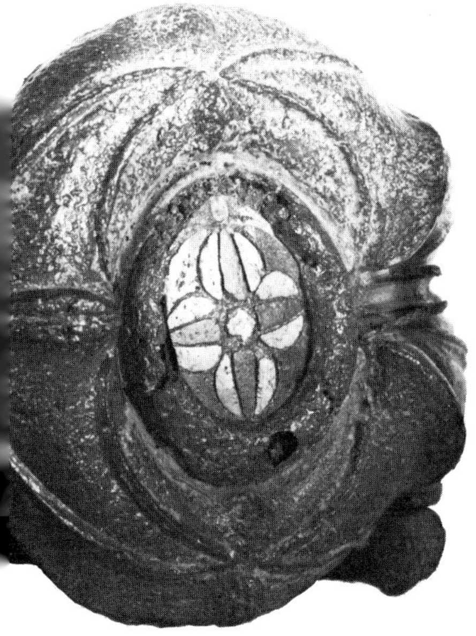

116

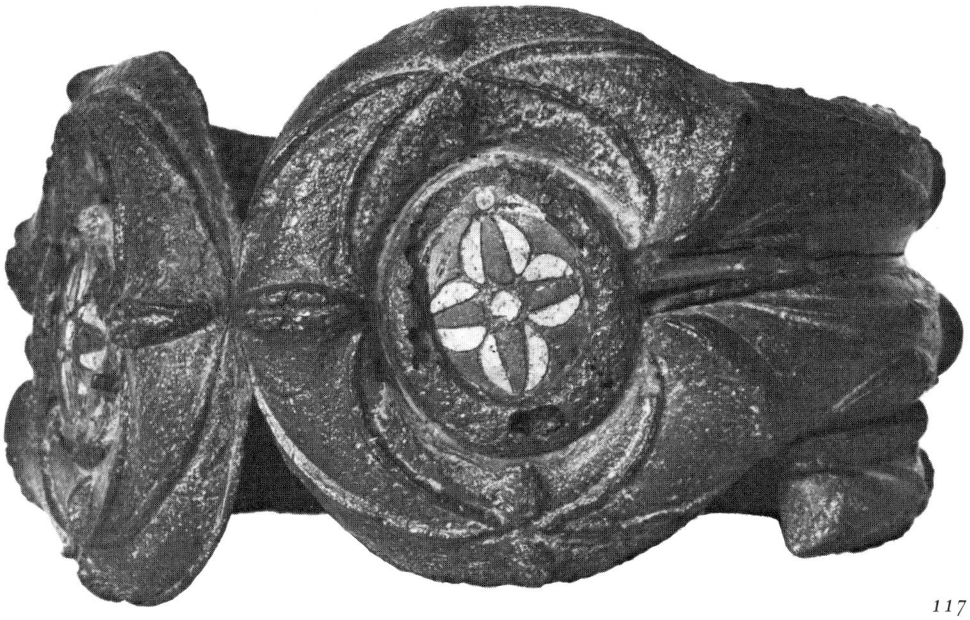

117

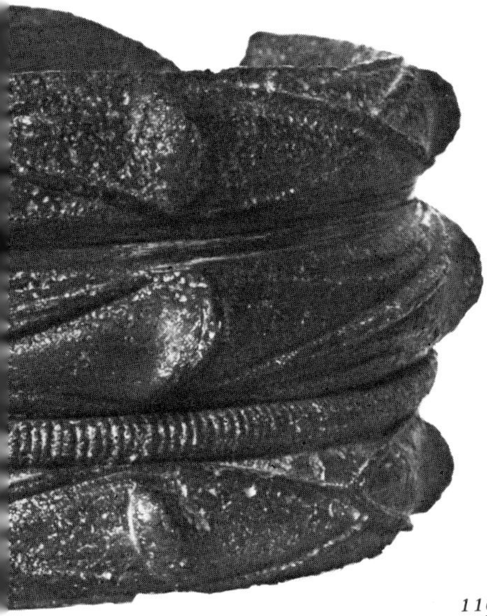

119

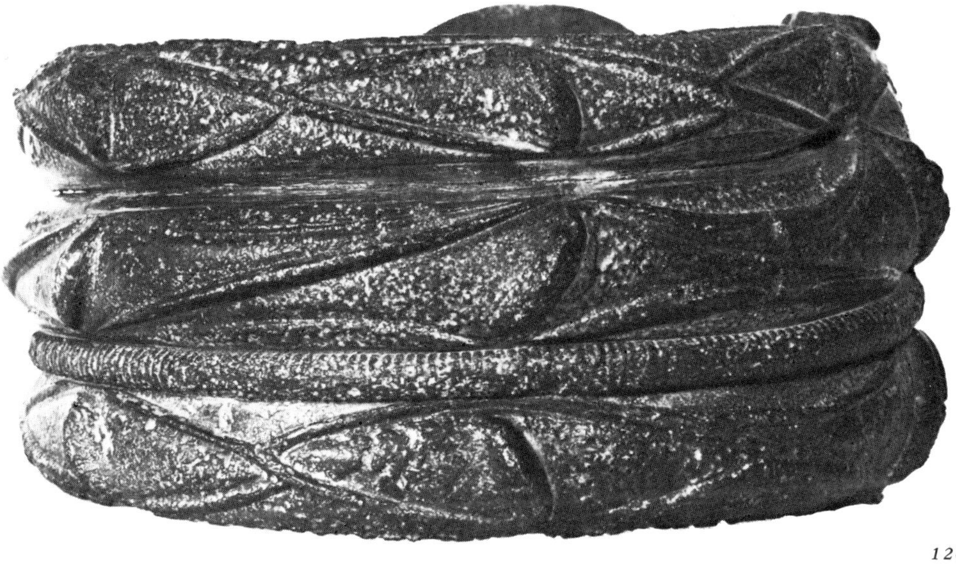

120

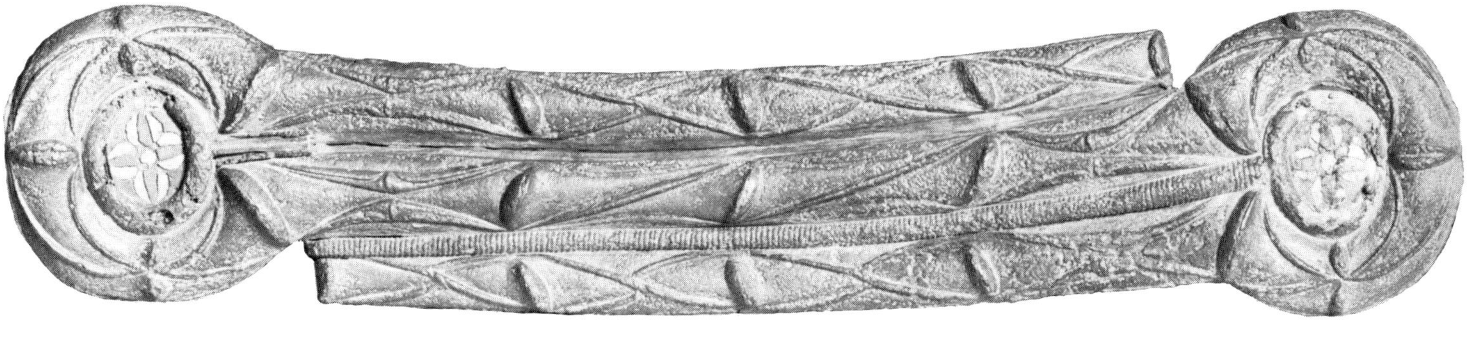

122

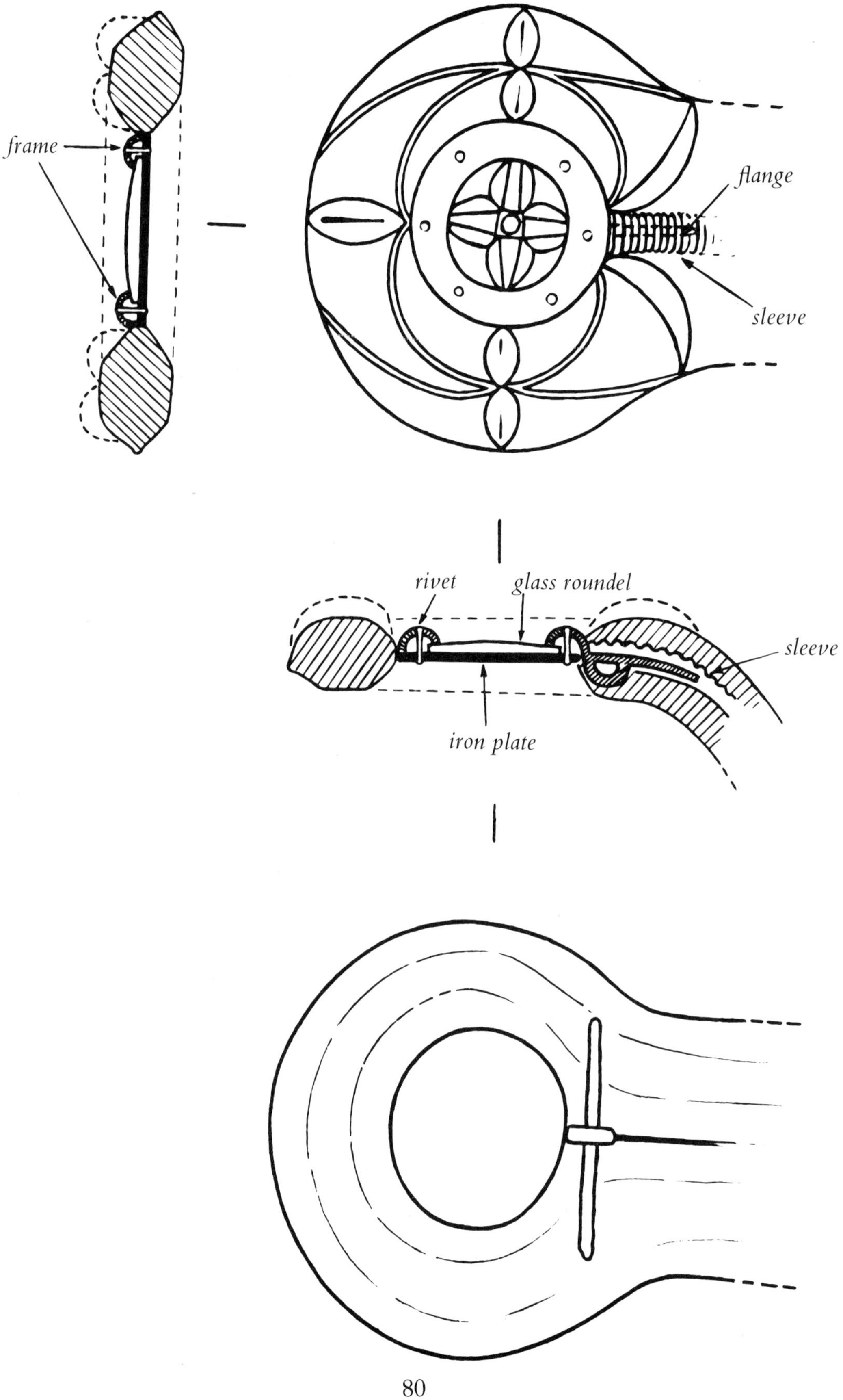

123

Technical comments

Recently a scientific examination has been carried out on both the Castle Newe and the Drummond Castle armlets by the British Museum Research Laboratory. This examination has clarified many of the problems concerning these pieces, notably regarding their method of manufacture and also to indicate that the inset decorations on the terminals are glass, not enamel as hitherto thought. The Laboratory Report comments that:

'The bodies of the armlets are made essentially of a copper–zinc–tin alloy with traces of other metals, the presence of which is probably fortuitous, including lead, silver, nickel and iron. The Castle Newe pair could be more accurately described as bronzes, i.e. copper alloyed with tin but containing a small amount of zinc whereas the Drummond Castle pair are brasses, i.e. copper alloyed with zinc but containing a small amount of tin. The chemical compositions of the Castle Newe pair are sufficiently alike to suggest that both were cast from the same batch of metal, although this is not true of the Drummond Castle pair which show significant compositional differences. One of the latter (Reg. No. 38,7–14,3a) was poorly cast, for there are at least three casting flaws on the armlet which were repaired by casting-in at some later stage during its manufacture.

'As regards the method of fabrication, it is suggested that blanks were cast, very roughly to a U-shape, possibly with those parts of the design in highest relief indicated in the casting. The rest of the design was then raised by repoussé and chasing. There are signs of flow-over of metal and under-cutting at the cross over points in the X-shaped parts of the design and disturbed metal is associated with the oval-shaped protrusions which were shown by metallographic examination to have a worked and annealed structure. At some stage the terminals were bent round, roughly through 45° as indicated by some hammering marks which are visible on the inner surfaces. During the various stages in the fabrication the metal was heated where necessary to anneal it.

'Both the Drummond Castle armlets and one of the Castle Newe pair are inset with roundels containing yellow and red glass. The Drummond setting consists of a circular brass frame of semi-tubular section surrounding the brass plate containing the glasses which is backed by an iron plate, now almost *121*
entirely corroded; the whole structure is held together by brass rivets which pass right through the frame to the back of the setting. The settings are located on openings on the terminals of the armlets and are retained in position by a brass pin passing through a loop on the underside of an extension of the frame of the setting. The colorant and opacifier employed in the yellow glasses of the Drummond Castle armlets was shown by X-ray diffraction to be cubic lead–tin–oxide and in the red glass was shown to be cuprite.

'The one surviving roundel in the Castle *IX*
Newe armlet is constructed in a similar manner with a frame, iron backing and glass but is retained in position in a different manner. It rests against the inside surface of an opening on the terminal and was probably held there by three iron pins located in holes round the circumference of each setting. Notches cut into the edges of the armlets contain iron corrosion which also extends to the back of the settings. This may be the remains of an iron strip which bridged the back of the settings. The colorant and opacifier used in the yellow glass was found to be lead antimonate and in the red glass was shown to be cuprite.'

Bibliography

Guide to Antiquities of the Early Iron Age in the Department of British and Mediaeval Antiquities, British Museum, London, 1925, pp. 155–6, fig. 186 (Drummond Castle armlets).

Later Prehistoric Antiquities of the British Isles, London, 1953, p. 64, no. 1, pl. xiv (Castle Newe armlets).

J. B. Davis, *Proc. Soc. Antiqs. Scot.* 6 (1864–6) p. 13, pl. III (Castle Newe).

William Jerdan, *Archaeologia* 28 (1839), p. 435 (Drummond Castle armlets).

J. M. Kemble, *Horae Ferales*, London, 1863, p. 183.

Morna Simpson, 'Massive armlets in the North British Iron Age', *Studies in Ancient Europe*, Leicester, 1968, p. 235.

J. A. Smith, 'Notice of a massive bronze "Late Celtic" armlet and two small objects of bronze (horse trappings) found with a Roman patella at Stanhope, Peeblesshire in 1876, with an account of other bronze or brass armlets found in Scotland', *Proc. Soc. Ants. Scot.* 3, n.s. (1880–81), pp. 316ff. (p. 330, fig. 10 for Castle Newe, and pp. 341ff. for Drummond Castle).

CHAPTER NINE

THE AYLESFORD BUCKET

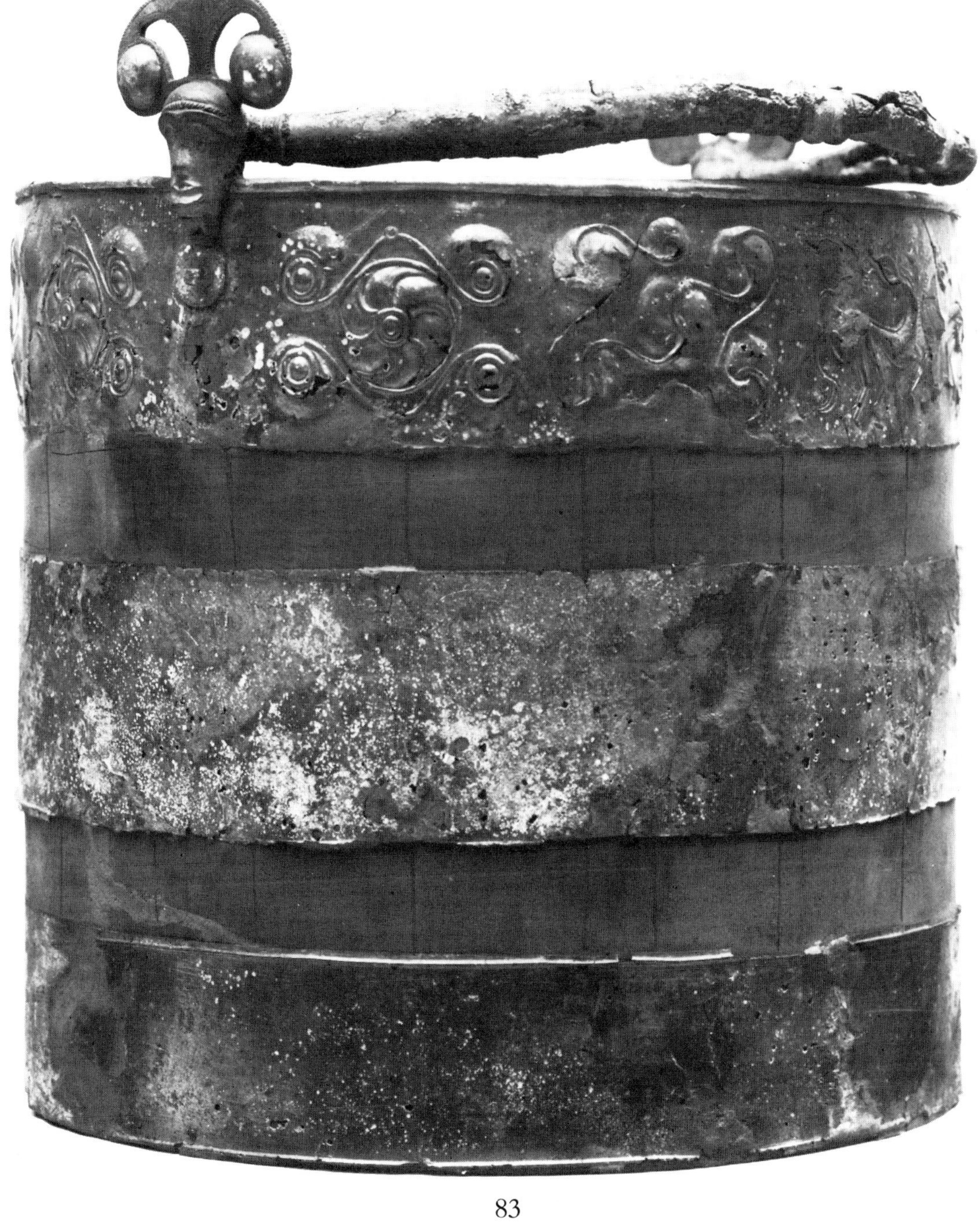

124

The Aylesford cemetery was found accidentally in 1886 and is one of two large Belgic cemeteries in Kent after which the Aylesford-Swarling Culture is named. Burials in these cemeteries were made in flat graves into which the cremated remains, in various containers, were placed. The Bucket came from Grave Y, which was the richest of the graves in the Belgic cremation cemetery at Aylesford. It had been deposited in a 'burial pit' 1·19 m. deep and it contained burnt bones and two bronze brooches.
125 Also in the grave were a bronze jug and skillet and four pots – a pedestal urn, a cordoned bucket-shaped pot and two jars. Graves with the same burial rite and containing the same kinds of pottery, bronze vessels and brooches also occur in Hertfordshire and Essex (cf. the graves from Welwyn, p. 93). By comparing the bronzes with similar types from Ornavasso in North Italy and other continental examples, the main (or 'middle') group of Aylesford-Swarling burials may be dated within the period 50–10 BC.

124 The present form of the bucket is a reconstruction made during the 1880s. It has been suggested that originally it stood on three feet. The decorated bronze band, the handle and its mounts are certainly in their original form and give a diameter of 26·5 cm. for the vessel. The body of the bucket was built up of wooden staves, but the width of these is uncertain.

The handle is made of an iron rod cased in bronze and has a stud at each end which pivots in a hole behind the head mount. On either side of the centre there is a decorative moulding.

Both handle-mounts are in the form of
I human heads, having long faces tapering to a square chin. The eyes are almond-shaped and
126, 127 protuberant, and the noses are long, narrow and flat. Beneath slot-like mouths the chins are sharply jutting, one having a groove round its point. Each head is shown wearing a cap or helmet with a moulded band across the brow which is continued across the back of the head. On the crown of each head is mounted a transverse crescentic crest with a knob at each end. At the time of its burial neither head mount was securely attached to the bucket.

The bronze band with repoussé ornament *131*
carries three motifs:

1. Five low bosses linked by a curving ridge *128*
which ends at the top and bottom in fan-shaped terminals. A similar motif occurs on a sword-scabbard from the Swiss Iron Age site of La Tène.

2. A large low boss having at the centre two *129*
concentric ridges from which curved ribs extend to a ridge round the circumference. Above and below there are arched ribs with a small circle in the centre of each, while at each end there is a curved 'birds' head' terminal surrounding a raised ring and central boss.

3. A pair of confronted animals with their *130*
heads turned backwards. These are shown in a very stylized form and are not certainly identifiable. Perhaps they should be regarded as horses. The lips of these creatures are expanded into a pair of crescentic projections, the eyes are pointed ovals and on the head of each is a plume-like topknot growing backwards. A mane-like ridge stretches down from the back of each head. The creatures have spindly legs with small feet and a spur above each foot. The tail of each creature is bifurcated, each point ending in a feather-like terminal.

These animals on the Aylesford Bucket may be compared with representations of animals found on Gaulish coins belonging to the tribe of the Remi.

Bibliography

A. Birchall, 'The Aylesford-Swarling Culture: the problem of the Belgae reconsidered', *Proc. Prehist. Soc.* 31 (1965), pp. 203–49, 302, fig. 7.

Guide to Antiquities of the Early Iron Age in the Department of British and Mediaeval Antiquities, British Museum, London, 1925, pp. 124–9, figs. 134–6.

Later Prehistoric Antiquities of the British Isles, London, 1953, p. 70, pl. xxi.

A. J. Evans, 'On a Late Celtic Urn-Field at Aylesford, Kent', *Archaeologia* 52 (1890), pp. 317–88.

J. V. S. Megaw, *Art of the European Iron Age*, Bath, 1970, no. 187.

I. M. Stead, 'The reconstruction of Iron Age Buckets from Aylesford and Baldock', *British Museum Quarterly* 1971, pp. 250ff.

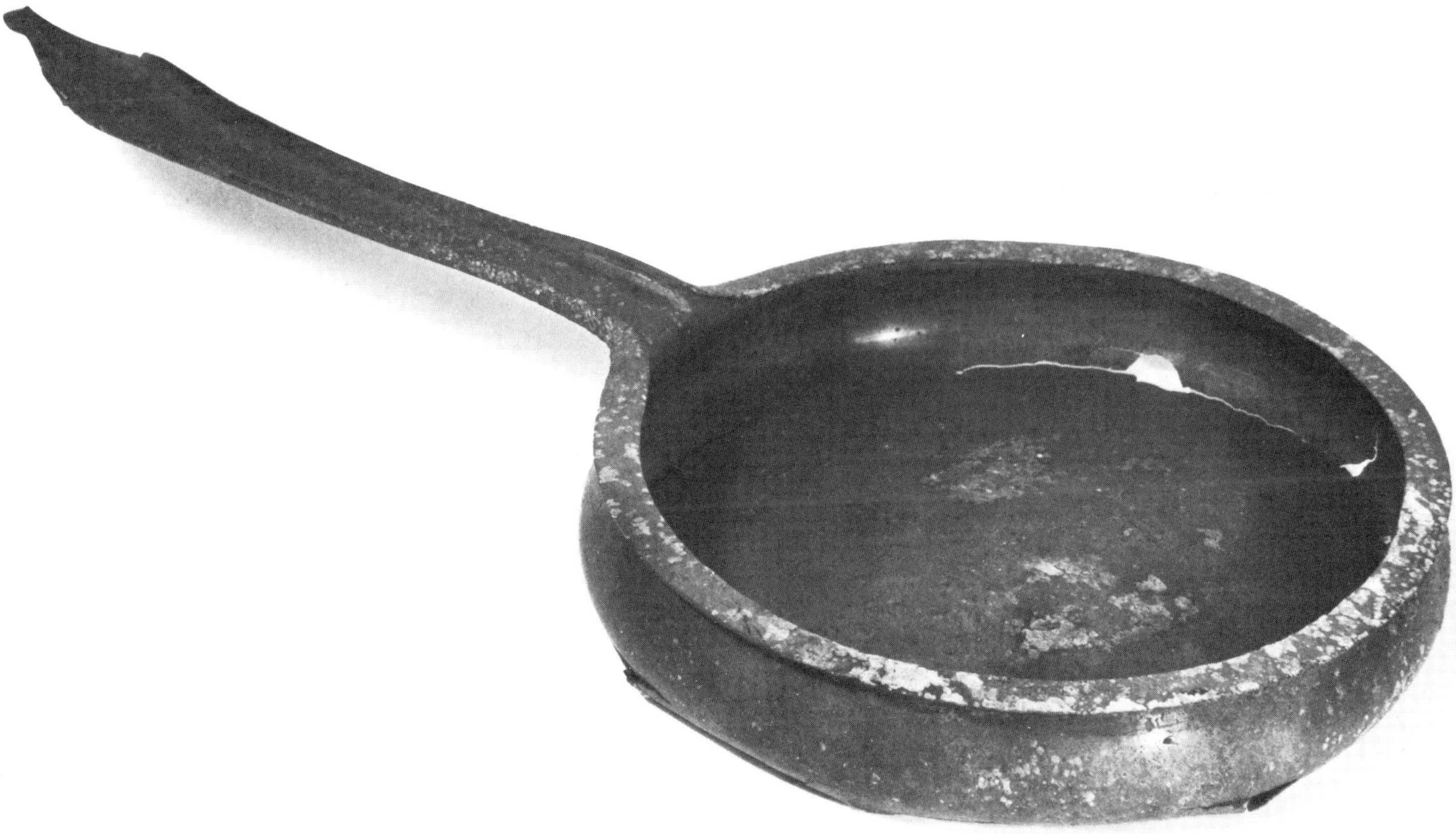

125

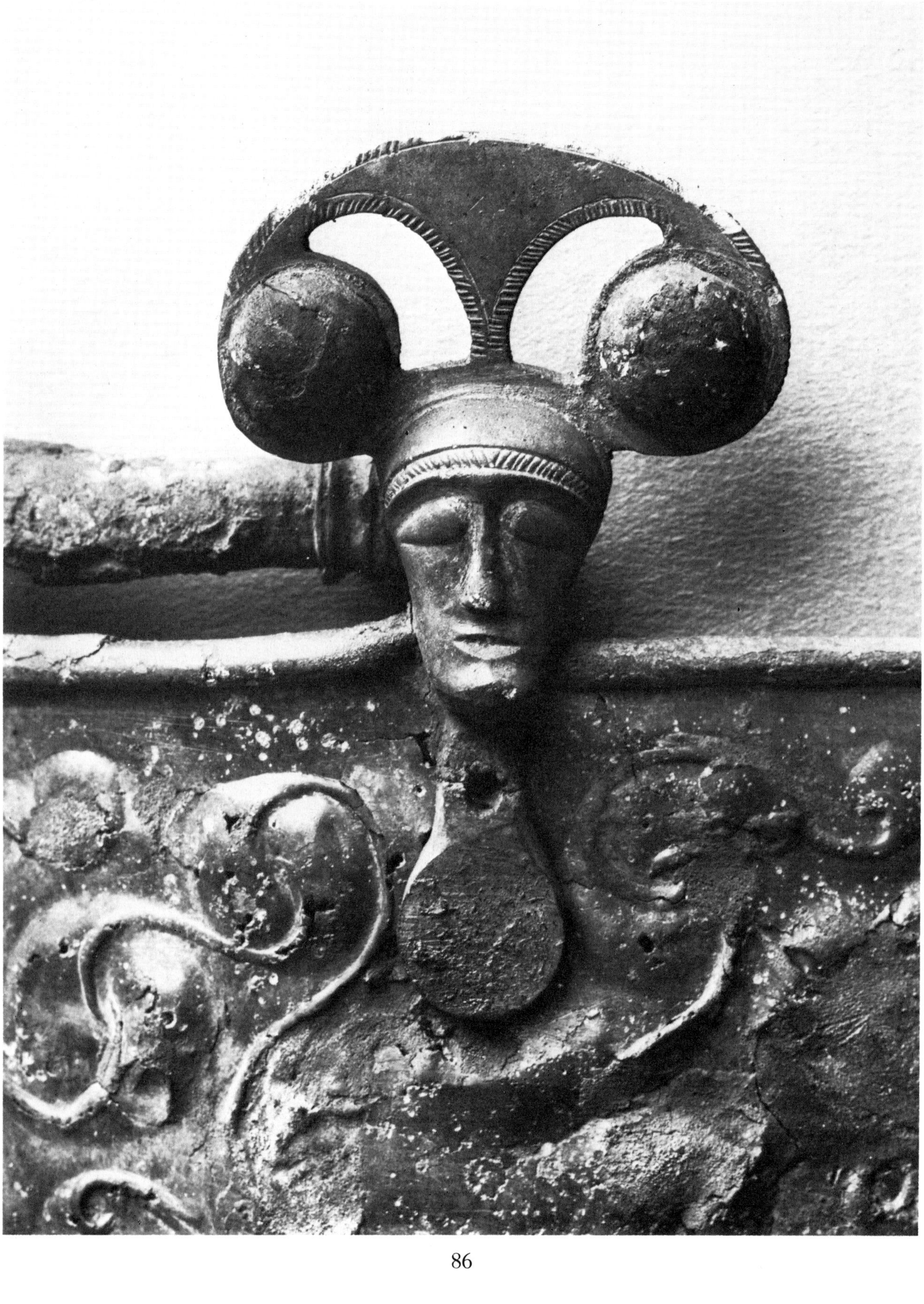

126

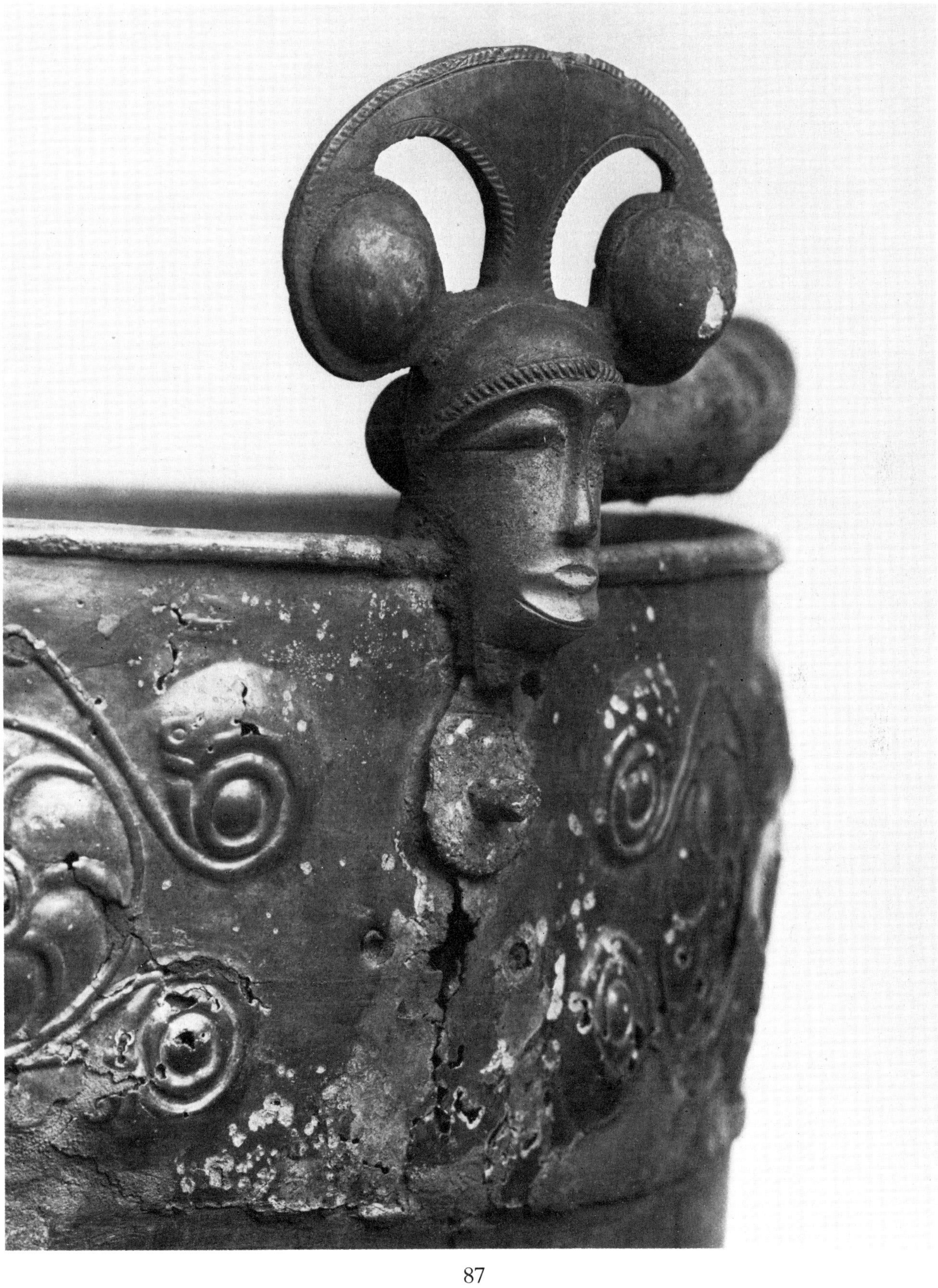

127

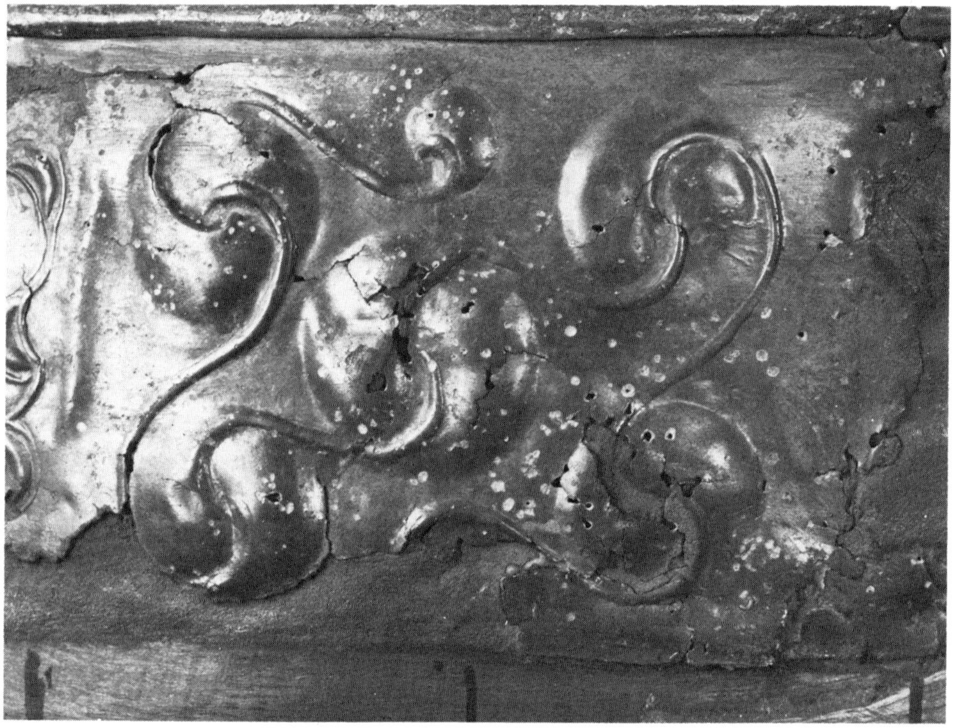

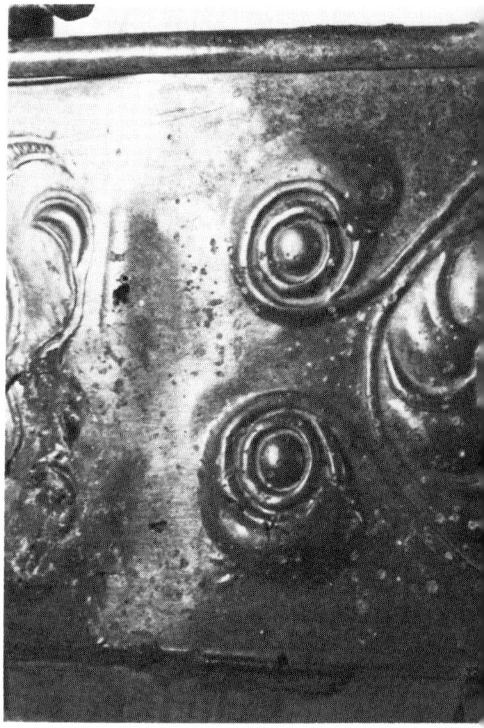

128

131

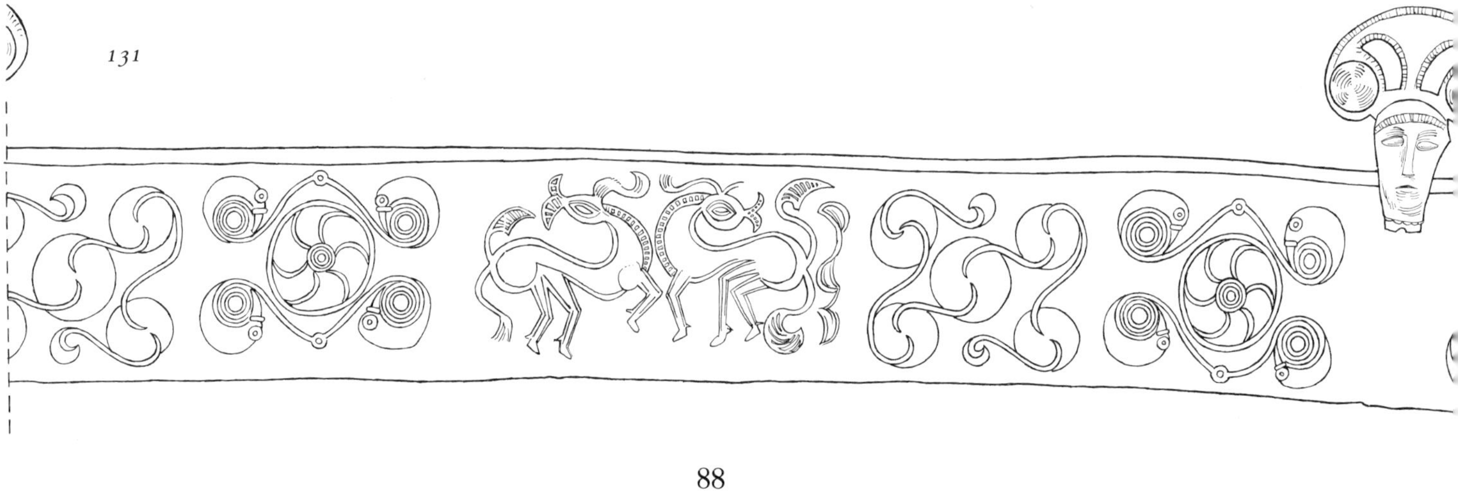

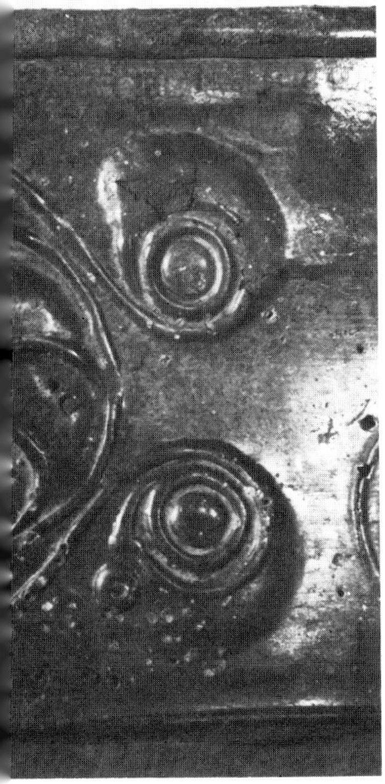

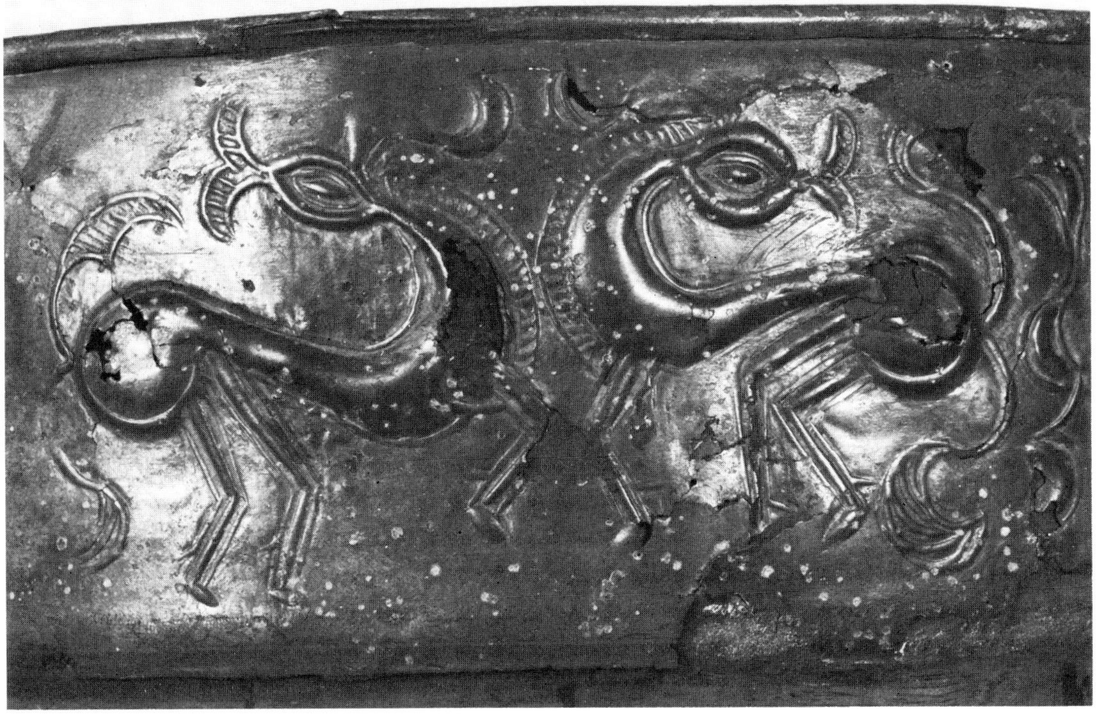

129

130

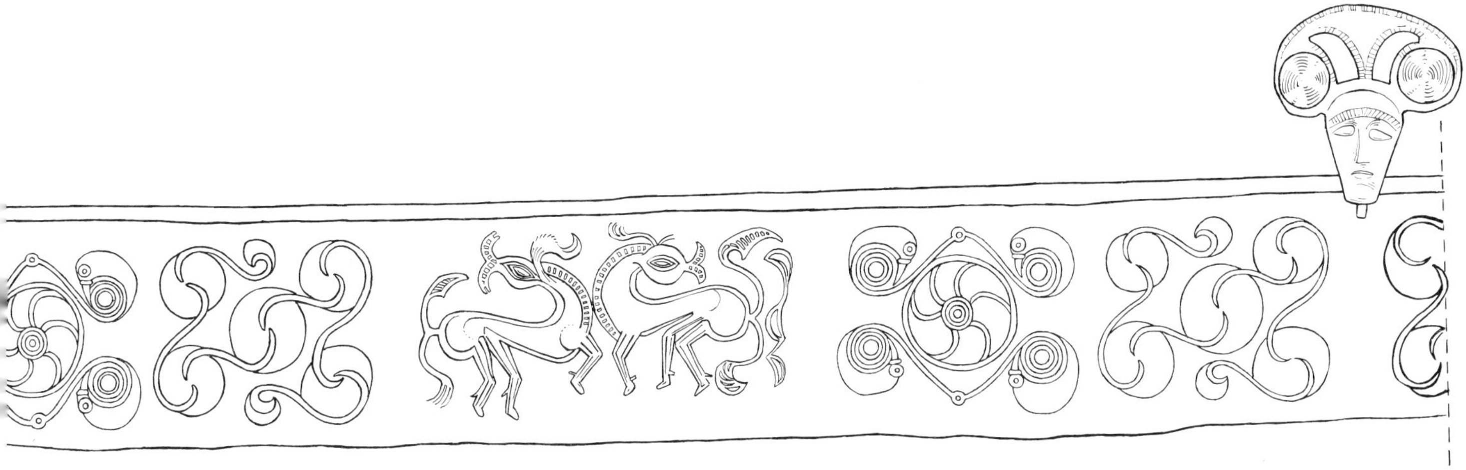

CHAPTER TEN

THE WELWYN BELGIC BURIALS

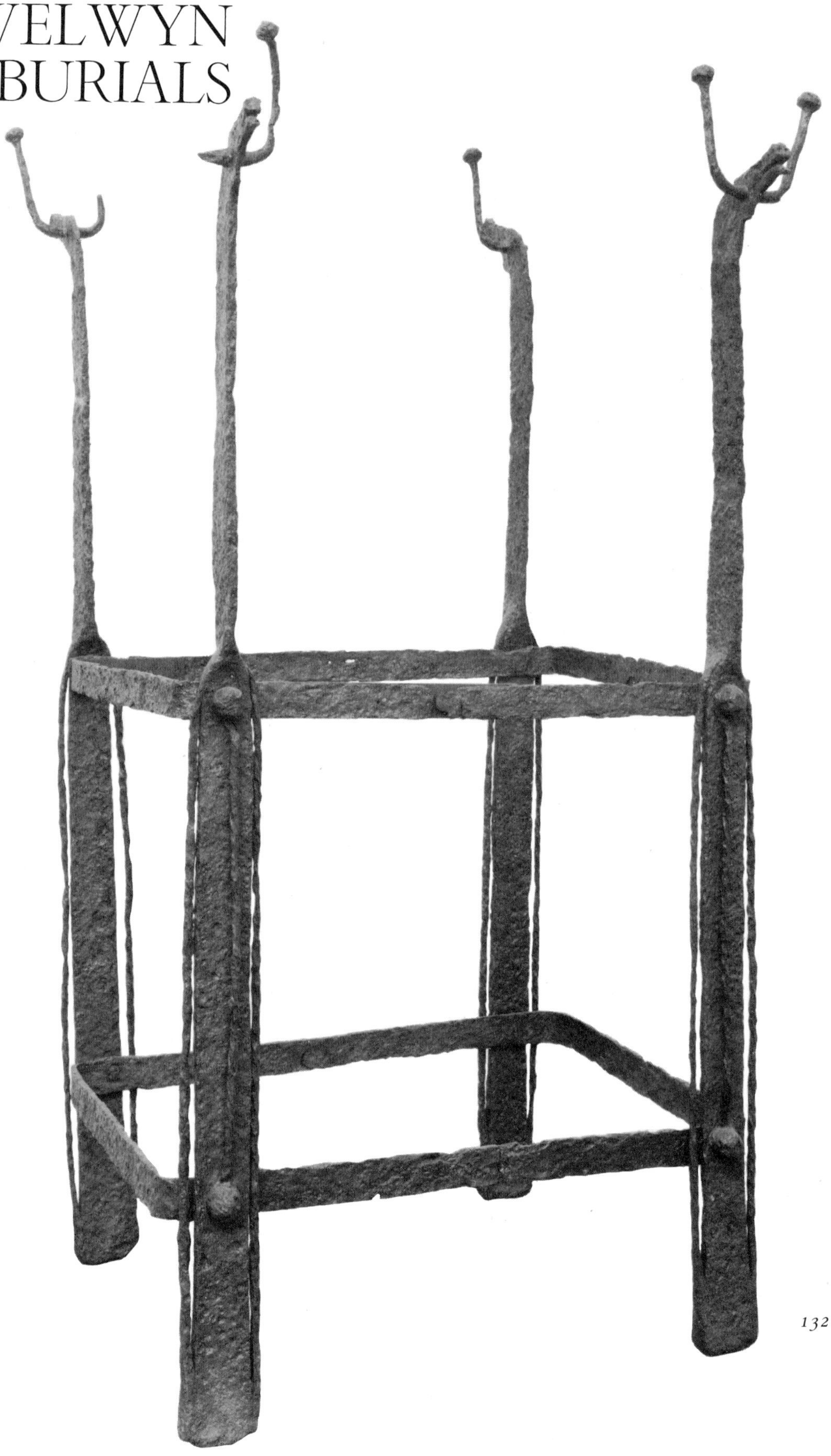

The Belgic burials from Welwyn, Hertfordshire, belong to a well-defined group of La Tène III graves in Britain, which includes in the immediate vicinity of the Welwyn burials a rich grave recently excavated at Welwyn Garden City and also one at Hertford Heath. These 'Welwyn-type' burials are characterized by cremations deposited in large rectangular graves without covering mounds. A quantity of pottery is always present, which includes at least one amphora. Some imported metal or glass vessels are also usually present. These burials may be divided into two chronological groups, those of Phase I being represented by the Welwyn graves with bronze vessels of 50–10 BC. Phase II dates from about 10 BC to about AD 50. Welwyn-type graves are one form of the rich burials associated with the Aylesford-Swarling Culture (see p. 84 above).

Welwyn-type burials commonly contain
137 iron fire-dogs of the type found in one of the
Welwyn vaults. Such fire-dogs have also been found in contexts not always established as funerary, but on the basis of examples found in archaeological contexts the whole series may be dated from the mid-first century BC to the early second century AD. Nearly all the British examples are of Piggott's type A, the large type placed across the front of the hearth. Close parallels exist from Northern France and Germany but the ultimate prototype of these objects may have been Etruscan. The quad-
132, 133 rangular frame from Welwyn is, however,
unique. It is worth noting a Continental find at Kappell (Dürnau on the Wedersee), where there was a large hoard of metalwork, scrap or votive in character, associated with a late La Tène jug of the same type as those from the Welwyn graves and that associated with the Aylesford Bucket, i.e. dating from about 50–10 BC. The Kappell hoard included a fire-dog of the same form as the British type A and a remarkable quadrangular frame, crowned with four eagles' heads.

The Welwyn Belgic burials were found accidentally during the digging of a road cutting in 1906. Apart from two separate burials the finds were contained in two 'vaults'. The first 'vault' contained an amphora; an iron
fire-dog with (?) ox-head terminals, each of *136, 137*
which has the remains of a mane-like fringe on the neck; the foot, handle and part of the body of a bronze bowl; three bronze masks about 3·8 cm. high representing human faces in a characteristic Early Celtic style; the handle of a bronze jug of the same type as that found with the Aylesford Bucket (p. 84); a pottery *tazza* (footed cup), and the base of a pottery pedestal urn.

In the second 'vault' were five amphorae and
the wrought iron frame. The latter consists of *132, 133*
four uprights with (?) ox-head terminals at *135*
the top of each, the uprights are joined by rectangular pieces of strip iron. The maximum height of the uprights is 1·69 m. and the horizontal dimensions of the structure are 63·3 cm. by 71·5 cm. The lower part of each upright is a massive bar 11 cm. wide by 4·5 cm. thick; the upper part is turned at right angles to these with each horned head looking outwards over the lower faces of the uprights. Twisted
bars are attached to each edge of the lower *134*
sections. The horizontal strips are attached to the uprights by rivets with large bossed heads on the outside and these are joined by twisted bars running up the face of the upright. Altogether the frame is a *tour de force* of wrought ironwork without equal in the European Iron Age.

Also in the second 'vault' was a bronze skillet of the same form as that found with the

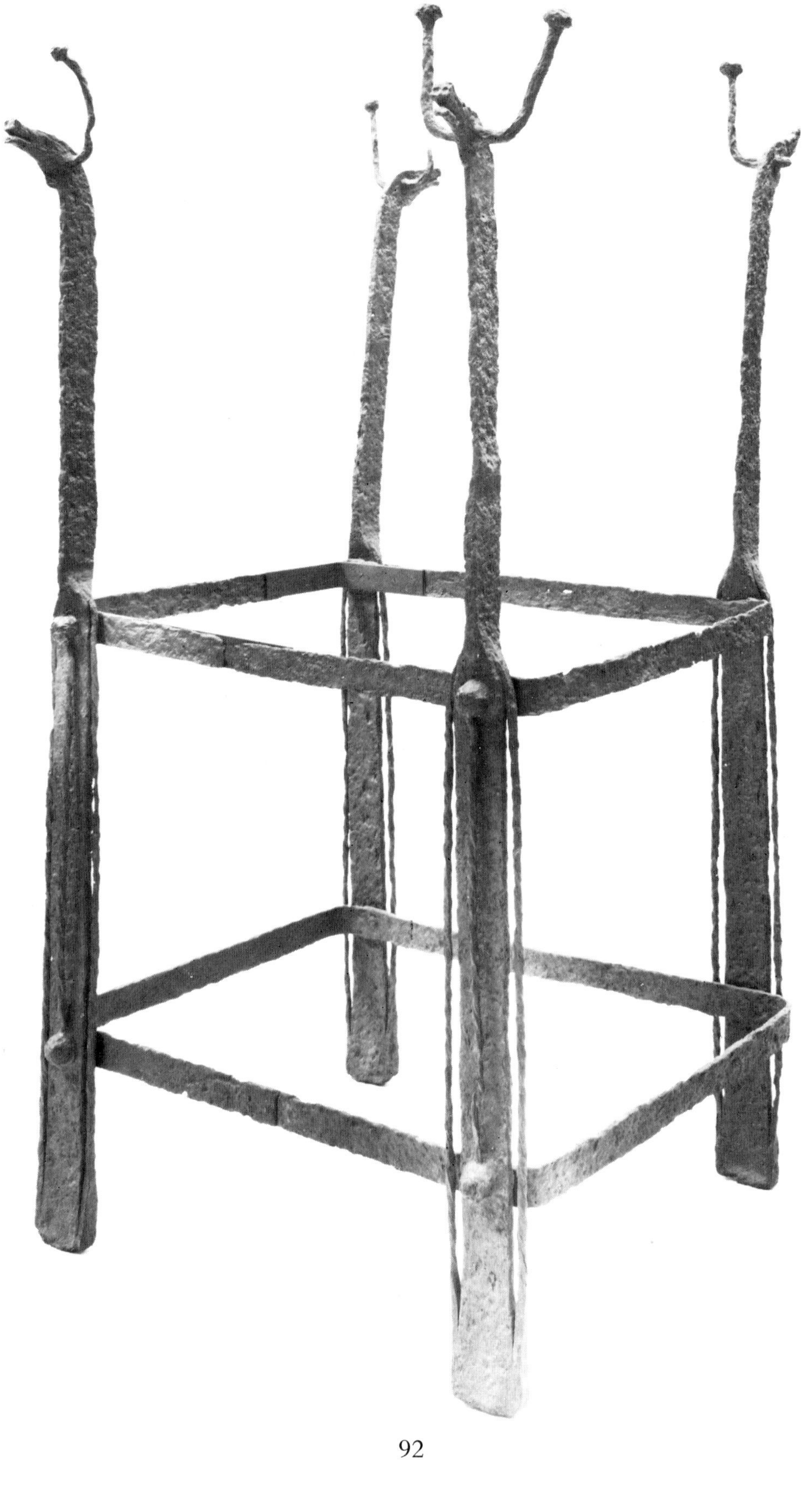

133, 134

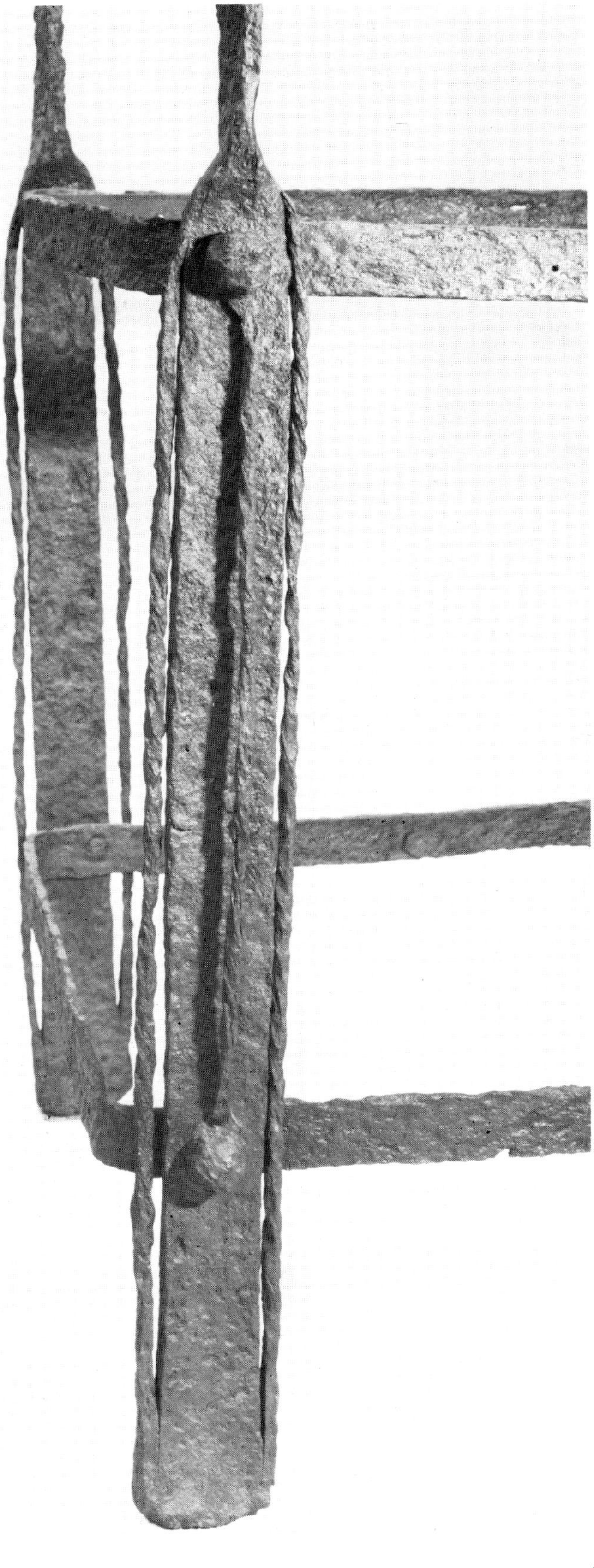

Aylesford Bucket (p. 84) complete with a bird-head terminal in the form of a reversed 'S' below the tip of the handle; the handle of a bronze jug of the same form as that found with the Aylesford Bucket; a wooden tankard with a decorated bronze handle; a bronze ring with peripheral groove and tang ending in a large domed head, perhaps the handle for the lid of some vessel; a pair of silver cups of Roman manufacture, probably of the late first century BC which had been imported from the Continent; bronze domes of unknown use, two about 2·2 cm. in diameter and about fifteen 3·8 cm. in diameter; a pottery pedestal urn and a pottery *tazza*. 125

Bibliography

J. W. Brailsford, 'A corrected restoration of the Belgic iron frame from Welwyn', *Antiquaries Journal* 38 (1958), pp. 89–90.

A. Birchall, 'The Aylesford-Swarling Culture: The problem of the Belgae reconsidered', *Proc. Prehist. Soc.* 31 (1965), pp. 241ff.

S. Piggott, 'Firedogs in Iron Age Britain and beyond', in *The European Community in Later Prehistory*, ed. J. Boardman *et al.*, London, 1971, pp. 245–70.

R. A. Smith, 'On Late Celtic Antiquities Discovered at Welwyn, Herts.', *Archaeologia* 63 (1911–12), pp. 1ff.

I. M. Stead, 'A La Tène Burial at Welwyn Garden City', *Archaeologia* 101 (1967), pp. 1–62.

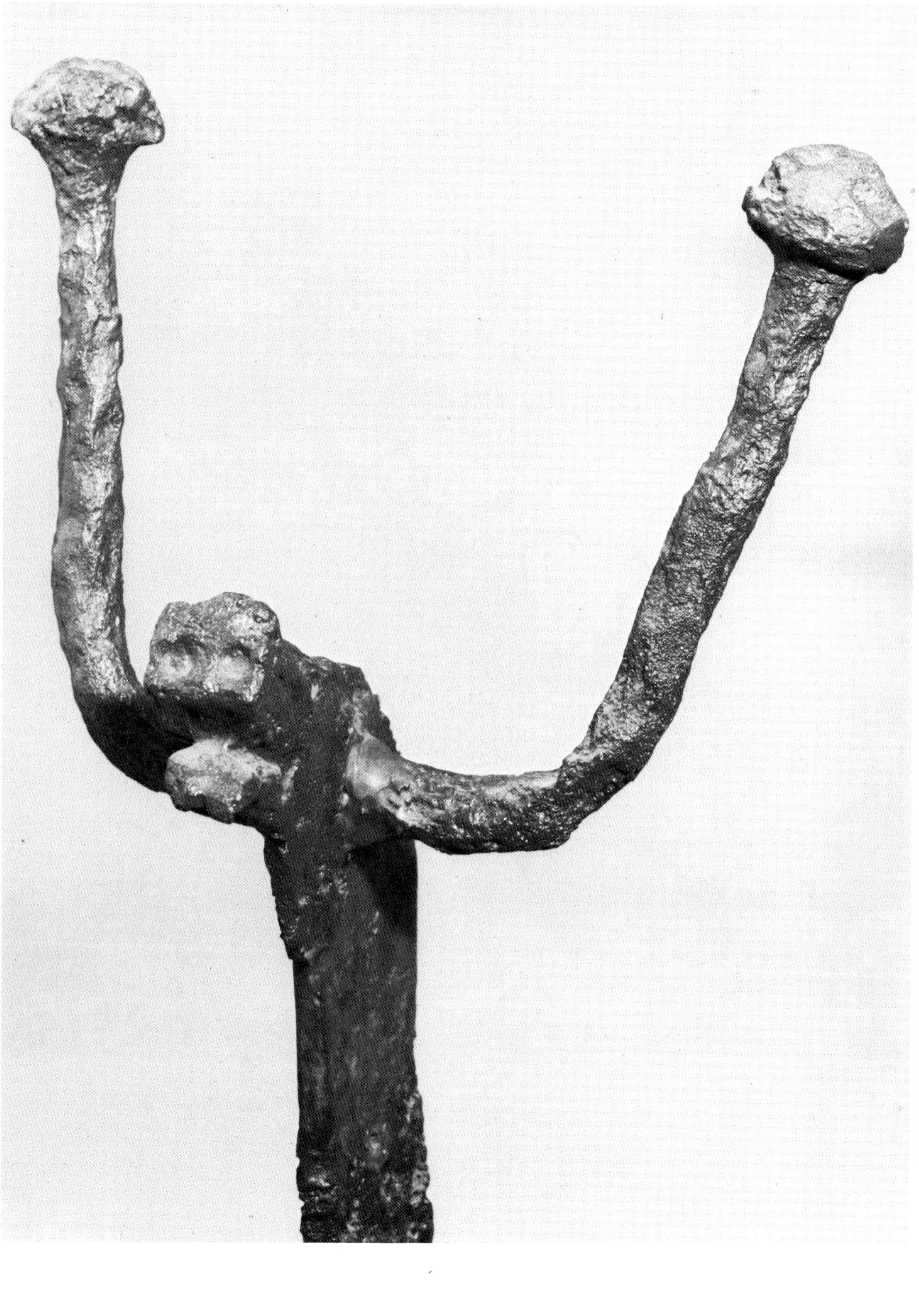

THE WELWYN FIRE-DOG

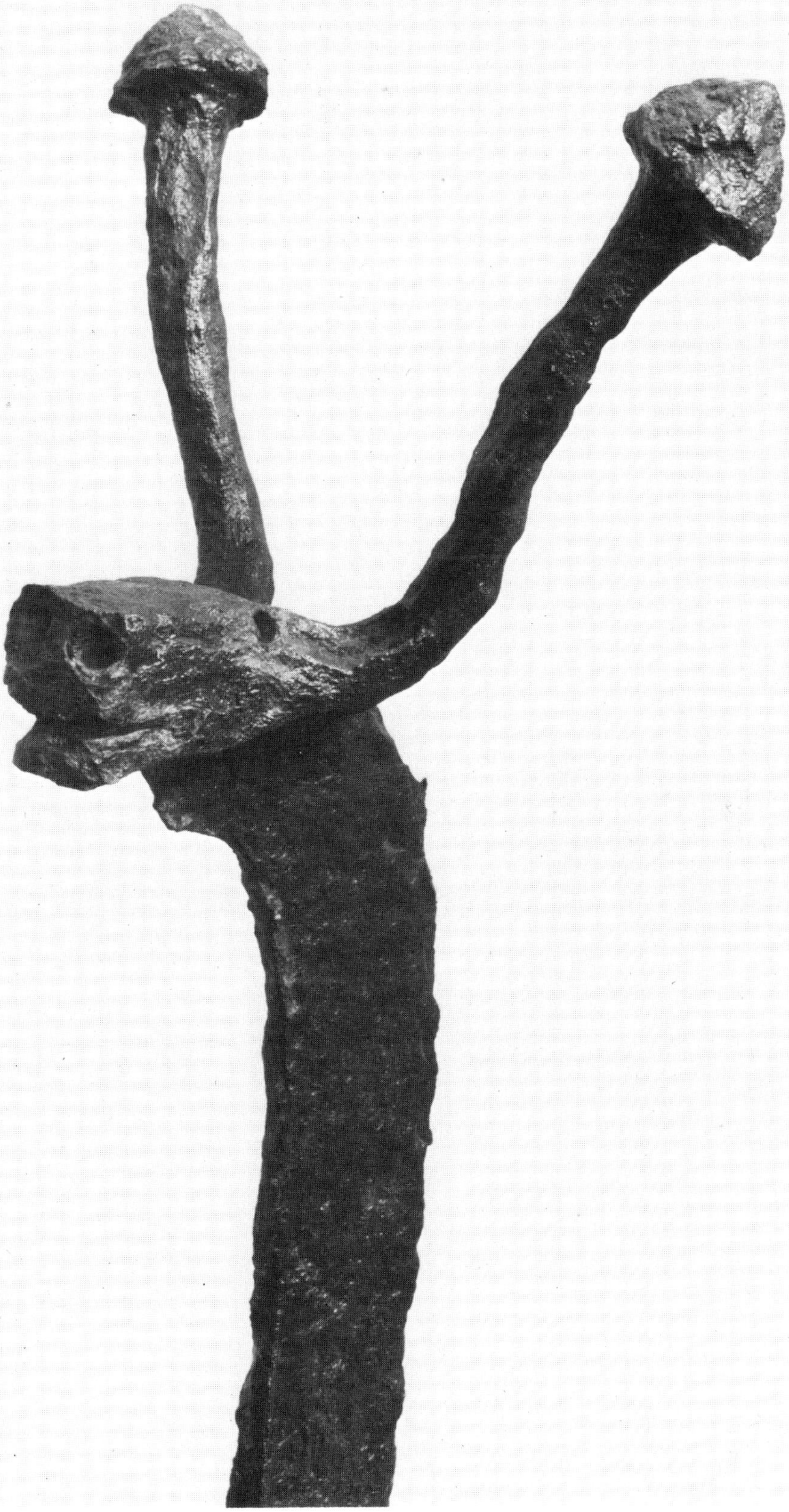

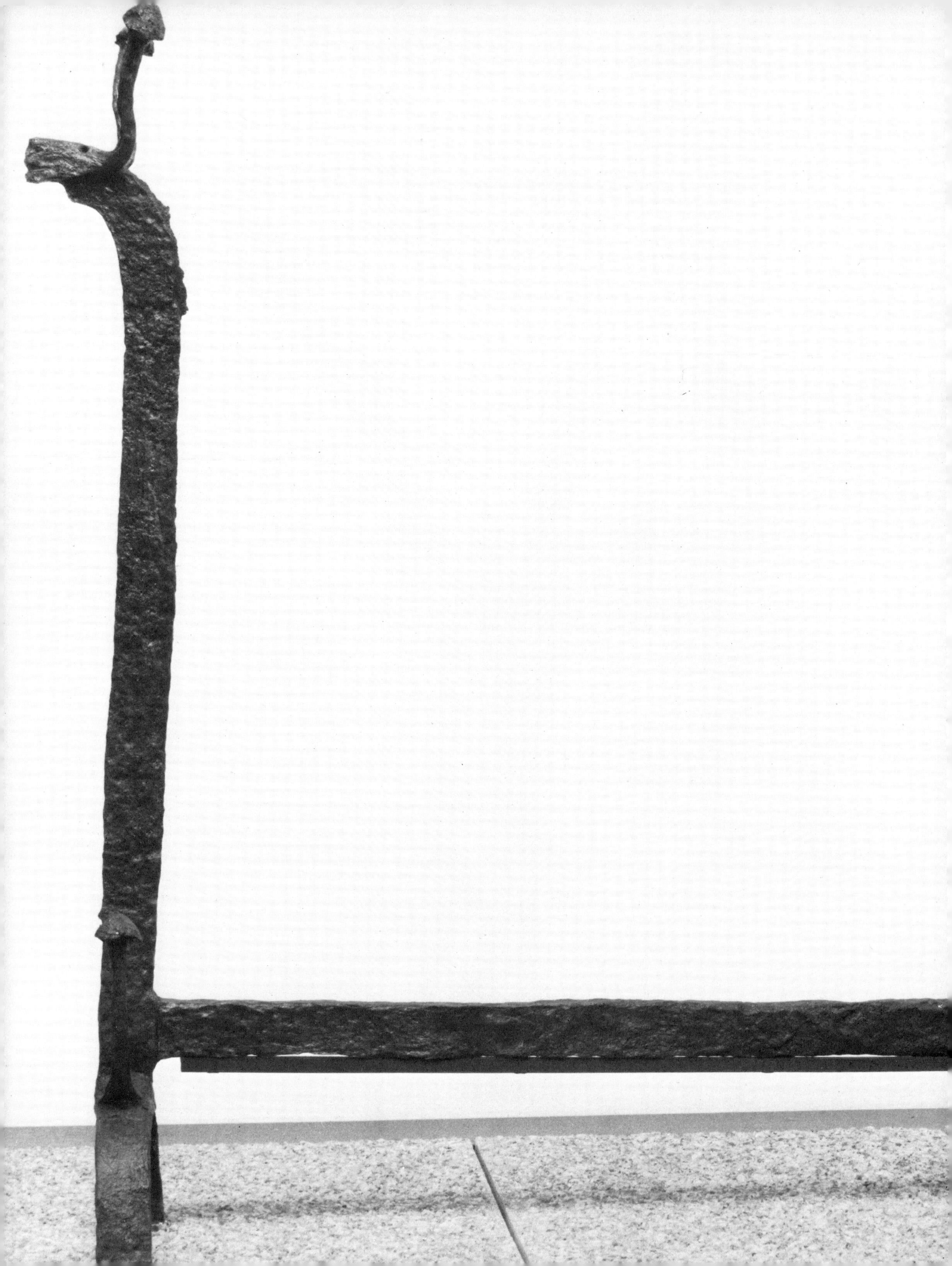

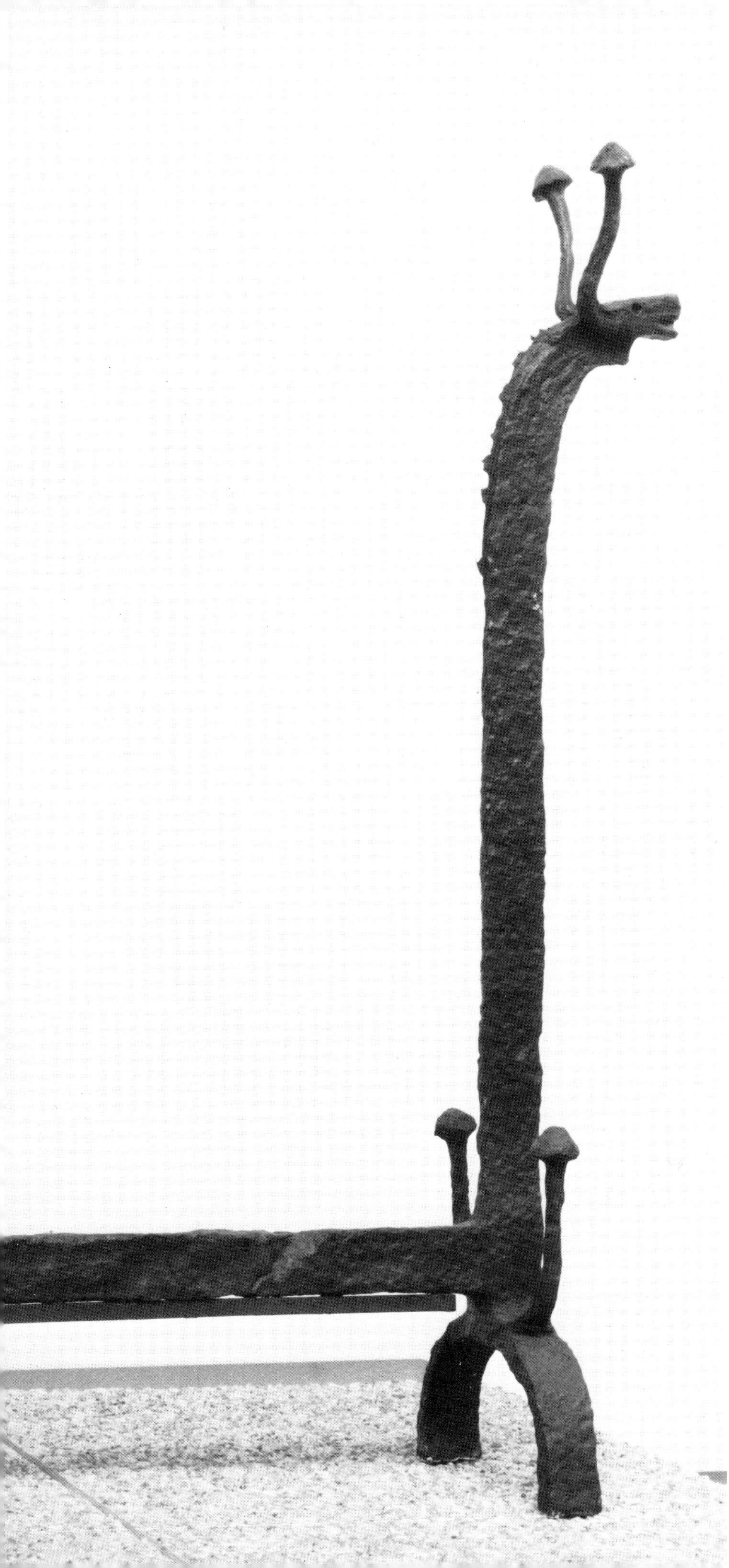

GLOSSARY

amphora: a large two-handled Greek or Roman coarse ware pottery vessel used for importing wine into Britain in the first century BC and later. See Welwyn-type Burials above.

chasing: decoration executed by means of a hammer and punch (*cf.* engraving, below).

cire-perdue: ('lost wax') a method of casting in which a wax model of the object is covered with clay. This is then heated, the wax runs out leaving a cavity into which molten metal is poured. The mould must then be broken in order to extract the casting. It is therefore only possible to make one casting from each mould by this process.

cloisonné: a type of ornament where metal cells are filled with pieces of inlay cut to fit and cemented into place.

engraving: incised ornament executed by using a graver or sharp cutting tool (*cf.* chasing, above).

La Tène: the second period of the European Iron Age (after Hallstatt) named from a Swiss site. It is characterized by a Celtic culture notable for its outstanding artistic tradition.

palmette: a stylized foliate decoration originating in the Classical world as a fan-shaped cluster of radiating leaves. Derivatives are commonly used in Early Celtic Art.

pelta: a motif of basically crescentic form originating in the Classical world. Often found used in mirror decoration, a typical pair may be seen above the handle mounting of the Desborough Mirror, Ill. 95.

repoussé: relief ornament formed by hammering up the design from the underside of a metal sheet.

torc: a decorated metal collar. Torcs were worn as a badge of rank amongst the Celts.

umbo: the central round boss of a shield.

INDEX

Roman numbers refer to the colour plates, those in italic to black-and-white illustrations; all other references are to ordinary page numbers.